PENGUI

Hell-hole
of the Pacific

Richard Wolfe completed a Bachelor of Fine Arts at Elam School of Fine Arts, Auckland, in 1972. Since then he has worked in museums as a display artist and curator of display, and as a freelance curator and writer. He published his first book *Well Made New Zealand: A History of Trademarks* in 1987. He has also published five children's books, including *Midnight at the Museum* (1997), all illustrated by his wife, the artist Pamela Wolfe. They live in Freemans Bay, Auckland.

Also by Richard Wolfe

Well Made New Zealand: A Century of Trademarks
New Zealand! New Zealand! In Praise of Kiwiana (with Stephen Barnett)
Kiwi: More than a Bird
At the Beach: The Great New Zealand Holiday (with Stephen Barnett)
All Our Own Work: New Zealand's Folk Art
Remember When . . . Our New Zealand 1900 to 1999
Kiwiana! The Sequel (with Stephen Barnett)
In My Day: Looking at New Zealand's Past
Classic Kiwiana: An Essential Guide to New Zealand Popular Culture
(with Stephen Barnett)
The Way We Wore: The Clothes New Zealanders Have Loved
Auckland: A Pictorial History
The Time of Our Lives: Growing up in New Zealand
Moa: The Dramatic Story of the Discovery of a Giant Bird
A Noble Prospect: 75 Years of the Auckland War Memorial Museum Building
On Active Service: New Zealand at War

Children's Books
(illustrated by Pamela Wolfe)
Midnight at the Museum
Mouse Opera
Mouse Hotel
Walter's Planet
Mouse on the Moon

Hell-hole of the Pacific

RICHARD WOLFE

PENGUIN BOOKS

PENGUIN BOOKS
Published by the Penguin Group
Penguin Group (NZ), 67 Apollo Drive, Rosedale,
North Shore 0632, New Zealand (a division of Pearson New Zealand Ltd)
Penguin Group (USA) Inc., 375 Hudson Street,
New York, New York 10014, USA
Penguin Group (Canada), 90 Eglinton Avenue East, Suite 700, Toronto,
Ontario, M4P 2Y3, Canada (a division of Pearson Penguin Canada Inc.)
Penguin Books Ltd, 80 Strand, London, WC2R 0RL, England
Penguin Ireland, 25 St Stephen's Green,
Dublin 2, Ireland (a division of Penguin Books Ltd)
Penguin Group (Australia), 250 Camberwell Road, Camberwell,
Victoria 3124, Australia (a division of Pearson Australia Group Pty Ltd)
Penguin Books India Pvt Ltd, 11, Community Centre,
Panchsheel Park, New Delhi – 110 017, India
Penguin Books (South Africa) (Pty) Ltd, 24 Sturdee Avenue,
Rosebank, Johannesburg 2196, South Africa

Penguin Books Ltd, Registered Offices: 80 Strand, London, WC2R 0RL, England

First published by Penguin Group (NZ), 2005
This Print on Demand digital edition created by Penguin Group (NZ), 2008

Copyright © Richard Wolfe, 2005

The right of Richard Wolfe to be identified as the author of this work in
terms of section 96 of the Copyright Act 1994 is hereby asserted.

Designed by Mary Egan
Typeset by Pindar NZ
Printed in Australia by McPherson's Printing Group

ISBN 978 014 301016 6

A catalogue record for this book is available from the
National Library of New Zealand.

www.penguin.co.nz

CONTENTS

INTRODUCTION

'Hell-hole of the Pacific' may qualify as New Zealand's first local slogan. Long before other parts of this country began promoting themselves as the 'River City' or 'Garden City', for example, Kororareka was well known for its own particular attractions. Those of us who missed the action may now wonder just how justified that redoubtable reputation was. Was the place really as bad – or, depending on your point of view, as good – as was claimed? I intend to look at the surviving reports, and then see how Kororareka compared with other 'colourful' spots around the Pacific.

Visiting modern-day Russell, it is difficult to imagine the drunken and licentious goings-on when the town was known as Kororareka. Reports of it in its hey-day varied considerably. As they say, you probably had to be there, while timing was also important. The more boisterous the evening's activities, the quieter things were likely to be the morning after, as revellers recovered. And unlike today, things didn't necessarily let up on Sundays, for drunken antics were known to disrupt church services. But while the town surely 'rocked' at times, such unbridled activity could not be sustained and there were periods of unnatural and ominous calm.

In one sense there was a fine line between the forces of good and evil at Kororareka, with godliness (represented by the missionary enclave at Paihia) and wickedness separated by a narrow strip of water. Those gentlemen had an uphill battle, attempting to undo some well-worn traditions. The Reverend Henry Williams, who had been a midshipman in the Royal Navy, would have known better than most what sailors were capable of. Missionary efforts to prepare souls for the life hereafter conflicted with more earthly desires – on one side, for physical pleasure, and on the other, for the material benefits such contacts could bring.

Irrespective of the accuracy of Kororareka's unsavoury reputation, it is easy to see how it came about. Thanks to its sheltered harbour, plentiful supplies and proximity to the whaling grounds, the town had just about everything a sailing master could want for. There were added incentives, including grog-shops and a willing female population. It was both a convenient destination for escaped convicts from across the Tasman and a popular place to jump ship, with its dense hinterland and lack of authority for those choosing to live outside the law.

Prostitution was a primary employer in Kororareka in the 1830s, some 170 years before the profession was legalised in this country. For sailors arriving on the stinking confines of whaling ships, the Bay of Islands and its welcoming canoes of women must have seemed more like a slice of heaven than a hell-hole. The arrival of British authority in 1840 marked the beginning of the end of this boisterous period, but there was at least one more dramatic chapter to be played out. In March 1845 Kororareka added to its list of achievements with what was probably the most spectacular man-made destruction of a town in New Zealand history. Not surprisingly, some suggested that the hand of God played a part in the removal of this blighted spot from the map. But whoever was responsible, the old town had gone. I hope we can now decide whether its reputation, at least, has survived intact.

Hell-hole of the Pacific might be seen as a logical development of my previous book *Moa*. A number of leading players in the identification of this extinct bird also feature in the story of Kororareka, among them the versatile Joel Polack, the brothers Henry and William Williams, and missionary printer William Colenso. Common to the stories of the moa and Kororareka are personal rivalries and disagreements. Colenso, whose press was a vital weapon in the war against wickedness, would never accept that Polack was the first to publish a reference to the moa. Meanwhile, the latter had a famous disagreement with another early settler, Benjamin Turner, who also had his own version of the town's early history. Another individual with some connection to both stories was Everard Home, commander of the frigate *North Star*. This ship played a dramatic role in the Bay of Islands in 1845–46, and on its return to England carried what another missionary mistakenly claimed was the first moa bone to have been discovered. Dumont d'Urville, who made three visits to the Bay of Islands, also had a slight moa connection, for while at Paihia he was presented with a specimen of the kiwi, the living relative of the extinct bird. The same places, as well as people, feature in both stories. Important moa remains were found at Waikouaiti, a spot which some maintained was every bit as bad as Kororareka when it came to human behaviour.

For this opportunity to tackle the story of Kororareka I am once again grateful to Geoff Walker, Rebecca Lal and all the people at Penguin. I also thank the following for their advice and assistance: my editor, Stephen Stratford; Heather Lindauer and staff at Russell Museum, Russell; Judith Bright and Eddie Sun, Kinder Library, St John's College, Auckland; Marian Nee and Bruce Bolland, Auckland Catholic Diocesan Archives; David Verran and staff at Auckland Research Centre and Special Collections, Auckland Central Library; Elizabeth Ellis, Mitchell Librarian, State Library of New South Wales, Sydney; the Hon. Rick Barker, Minister for Courts; staff at Auckland Art Gallery Library, Auckland War Memorial Museum Library, and Archives New Zealand, Mt Wellington, Auckland and Wellington; National Archives, Kew, London; the British Library, London; Historic Places Trust, Auckland; Bryan Harold, Moa-hunter Books, Ponsonby, Auckland; Kate Martin, Pompallier, Russell; Linda Thomas and Juliet Hawkins, Marion Davis Library, Auckland Hospital; Michael Bassett, Simon Best, Max Cryer, Christopher Johnstone and Nigel Prickett. For permission to reproduce the plan of Kororareka from her 1979 book *Brind of the Bay of Islands*, I thank Mrs J Chisholm, and also Mrs M V Hedges for the re-use of the same item, drawn by Murray V Hedges from the original in the Alexander Turnbull Library, Wellington. I also thank Angela Middleton for permission to quote from her paper, 'Early Nineteenth Century Globalisation: A Maori Response in the Bay of Islands, New Zealand', and David Caughey for allowing me to quote from his paper 'In Search of Samuel Ford 1811–1876'.

Richard Wolfe
April 2005

1

BACK TO THE SEA

ON THE OCEANS OF ABUNDANCE

For this scarcity of animals upon the land, the sea,
however, makes an abundant recompense . . .[1]

Sometime during the Eocene period, about 54 million years ago, a large, furry and hyena-like mammal tested the waters in India, and what followed may qualify as the most remarkable case of an animal returning to its roots. India at that time was an island, yet to connect with the Asian mainland and partly covered by swamps and coastal seas. This enterprising beast, now known as Mesonychid (pronounced *mez-o-nek-id*), found itself increasingly surrounded by water and took the unlikely step of returning to the ocean from which all life had evolved, some 2.5–3.5 billion years earlier.

In the ocean Mesonychid began the first of many gradual changes on the way to what would eventually be recognised as a whale. The early links in this evolutionary chain looked progressively less like terrestrial animals and more like sea creatures. Legs became shorter and paddle-shaped, hooves morphed into flippers, nostrils moved to the top of the snout to allow for more effective breathing at sea, while bodies acquired thick layers of fat or blubber and streamlined forms. Necks became shorter and stiffer and, at the other end, tails grew muscular to provide a powerful form of propulsion.[2]

As Mesonychid adjusted to sea life, dramatic changes were also taking place to its environment. Two super-continents, Gondwana and Laurasia, were partners in what has been described as a 'global elephantine waltz'.[3]

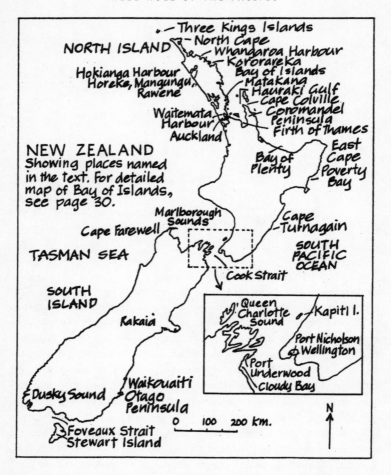

This was no elegant affair; more of a slow-motion bump and grind, as land masses powered by unimaginable momentum ploughed into one another with earth-shattering results. In time, Gondwana broke up to produce Africa, South America, India, Antarctica and Australia, and then about 85 million years ago the Tasman Sea opened up between Australia and New Zealand. The channel between New Zealand's two main islands was then discovered by descendants of Mesonychid and *Basilosaurus*, the southern right whales, which migrate to this country's coasts at the beginning of May each year.[4]

Whales became supremely adapted mammals, at the top of their food chain. As unlikely as it may seem, their closest living relatives remain on dry land and include the cow, camel and hippopotamus. Although they had evolved in the relatively undisturbed environment of the oceans, whales would eventually have to contend with the arrival of another highly developed mammal, and one with an unfair advantage. Their fateful meeting in the Pacific had its origins in January 1769, when Lieutenant James Cook rounded Cape Horn and passed through the Strait of Magellan.

Cook now directed the *Endeavour* north-west across the Pacific towards Tahiti, where he observed the transit of the planet Venus across the face of the sun. He then began his second assignment for the Admiralty, the search for the alleged great southern continent, *Terra Australis Incognita*. On 13 July 1769 the ship left Tahiti, sailing southwards to just beyond the 40th parallel of latitude before gales forced it to turn to the west. By early September there were signs that land was near, among them the sighting of a seal 'a Sleep upon the water'. Cook noted that these 'creators' held their fins in a manner he hadn't seen before, and reckoned they never went 'out of sounding', or far from land. Over the next few days the crew saw increasing amounts of marine life, including a large number of 'Porposes', now identified as southern right whales, followed by more seals, along with seaweed and barnacle-encrusted wood. By 6 October the water was increasingly 'paler than common', although the men could not touch the bottom – or 'find ground' – with 180 fathoms (330 metres) of line.[5]

At 2 p.m. on Saturday 7 October, New Zealand was spotted from the masthead. The *Endeavour* spent two days in what was named Poverty Bay, before sailing south and then beginning an anticlockwise circumnavigation of the North Island. The ship rounded East Cape and crossed the Bay of Plenty, and beyond the Coromandel Peninsula it turned into the Hauraki Gulf and the Firth of Thames. It then sailed north along the east coast, passing the Waitemata Harbour. When fresh gales were encountered further north at Cape Brett, Cook took shelter in a bay some two leagues to the west. The *Endeavour* remained here, anchored at the south-east tip of Motuarohia Island – later known as Roberton Island – from 29 November until 5 December 1769. After some initial skirmishes with the local inhabitants, relations became cordial and trading took place, with Cook recording that some 400 Maori gathered about the ship in their canoes. He saw numerous villages about the bay, with cultivated gardens and grass which sailors went ashore to cut for the *Endeavour*'s sheep. But two crew members who dug up 'potatoies' from a native garden received half a dozen lashes at Cook's order,[6] while three other men got a dozen each for establishing an inauspicious first for the district, being caught in possession of – and under the influence of – alcohol, in this case the ship's rum cask.[7]

This bay offered a good source of fresh water, so all the *Endeavour*'s casks could be filled. The crew also gathered a large quantity of the locally grown 'sellery', an important anti-scurvy measure and part of the on-board breakfast when boiled up with oatmeal and 'portable soup'. Cook named this spot the Bay of Islands on account of the large number of islands which lined its shores, providing 'several safe and commodious harbours where in is room and depth of water sufficient for any number of Shipping'. Although he did not make an accurate survey, he was sure it offered a 'good anchorage' with 'every kind of refreshments for Shipping'. Root crops were not then in season, but fish were in plentiful supply. The crew bought quantities from Maori, including the largest mackerel Cook had ever seen. He observed that the local inhabitants were far more numerous than in any other part of the country he had yet visited, occupying the islands as well as the mainland. And while he saw a number of fortified strongholds, the residents appeared to live in a state of friendship.[8]

On 6 December the *Endeavour* left the Bay of Islands, but not before scraping its bottom on what Cook would call Whale Rock (Te Nunuhe). The ship carried on northwards, around the top of the North Island and down the west coast, and on 15 January it reached a 'very snug' spot to be named Ship Cove in the Marlborough Sounds, at the north-eastern corner of the South Island. It lay within Queen Charlotte Sound, which Cook – its first European visitor – named in honour of the wife of George III. On 31 January 1770, on nearby Motuara Island, Cook took formal possession of the South Island in the name of his King. He established good relations with local Maori, and found plentiful supplies of food, wood and fresh water. It was a safe harbour located in a central position, midway between the Southern Ocean and the Pacific Islands, and would make a good forward base for future explorations.

Refitted and provisioned, the *Endeavour* then negotiated its way between the North and South islands, via a passage that was named Cook Strait. The expedition continued northwards before doubling back at the appropriately named Cape Turnagain and beginning a clockwise circuit of the South Island. Off the south-east coast, further evidence of a rich marine life was sighted, including several whales, seals and a penguin.[9] On 1 April 1770 Cook left New Zealand at Cape Farewell, sailing for the east coast of New Holland (Australia), before heading back to England.

Such was the interest in Cook's exploits that the first printed account of his voyage appeared barely two months after his return home. Published anonymously and preceding the official account by almost two years, it quickly enjoyed a second edition, as well as translations in German and French. The official account, along with those of three other navigators, would be edited by John Hawkesworth, an eminent London author. By the time his three-volume work appeared,[10] Cook was at sea again. Thanks to the success of his first venture, the Admiralty appointed him to lead a second expedition, to circumnavigate the globe as far south as possible to continue investigating the existence of the elusive southern continent. On 13 July 1772, exactly one year after he had stepped ashore from the *Endeavour*, Cook left Plymouth Sound, now captain of the *Resolution*, and accompanied by the *Adventure* under the command of Tobias Furneaux. The two ships headed south, and in January 1773 became the first European vessels known to have crossed the Antarctic Circle.

On 26 March 1773 the *Resolution* anchored in Dusky Sound and the crew now had ample opportunity to experience New Zealand's marine life at close quarters. They soon saw a large number of seals on a nearby rock; Cook noting with satisfaction that one 'afforded us a fresh Meal'. A few days later some of the men in the pinnace – the ship's small boat – killed three more, one now providing 'much sport' in the process. On 13 April they rowed to some other outer islands and killed another fourteen, and could have got many more had they been able to land safely. These animals were found to be 'excellent eating', their flesh being 'not a bit inferior to the finest Beef Stakes'. In addition, seal harslets – the edible viscera including the heart and liver – were considered a good substitute for those of a hog. Assistant naturalist Anders Sparrman, who claimed that liver disagreed with him, suggested that it be braised with cherry sauce, a culinary tip which seems to have been taken up by others. The blubber or 'fatt' from seals – which Sparrman referred to quaintly as 'sea-bears' – was substituted for 'oyle' in lamps, while the skins were used for rigging. And in what would later prove an unfortunate asset, these southern animals had finer skins than their European cousins, resembling those of an otter.[11]

Cook ventured that the human inhabitants of this isolated part of New Zealand would never go hungry, as 'every corner of the bay abounds with fish'.[12] His crew sampled some of its other edible resources at 'Lunchen Cove', so named after a group who dined here on 'Craw fish' (crayfish) beside a pleasant brook under the shade of the trees.[13] In late April the *Resolution* had to leave such tasty attractions behind when it headed to Queen Charlotte Sound for a planned rendezvous with the *Adventure*. Before departing from Dusky Sound, Cook produced a detailed map of the area, which would prove extremely useful to its next influx of visitors – sealers and whalers.

On 7 June Cook left Queen Charlotte Sound for a winter voyage of the Pacific that took in Tahiti and Tonga, which he named the Friendly Isles. He returned to his New Zealand base on 3 November 1773, and three weeks later embarked on a summer voyage, this time an exploratory sweep of the southern latitudes of the Pacific. By the second week of December the lack of any further sightings of seals or penguins led Cook to conclude that those they had seen earlier were natives of New Zealand, or had 'retur[n]ed there when nature made it necessary for them to be on land'.[14] They now saw some larger denizens of the deep, including an 'extraordinary fish of the Whale kind', described as 'about twelve yards long, with an oblong blunt head, on which were two longitudinal furrows, and as many upright ridges. It had small eyes, two semilunar apertures, from whence it occasionally spouted the water, and was mottled all over with white spots.' This 'extraordinary' creature was 'intirely unknown' before, and while some called it a 'Sea Monster' it was probably a sperm whale.[15] By late January 1774 the *Resolution* had crossed the 'Antarctick Polar Circle' for the third time on this voyage, venturing further south than anyone had before, and Cook was now finally certain that no great continent existed.[16]

The *Resolution* reached Spithead, England, on 30 July 1775, just over three years after setting out. As before, such was the interest in the voyage that an anonymous and surreptitious account was published a full eighteen months before Cook's, this bootleg version now confidently dismissing the notion of *Terra Australia Incognita*.[17] Cook's own account appeared in 1777, by which time his third (and final) expedition was well underway. This two-volume publication also proved popular, going to four English editions in 1777 alone, and translations in German, Swedish, Russian and other languages.

Publicity surrounding Cook's explorations drew attention to the rich resources of the southern oceans. During the third voyage his men also saw evidence of whales in the north-east Pacific, with Captain Charles Clerke of the *Discovery* noting the importance of oil extracted from blubber in the diet of the inhabitants of Nootke Sound, Vancouver Island. He described it as 'by no means ill-flavoured or disgusting to the Palate' and purchased some 100 gallons, although for lamp-burning rather than dietary purposes. In a premonition of developments elsewhere in the Pacific, he also recorded that the natives in canoes, armed with bone- and shell-tipped harpoons attached to large buoyant bladders, chased these 'enormous Animals' to exhaustion.

On his first visit, James Cook was impressed by New Zealand's natural features. According to Hawkesworth's account, Joseph Banks, botanist Daniel Solander and 'every other gentleman on board' were of the opinion that all kinds of European plants would flourish in this country. It seemed that people from Europe would also do well there, and with 'a little industry' would soon acquire 'not only the necessities, but the luxuries of life in great abundance'.[18] But before that happened there would be an abundance of another kind.

With the loss of its American colonies following the recent War of Independence, Britain was in need of land for a different form of emigration – that of a troublesome underclass. It determined to establish a penal colony in New South Wales, and the First Fleet of some 300 soldiers and 700 convicts arrived there in 1788. Before long, this programme of transporting undesirables became inextricably linked with whaling. With the intensification of the industry in the Atlantic in the eighteenth century, traditional grounds close to shore had become depleted. British whalers needed to extend their range, but Cape Horn and the Cape of Good Hope represented natural obstacles, while certain areas of ocean beyond were the exclusive economic preserve of the East India Company. Even so, there was little profit in such long journeys without an outgoing trading cargo. But now there was one that was conveniently beyond the control of the East India Company: convicts for New South Wales. When the Third Fleet sailed for that distant human dumping ground in 1791 it included five whalers, among them the *Britannia*, under Thomas Melville. Although he didn't see many whales on the journey out, within half a day's sail of Sydney he reported vast shoals of the animals, visible from midday until after sunset and for as far as he could see from the masthead. Melville unloaded his 'live Lumber' in Sydney as quickly as he could so he could return to the 'fishery', and was closely followed by Eber Bunker in the *William and Ann*. In his first encounter with this new and rich resource, Melville managed to kill seven whales in less than two hours, although a sudden squall prevented him from securing all but two. Despite the weather, he was convinced of the great potential of the local whale fishery.[19] Bunker became the 'Father of Australian whaling', and when he took the *William and Ann* across the Tasman and into Doubtless Bay in 1792 that ship qualified as both the first whaler off the New Zealand coast and the first to make a commercial voyage here.[20]

In that same year Captain William Raven visited Dusky Sound in the *Britannia*, depositing the first sealing gang on the coast of New Zealand. The ship had been charted for a voyage to the Cape of Good Hope via Cape Horn, and on the way left a party of men to collect skins for the lucrative Chinese market. Three years later, and nineteen years after Cook's visit, a second *Endeavour* – an elderly East Indiaman – also came to Dusky Sound. On 19 September 1795, the day after clearing Port Jackson, the crew of this ship found that some forty men and one woman had secreted themselves on board. It turned out that four of them were carpenters and would later prove useful, but the fourth officer's account of the incident suggested that contrary to how it might seem these stowaways had not been intentionally concealed. Already, trans-Tasman shipping was an obvious escape route from the penal colonies of Australia. This *Endeavour* was also plagued by thievery, with even the ship's company under a cloud of suspicion. In the fourth officer's view this hardly set a good example, especially for the unofficial passengers he termed 'Sydnians'. Apart from carrying stowaways and thieves, the ship had the further distinction of being the first shipwreck in New Zealand. But it was less of a wreck and more of a scuttle, for it had developed leaks during a heavy gale in the Tasman and after a survey it was abandoned in Dusky Sound.[21]

Initially, Dusky Sound provided easy pickings for sealers. The trade quickly spread, to the islands in Foveaux Strait, Stewart Island, and the deep harbours perforating the south-western coast of the South Island. The early sealers were mostly from Australian ports, but American vessels began arriving around 1804, and spreading to the Sub-Antarctic Islands. The sealing boom was spectacularly short-lived in New Zealand, rising and collapsing in little more than five seasons, from 1804 to 1809. The total number of known sealing voyages in New Zealand waters before 1800 is only three, while there were seven more before 1805, thirty-six more in the next five years, and – reflecting the decline – only twenty-two more in the decade to 1820.[22] As for the wholesale slaughter of the seals, in 1935 Auckland Museum zoologist Robert Falla suggested there had been 'no more regrettable happening in animal history'.[23]

Transportation to Australia brought individuals who, upon gaining their freedom, might be able to exploit opportunities which brought them to New Zealand. But the growing population back in the penal colony needed a second chaplain, leading to the arrival in March 1794 of Samuel Marsden, who later played a major part in the introduction of organised religion to New Zealand. He was based at Parramatta, some fifteen miles from the main settlement at Sydney Cove in Port Jackson. Morality and punishment were obviously important matters and he drew up what Robert Hughes has described as an 'inspired piece of creative bigotry', a register that classified every woman in the colony, except for a few widows, as either 'married' or 'concubine'. His statistics, which suggested the latter far outnumbered the former, were grossly distorted by his unwillingness to recognise any marriages not performed by the Church of England, and automatically blighted women who married within other faiths.[24] At the same time, moral disapproval of the lower classes made 'prostitution' synonymous with 'cohabitation', and the term was applied judgmentally to extramarital relationships.[25]

In April 1806 the brig *Venus* sailed from Port Jackson for Hobart Town in Van Diemen's Land (Tasmania). From there it continued to Port Dalrymple (now Launceston) in the northern part of the island, intending to sail south to make contact with sealing gangs. Instead, it was taken over by a mutinous crew led by a transported deserter from the Royal Navy. Among the other brigands was one who conformed to the classic pirate image with large earrings and his hair tied back, and two women convicts. One of these was identified as Charlotte Badger, a one-time 'notorious London prostitute' and pickpocket who had been sentenced to seven years' transportation.[26] Having little choice as to where they might now go, the mutineers headed for the relative safety of New Zealand, putting in to the Bay of Islands. Some on board, including the two women, opted for shore life while the *Venus* continued down the coast, carrying two Maori women against their wishes and kidnapping others on the way. These actions would have grave consequences much later, when Bay of Islands Maori avenged the death of one of these women. The fate of the *Venus* is uncertain, although reports reached Port Jackson that it had been captured and burned by Maori who had also eaten her crew. Charlotte Badger may have continued living at the Bay of Islands, but became recognised as 'Australia's woman pirate'. Even then, it seems, enterprising individuals had to cross the Tasman to achieve recognition in their chosen field.[27]

The penal colony of New South Wales was a likely source of labour for the sealing industry which, while not the most desirable form of employment, surely had some advantages over a convict lifestyle. Gangs were dropped off along the southern coasts of New Zealand, often for long periods. One ship involved in that business was the *General Gates*, and in June 1819 a number of convicts were enticed on board at Sydney by its unscrupulous captain, the impressively named Abimelech Riggs. He sailed for the Bay of Islands, where the ship was prepared for a sealing expedition to Dusky Sound. The crew soon found Riggs to be a hard taskmaster, liberal with both the lash and the irons. News that the ship was illegally carrying convicts reached the captain of the British warship *Dromedary*, also in at the Bay of Islands at the time. Although that captain had the power to seize the ship, he thought better of it on the grounds that in this land of potential treachery he could not spare the men. But when some of the convicts revealed the unacceptable recruitment methods employed on the *General Gates*, Riggs was arrested and his ship confiscated. However, by early 1821 he was reported to be back in business, still on the *General Gates* and still using convict labour.[28]

In the decade from 1816 there were 100 sealers 'permanently settled' in New Zealand,[29] but within a few years their once lucrative industry was fished out, a victim of its own initial success. Many of these men turned to the related business of 'shore whaling', based around the southern coasts of the country. Meanwhile, another aspect of the whaling industry would have serious implications for the northern part of New Zealand, with the Bay of Islands about to become its main commercial centre and largest permanent settlement. Perhaps the earliest account of that developing port is found in the first individual book to be devoted to New Zealand, published in 1807.[30] Its author, John Savage, spent two months in the Bay of Islands, and quickly appreciated both the appropriateness of its name and its advantages as a harbour. But he advised ships to be mindful of rocks covered at high-water, and suggested they have a pair of anchors ready in case of gusts of wind. When he arrived on the *Ferrett*, it was surrounded by a large number of canoes, each containing upwards of a dozen Maori. Savage found them friendly or, as he put it, not showing any 'symptom of savage ferocity'. Even so, he advised against allowing them on board until the ship had anchored, for fear that sailors might be distracted. And when they were permitted to do so he recommended that numbers be restricted, and that firearms should be kept handy, in case of any mischief.[31]

Savage was at the Bay of Islands well before any organised European settlement and saw several Maori villages and 'a great number of straggling huts'. Around the Bay were patches of cultivated ground, and the visitors enjoyed some of the local produce, especially potatoes. The soil was obviously highly productive, and Savage determined it to be a 'light vegetable mould'. Even at this early stage there was not much evidence of the original vegetation. The vicinity of the Bay was 'almost destitute of wood', although Savage was aware of 'immense forests' that lay further afield. The local Maori provided the *Ferrett* with ample supplies of seafood, of which Savage considered the oysters especially flavoursome, even if not fit for the London market on account of their irregular shells. There were also other attractive varieties of shellfish which, apart from being welcome additions to the dinner table, would be keenly sought after by keepers of curiosity cabinets.[32] As for larger marine life, Savage correctly predicted the growing importance of the Bay of Islands for the whaling industry on account of its natural resources, safe and capacious harbours, and proximity to the 'fishing' grounds.[33] But he was also mindful of the downside of contact, suggesting that diseases introduced by visiting ships might 'entail misery upon the future population of a healthy and happy country'.[34]

While in New Zealand Savage learned of a fugitive European who had been put on shore for 'mutinous or improper conduct'.[35] This individual avoided all contact with other Europeans, and retreated to the interior of the country when a ship turned up. He appeared to be spoken well of by local Maori, and had adopted their manners and customs. Savage saw his adopted

Maori wife, along with one of their children, who had a Maori complexion and light flaxen hair. It is likely that the father was convict sailor James Cavanagh, who had crossed the Tasman on the New South Wales government brig *Lady Nelson* in 1806. When the ship anchored offshore near the Cavalli Islands to replenish wood and water, Cavanagh abandoned it and fled inland, becoming a Pakeha Maori and the first known European to live in the region of the Bay of Islands.[36] Others would follow, although most were drawn to the growing settlement in the area rather than the prospect of going native in the bush.

Savage had a high opinion of the original New Zealanders, regarding them 'in all respects a superior race of Indians'. He seemed to have colonisation in mind, seeing them as providing a cheaper labour pool than was available in other colonies, and confident they were 'capable of instruction'.[37] But by the time of his visit there was already a history of 'disagreements' between Europeans and Maori. Savage believed that many of these were the result of the new arrivals' sense of superiority, and any cruelty either had experienced at the hands of the other was often in revenge for previous injuries.[38]

The most outrageous of these earlier confrontations between Maori and Europeans had been the massacre of the French navigator Marion du Fresne and twenty-six of his men in 1771 at Te Hue Bay, Bay of Islands, but that would soon be matched by another for viciousness. News of this particular incident was first taken to the outside world by another early visitor to the Bay of Islands, Alexander Berry, who may have also been the first to record the name of its main settlement. It was here, according to Maori history, that a young chief had lain badly wounded in battle, and in an effort to speed his recovery a woman from his tribe brought him a broth made from the flesh of the little blue penguin. He was so taken by this delicacy that he commented in gratitude: 'Ka reka te korora!' ('How sweet is the penguin!') As a result, the bay where that chief was given the restorative elixir became known as Kororareka.[39]

In early March 1809 the trader *City of Edinburgh* under Alexander Berry anchored off Te Puna, the village of chief Te Pahi in the north of the Bay of Islands. Berry went south to Kawakawa, in the 'spar district', to meet chief Tupe and arrange delivery of some timber, which was felled on the banks of a creek several miles beyond the village and rafted back to the ship. Tupe – whom Berry reported was in the possession of muskets and traded with whalers – also guided the *City of Edinburgh* safely to Kororareka, the village of his brother Tara and an excellent and sheltered anchorage. Because the ship had sprung a few leaks, Berry decided that these should be fixed before the voyage out. Aware of the region's reputation for savagery, he was initially nervous about carrying out this work at Kororareka, but repairs were soon underway on the beach.

While this was going on, Tupe and Tara had arranged the construction of a small cottage on the beach for Berry. However, the wary captain preferred to remain on board until the ship had keeled over at an uninhabitable angle. On his first night ashore he was struck by the stillness of the bay, the only sounds were the 'roar of the reef' and the cries of morepork in the bush. When the repairs were complete, celebrations were attended by the crew and local Maori. In a hint of things to come, a mock English duel was fought with pistols on Kororareka Beach, followed by a dramatic Maori fight in which one man was wounded.[40]

In late May 1809 the ship-shape *City of Edinburgh* left for the tropics. But it was back five months later with less sandalwood than planned, so Berry now hoped to top up his cargo with kauri. He decided against entering Whangaroa Harbour, on account of both unfavourable winds and the insistence of Maori on board who feared an attack. He changed course for the Bay of Islands, and back at Kororareka he met up with Tupe and Tara and his request for kauri was quickly attended to. But Berry now began to hear reports of a terrible massacre that had recently taken place at Whangaroa.

While the *City of Edinburgh* was in the tropics, the *Boyd* had arrived at Port Jackson from London, transporting convicts and a detachment of soldiers. It then sailed on for Cape Town, carrying some seventy people and a cargo of coal, whale oil and seal skins, and on the way called in at Whangaroa Harbour for kauri. The captain and some of the crew went ashore to inspect timber, and were set upon and murdered by Maori. The attackers then took over the ship, murdering most of the passengers and crew, and accidentally igniting a gunpowder cask, with further disastrous consequences. The massacre of the *Boyd*, which had been in reprisal for earlier mistreatment of Maori chief George (also known as Tara and Te Ara, and not to be confused with the Kororareka chief), quickly became front-page news in Sydney.

The fate of the *Boyd* and its passengers and crew increased New Zealand's reputation for savagery and treachery. Such incidents were of concern in

Britain, but were hardly confined to this corner of the Pacific. On the Caribbean side of the Central American isthmus was another area whose frightening reputation had been established much earlier. The Bay of Honduras had been settled by shipwrecked English seamen since the 1630s and, like New Zealand, had rich timber resources – in this case, forests of mahogany. These Caribbean coasts were also known as hangouts for pirates and buccaneers and, in 1817, as a consequence of 'grievous Murders and Manslaughters', the British government passed legislation to ensure that those responsible might be tried and punished. The new act recognised that offences had recently been committed in other regions, most notably the South Pacific Ocean, and 'the islands of New Zealand and Otaheite'. The offenders were the masters and crews of British ships, and deserters, whose behaviour had impugned the name and character of British and other European traders. Because of the difficulty of bringing those presumed guilty to trial, such offenders had previously got off free, but now any such miscreant, whether in one of the above-mentioned places, on a British ship (or having quitted it), or on any of His Majesty's 'Islands, Plantations, Colonies, Dominions, Forts or Factories', might – if caught – expect to be tried, judged and punished.[41]

But the outrages continued, and an 1823 House of Commons inquiry into the economy of New South Wales was more specific about the cause and location of such offences. Those most to blame were whalers engaged in the South Sea fisheries, and the place where this 'violent and unpunished outrage' most frequently resulted in 'savage and indiscriminate revenge' was New Zealand. This particular report was concerned with the economic repercussions of such incidents, noting that the 'outrages' committed by the crews of vessels and the 'spirit of vengeance' that followed had caused a decline in trading activities in the South Pacific. The situation in New Zealand was made worse by the supply of firearms, 'instruments of destruction' which fed the 'warlike and hostile spirit of the native tribes towards each other'. Maori enthusiasm for acquiring such weapons put them in a powerful bargaining position: no food would be traded unless guns were part of the deal. The report also recognised the influence of another important group of Europeans who had recently settled in New Zealand – the missionaries. It was suggested that if these gentlemen were to encourage Maori to cultivate their land so that they might see the practical benefits of the arts of civilisation and commerce, they might be turned away from the pursuits of war and plunder.[42]

Before long, the first significant European settlement in New Zealand began acquiring a certain reputation. To a large extent this was inevitable, given its location and the sort of individuals it attracted. But while Kororareka most certainly did become a boisterous sailor town, on one level the goings-on here could hardly compare with those encouraged in other places across the Tasman. The first and worst of these was a penal settlement founded in 1821 on Tasmania's west coast. This prison, on a small island in the middle of an almost inaccessible and gale-swept Macquarie Harbour, was selected by the British government to provide new levels of terror for the most unmanageable of its convicts. Men lived and died there like animals, at the hands of whip-wielding overseers. It quickly became known as 'Hell's Gates', and for ten years was said to be 'the worst spot in the English-speaking world'. Some prisoners managed to escape, but those who did mostly perished or were recaptured and hung. A few also met their fates at the hands of their desperate companions, being murdered and even eaten on the run. But Macquarie Harbour was not alone: Port Arthur in south Tasmania was established as a settlement for male convicts in 1833 and quickly earned its own reputation as 'hell on earth'.[43] Those who managed to get away from such places might hope for some sort of relief among the sealing gangs camped around Bass Strait, between Tasmania and the mainland. Robert Hughes described the members of those scattered communities as 'the scum of the System, escaped convicts gone wild on a bitter shore'. Here, desperate and lawless bolters from society had formed 'bloody, troglodytic island colonies', taking black women from their tribes for sex and for their skill at catching seals.[44]

In 1823 the House of Commons committee of inquiry heard that the lawlessness in New Zealand and New South Wales was not helped by the lack of an effective symbol of British authority, such as a ship of war. Later that year such a vessel was dispatched, but by another country with an interest in the South Pacific.[45] France was now also considering the establishment of a penal colony, and Louis Isadore Duperrey was sent on the twelve-gun corvette *Coquille* to investigate such possibilities. His second-in-command was Jules Sébastien César Dumont d'Urville, who would eventually make three visits to the Bay of Islands. The first was on 3 April 1824 when the

Coquille was greeted by large numbers of local Maori. On his return to France d'Urville recommended that penal colonies be established in both West Australia and New Zealand, but any such plans were now forestalled by Britain's initiatives. In the meantime d'Urville planned his own voyage of exploration, and the *Coquille* – now renamed *Astrolabe* – departed from Toulon in April 1826.

While an increasing number of visitors were coming to the Bay of Islands, traditional Maori life continued, now absorbing new and influential elements into the local culture. The most obvious and dramatic of these was the musket, which may have been first used in battle here around 1807. Tribal alliances were changeable and military campaigns complex, involving many different events, hapu and groups interconnected by marriage. Another new influence – and additional source of conflict – was access to trading posts where European goods could be exchanged for Maori produce. Local agriculture enjoyed a spectacular growth to satisfy the new demand, with missionary Samuel Marsden estimating a ten-fold increase in production from 1814–15 and 1819, thanks mainly to the introduction of iron tools.[46]

Although Cook had described a peaceful situation at the Bay of Islands in 1769, territory was probably already changing hands through regular campaigns and conquests. Waimate, inland from Kerikeri, was one such fought-over area, with its fertile soil and rich fish and bird resources. These conflicts redistributed the population of the Bay of Islands, generally eastwards. Marsden saw dramatic evidence of this in 1819 in the form of once strongly fortified villages that now lay uninhabited. Concurrent with these battles were external wars, with invasions by war parties from the south, part of an extensive history of aggression between Northland tribes and Ngati Paoa of Tamaki–Hauraki and Ngati Maru of Hauraki–Thames. Such hostile expeditions were inevitably followed by reprisals for the obligatory utu.[47]

Matters came to a head in 1826 when Paroa, some thirteen kilometres south-east of Kororareka, was attacked and destroyed by an alliance of people from Waimate–Kerikeri. This had previously been a popular anchorage, but Kororareka was now favoured by shipping, having the added advantage of the protective presence of the mission across at Paihia.[48] It was during this unsettled period that Dumont d'Urville made his second visit, the *Astrolabe* entering the Bay of Islands on 12 March 1827 and mooring near the same spot it had occupied three years earlier as the *Coquille*. D'Urville was surprised that no canoes came out to meet him on this occasion, until he realised that the Bay had been wracked by warfare. He noted that the pa near Paroa – which he had seen in 1824 – was now abandoned. To avoid trouble during his week-long stay he required all contact between sailors and Maori to be kept to a minimum. However, he was aware that upwards of fifteen women visited the ship every day, being brought on board and distributed by a chief who also took payment for their services. '[W]hether they liked it or not' these young women were passed 'on to everyone in turn', and the captain also noted that many of the men suffered 'terrible consequences' as a result of such activities.[49]

Canoes also came alongside the *Astrolabe* offering potatoes and vegetables, but would now accept only gunpowder in exchange. D'Urville noted the detrimental effect that contact with whaling crews and other undesirable types had had already on the Maori population. He learned much about the Maori from the English missionaries, although he felt the latter gentlemen would be better off applying their efforts somewhere else, perhaps further south. While his crew went ashore – ostensibly to wash their clothes – d'Urville went pig-hunting for fresh pork and admired the region from a vantage point. He saw a great future for this harbour as a result of the development of New South Wales, and suggested it would rate behind only the Hauraki Gulf and Cook Strait in terms of places visited by Pacific shipping. It would in fact become second-to-none in terms of New Zealand ports, and among the many captains who made return visits was Dumont d'Urville himself.[50]

2

A DARK BENIGHTED LAND

MUSKET SHOTS ACROSS THE BAY

Within these two months we have seen a comet and felt the
shock of an earthquake.[1]

Phillip King, lieutenant-governor of the penal colony of Norfolk Island, had
high hopes for a locally grown plant. He envisaged an industry based on flax
fibre, able to supply the huge maritime demand for ropes and canvas. Aware
of both the abundance and the use to which the same plant was put in New
Zealand, in 1793 King authorised the kidnapping of two young Maori men,
Tuki Tahua and Ngahuruhuru, from the Cavalli Islands, north of the Bay of
Islands. They were taken to Norfolk Island with the intention of training
convicts in the art of flax processing. But the plan failed because of a division
of labour in Maori society; the preparation of flax was regarded as women's
work and so the two co-opted men knew nothing about it. But King did not
give up, and soon had another suggestion for a likely labour pool for his
planned industry. In 1805 he noted that a large number of whaling ships had
visited the Bay of Islands during the previous four years, and to his knowledge
there had been no altercations with Maori. This seemed to augur well for that
part of the country becoming a safe and reliable port for whalers. As well as
obtaining wood and water, King suggested these men might also barter for
large quantities of processed flax. Then, if provided with suitable machines,
and when not occupied with whaling, they could convert the fibre into rope.
Mindful of conditions on board ships, the enterprising governor even

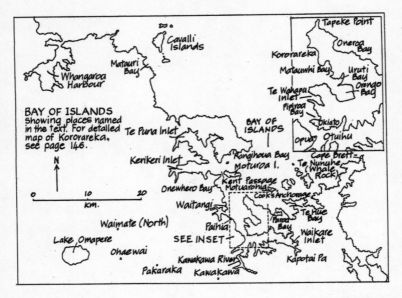

BAY OF ISLANDS
Showing places named in the text. For detailed map of Kororareka, see page 146.

suggested that the leakage of whale oil would not be a problem. In fact, it would be an advantage, adding further to the strength of the rope.[2]

Other early Maori contacts with European shipping were more voluntary than those of Tuki Tahua and Ngahuruhuru. In 1805 the New South Wales government vessel *Lady Nelson* sought shelter in the Bay of Islands, and Nga Puhi chief Te Pahi was able to sail to Norfolk Island with his four sons. From there they went on to Sydney, where Te Pahi met Samuel Marsden. Encouraged by the success of recent missionary endeavours in Tahiti, the ambitious Marsden now turned his mind to the challenge presented by the indigenous population of New Zealand.

There was little early support for Marsden's plans for putting New Zealanders on the road to spiritual enlightenment. In addition to reports of the wild nature of their country, there was a feeling that these people were beyond all hope when it came to matters of religion and morality. A safe alternative to exposing missionaries and their families to the dangers of cannibalism and treachery in New Zealand was to bring Maori to New South Wales. Marsden therefore established a seminary on an estate of about 100 acres at Parramatta, to instruct young men in 'various labours of the garden and the field', and by 1815 he had eleven individuals in his care.[3]

Te Pahi was the first influential Maori leader to visit New South Wales, and in 1806 returned home to Rangihoua on the north-eastern shore of the Bay of Islands, bearing gifts from Marsden. Along with fruit trees, pigs and fowls, he brought an invitation for other Maori to be sent across to acquire skills at the missionary establishment. But hopes for this planned alliance were short-lived, for Te Pahi was accused of responsibility for the massacre of the *Boyd*'s crew and passengers, a suspicion that was encouraged by Tara, chief of Kororareka, whose settlement was a rival anchorage to Te Puna. In a retaliatory attack on Te Pahi's island by crews of whaling ships, the chief was wounded, but escaped. But he was further wounded in later fighting between his people and those of Whangaroa, also caused by the *Boyd* affair, and died in 1810. Marsden's plans for New Zealand would now be delayed until he could obtain the necessary protection for his settlement.

In 1805 Te Pahi's nephew Ruatara had sailed from the Bay of Islands, crewing on the whaleship *Argo* to Sydney. From there he spent some six months in the South Sea fisheries on the *Albion*, and in 1807 travelled on the sealer *Santa Anna* to Norfolk Island. Here he endured a longer stay than intended, and when his ship eventually turned up it took him and its valuable cargo of seal skins on to England. Ruatara was disappointed in his hope to meet King George III, and was given a return passage to New Zealand on a ship taking convicts to New South Wales. Also on board was Marsden, who had been putting his case for establishing a New Zealand mission to his employers at the Church Missionary Society in London. Marsden took a personal interest in Ruatara, who by this stage was extremely ill, having suffered at the hands of European sailors. When the ship reached Sydney in February 1810 the reverend arranged for Ruatara to stay for several months at Parramatta, where he received agricultural instruction and other 'useful knowledge'.[4] Ruatara now offered to provide the much-needed protection for a mission station at Rangihoua, where he returned in 1812.

Unable to get leave of absence from the governor to travel to New Zealand, in June 1814 Marsden sent his assistants, the 'lay settlers' Thomas Kendall and William Hall, to view prospects for a mission station at the Bay of Islands. They travelled on the *Active*, under Captain Peter Dillon, a man who would later prove more of a hindrance than a help to the missionaries. On this occasion he was under Marsden's instructions that the main object of the voyage was to promote friendly relations with Maori. But there was a strong commercial component, for to help defray expenses Dillon was allowed to bring back as much flax as he could, along with any available spars, timber, pork, salted fish and rosin. Potatoes were also on the list, in which case the captain was instructed to bring them back in flax baskets, for they kept better that way. But there was to be no private trade with Maori and, in particular, no women were to be allowed on board. Instead, this voyage was 'for a particular object'.[5]

At the Bay of Islands Kendall and Hall met Ruatara at his 'principal hipwah [pa], or town, called Ranghee Hoo'.[6] They were also welcomed by chief Tara at his residence at 'Korreorahrekka', on the other side of the Bay. Kendall was presented with baskets of potatoes, and observed local villagers planting the next season's crop.[7] But he had a lucky escape as the *Active* was setting sail for Port Jackson, he was seated 'incautiously' on a 'closet' structure on deck when the main boom swung around and knocked him overboard. He couldn't swim, but fortunately Maori quickly rescued him from a 'watery grave'. Acknowledging that his life had been preserved through the 'kind instrumentality' of New Zealanders, Kendall now wished that the remainder of his life might be spent in 'humble endeavours to promote the Glory of God' among them.[8] But instead, his own moral character underwent progressive deterioration, leading to his suspension from the mission.

The *Active* returned safely to Port Jackson with encouraging reports. Far from molesting the visitors, the 'rude natives' had been extremely hospitable, and appeared delighted by the prospect of Europeans settling among them. Kendall and Hall reported on the 'beautifully picturesque' nature of that part of the country, blessed also with a soil that 'only required the hand of cultivation to produce every thing in the greatest abundance'. The climate was described as 'salubrious and inviting', and although it was mid-winter the only significant difference the visitors noticed was a 'few refreshing showers, which gave a mellow and vernal softness to the fields'.[9]

With Ruatara's support, Marsden could now begin planning his mission station in earnest. His hope was to 'erect the standard of Christ's kingdom' and to 'hear the sacred trumpet sound the glad tidings of salvation' in this country, the 'great Emporium of the South-Sea Islanders'.[10] This glorious undertaking would be made all the more easier by the purchase of the *Active*, intended to ensure both the safety and welfare of the missionaries, while operating as a coastal trader in New Zealand and collecting natural resources to take to the market in New South Wales.[11] Marsden also had the welfare of whalers in mind, believing that with the establishment of mission stations they would be safe when putting in to New Zealand for supplies. He now advised them against going to Port Jackson, where they were almost certain to be ruined from 'dangerous connections'. He believed it would be to the whaling industry's advantage if it assisted the mission in New Zealand.[12] But if he had hoped for the whalers' moral support he would have been gravely disappointed, for their ships brought commodities and sought services that were in total conflict with his lofty aims.

Apart from what he described as 'the unfortunate business of the *Boyd*', Marsden was concerned with 'customary predations' made by European vessels at the Bay of Islands. Such visitors were known for insulting and injuring Maori, and for seizing and carrying them off, both males and females. As a result, in 1814 Marsden succeeded in persuading Lachlan Macquarie, Governor of New South Wales, to require visiting British ships to obtain permission before any natives could be removed from the district or any sailors or others could land in that country. This permission was needed in writing, from both the local chief – or chiefs – and Thomas Kendall, who was sworn in as a magistrate. Macquarie also gave power and authority to Ruatara, Hongi Hika and Koro Koro, to assist Kendall in carrying out such duties. The official government order identified the three as Dewaterra, Shungie and Korra Korra, and advised that any offenders would be submitted to the 'utmost rigour of the law'.[13] Although Kendall did act on occasions in this capacity as New Zealand's first magistrate, his powers were for the most part nominal. Historian William Pember Reeves suggested that the granting of authority to the three Maori chiefs might have been an attempt to 'induce them not to eat' the fourth (European) member of this country's pioneering judiciary.[14]

With leave finally granted, Marsden made his first visit to New Zealand in December 1814. Also on board the *Active* on this voyage was John Lediard Nicholas, who decided to venture to this country because of his interest in its manners and customs.[15] Altogether the ship carried thirty-five persons, including two Maori crew and two from Tahiti, along with missionaries and their families, and eight Maori, among them the now authoritative figures of Ruatara, Hongi Hika and Koro Koro. There was also a 'heterogenous collection' of livestock and poultry that Nicholas suggested might bear a 'perfect resemblance to Noah's ark'.[16] Before their departure from Sydney, another ship arrived bringing pearl shells, pork and news that missionaries were succeeding in bringing civilisation to Tahiti.[17] But if Marsden was encouraged by such progress he faced a more immediate challenge. No sooner had the *Active* left port than a gale and heavy swell caused all those on board, including 'bipeds and quadrupeds' and 'brute species', to be violently seasick. Marsden suffered worse than most from 'convulsive retchings', while Kendall had the added discomfort of losing his wig over the rail while relieving his stomach.[18] Everywhere on deck were scenes of 'disgusting nastiness', but the queasy Marsden could not help marvelling at the intestinal strength of the Maori passengers, who regained their appetites and took with a 'voracious eagerness' to the tub containing the cook's slops.[19]

When they reached the entrance to the Bay of Islands, Nicholas was overwhelmed by the 'varied beauties of the scene' before him. Swelling rocks seemed to 'frown on the convulsions of the elements', while a Maori settlement and canoes in the harbour added to this 'extraordinary assemblage of views'.[20] Marsden followed Ruatara's knowledge of the harbour's hazards to bring the ship safely alongside the chief's residence at Rangihoua. Going ashore, Nicholas discovered gardens that looked more like the work of Chinese than 'cultivated barbarians'.[21] But it was the locals' turn to be astonished when the *Active*'s live cargo of cows and horses was landed, especially when Marsden gave a practical demonstration of riding one of the latter on the beach.[22]

Christmas Day 1814, also a Sunday, saw the voice of 'revealed religion' publicly raised in New Zealand for the first time. From a reading desk improvised from planks and an old canoe, Marsden addressed a congregation of Europeans and 'their dark fellow-creatures'.[23] This landmark sermon was delivered at Oihi Bay, a cove on the north-east side of Rangihoua Bay and to the east of Ruatara's pa, and now marked by the six-metre high Marsden Cross. On the morning of that first Sabbath observed in New Zealand, Marsden interpreted the fluttering English flag as 'the signal and the dawn of civilisation, liberty and religion, in that dark and benighted land'.[24] He now hoped that its inhabitants would soon 'shake off the shackles of superstition and barbarism, and render themselves worthy of ranking in the list of civilised nations'.[25]

With the spiritual foundations in place, the next step was the practical business of building the mission station. On Boxing Day the *Active* sailed south to the 'timber district' at Kawakawa, and Marsden, Kendall and Nicholas took a boat to visit Tara, at 'Corroradikee'. Nicholas described the chief as being at least seventy years of age, of cheerful disposition, and having only one eye. He welcomed them with a meal of sweet potatoes, and the visitors saw his crop of wheat raised from seed provided by missionaries on their previous visit.[26] They also saw one of his wives, a beauty familiar to visiting English sailors as a procuress, and therefore known as Mrs Goshore. Among other things she had a good grasp of English, having lived on board with the master of a Port Jackson ship for several weeks, and it was obvious that Tara preferred her and her 'fondling assiduities' to his older head wife.[27]

During Ruatara's absence in Sydney one of his wives had been seduced by a local tribal member who had sailed on British ships. Nicholas wondered why the missionaries weren't more concerned about the bad influence of sailors, a 'profligate class' and 'disgrace of the British nation'. For the moment Marsden was preoccupied with the dispensing of justice to the individual who had offended his friend and protector. When asked what sort of punishment would be appropriate, the reverend suggested a flogging with a cat-o'-nine-tails and, 'leaning to the side of mercy', recommended 'only' twenty lashes. In the event the adulterer got thirty but may have been grateful, for his crime normally attracted the death penalty.[28] Shipping was also responsible for 'the most wretched spectacle' Nicholas had ever seen. Two convicts, who had earlier stowed away on a vessel from Port Jackson bound for England, made their escape at the Bay. Recaptured and delivered to the *Active*, which had just arrived on its first visit, they preferred their chances of living among Maori to the fate that awaited them back across the Tasman. They escaped again, but their delusions of grandeur and unwillingness to work made them unpopular among the local population. Fearing for their safety they opted out of tribal life and sought the refuge of a cave, where they existed mainly on fern root. Before long the enfeebled and emaciated pair thought better of life on the run, and gave themselves up. In Nicholas' view, these 'walking spectres . . . bespoke the very last extremes of human misery'.[29]

Marsden and his entourage noticed that Maori women at the Bay of Islands who had had previous contact with crews of European ships no longer appeared timid or retiring. In fact, Nicholas felt their 'significant glances' suggested how much they desired what he termed 'a more intimate acquaintance'.[30] One who had enjoyed plenty of the latter was a 'damsel' named Mary, who had previously dispensed 'unlimited favours' among visiting Europeans. Marsden prohibited her from carrying out what Nicholas appropriately described as 'any intercourse' with the *Active*. Unable to trade her charms with sailors, this 'frail wench' believed that jealousy on the part of the missionaries' wives was the reason for her banishment.[31]

The site chosen for the mission at Rangihoua was steep but had the advantage of being among a friendly Maori population. Nicholas considered there were better locations, suggesting the neighbourhood of Lake Omapere to the south-west as an 'admirable situation for the seat of government, and chief town of the colony'. Mindful of the social problems such a settlement might face, he recommended that potential colonists should not be like the convict population of New South Wales, the 'most profligate and abandoned description of people in existence', who, he feared, would contaminate the morals of Maori and instruct them in 'the most depraved practices'.[32] Such concerns seemed justified, for on this voyage the *Active* had carried a convict stowaway, a 'worthless individual' whose provocation of a Maori resident at the Bay of Islands was about to lead to an exchange involving 'tremendous bludgeons' when Nicholas intervened.[33] The consequences of association with European shipping were now increasingly apparent, with Kendall noting that young Maori women were learning to curse and swear, while many had also contracted diseases, some perishing 'for want of knowing a remedy'.[34]

Upon Te Pahi's death in 1810 Ruatara became chief of Te Puna. He had previously spent some five months studying European agricultural practices at Parramatta, and been the recipient of numerous gifts as an inducement to provide the protection sought by the planned mission station. He returned to the Bay of Islands on 22 December 1814 to give his support, but a little over two months later he was dead. Noticing that the chief appeared to have a raging fever and heavy cold, John Nicholas recommended a 'dose of rheubarb'. The patient took it willingly, but to no avail. During another of his visits to the chief Nicholas obtained samples of a blue pigment Maori used for decorative purposes. He took it back to England where it was identified as manganese, the extraction of which became an important industry in the

Bay of Islands in the 1870s following the demise of the whaling trade.[35]

Despite the death of Ruatara, work proceeded at Rangihoua. It was a hive of industry, with William Hall soon having six pairs of sawyers at work, and sending some 4000 feet of 12 x 3 inch planks to Port Jackson to be sold by Marsden to support the mission.[36] The settlement also had blacksmiths' shops, and a school which opened in August 1816 with thirty-three pupils, aged from seven to seventeen and including orphans, slaves and several sons of chiefs. In an early report on progress Kendall wrote that his 'little wild pupils were all noise and play' with their 'incessant shouting, singing and dancing'. A decade later they were subjected to their first annual examinations, achieving 'highly satisfactory' results.[37]

Four years after the establishment of the mission station at Rangihoua, a second was opened some eight miles to the south-west at Kerikeri, in territory controlled by Hongi Hika. The Reverend John Butler was put in charge, and soon became aware of the practices of that powerful Nga Puhi chief. In October 1821 he sent the Church of England Missionary Society a description of his locality and its inhabitants that was anything but encouraging. He wrote: 'New Zealand is covered over with fern, weeds, brush, and woods; and the natives are covered with lice and filth to the last degree, and withal, a proud, savage, obstinate, and cruel race of cannibals.'[38]

Some months earlier, in March 1820, Thomas Kendall had gone to England with Hongi Hika and his nephew Waikato and had conferred with Professor Lee at Cambridge, establishing the grammar and vocabulary of the Maori language on 'scientific principles'. This increased understanding led to the gradual acceptance of modern spelling of words and place names that the early missionaries had struggled to commit to a written form. A 'new orthography' was announced about 1830, whereby the earlier interpretations of Kiddeekiddee, Pyhea, Rangheehoo, Wytanghee, Cowa Cowa and Korrorareka were now more recognisable as Kerikeri, Paihia, Rangihoua, Waitangi, Kauakaua and Kororarika, while the last two names still awaited a further slight transformation into Kawakawa and Kororareka.[39]

In 1823 the ranks of the Christian soldiers at the Bay of Islands increased with the appointment of thirty-year-old Henry Williams to take over the running of the missions. He sailed from England with his wife Marianne and three children, and was accompanied on the last leg from Sydney by Samuel Marsden, now on his fourth visit to the Bay of Islands. The missionary community would shortly increase further, for Marianne was six months' pregnant. The Williams family had an early hint of the challenges that lay ahead, for as they arrived at the Bay their ship had a narrow escape after striking a sunken rock. Safely ashore, Henry observed his 'new countrymen' and their 'reddled bodies and bushy hair', while Marianne described the Maori employed by the mission to row the boats as 'fine, intelligent, active looking lads', when compared to the 'sleepy, degraded and disgusting looking natives' she had seen at Port Jackson.[40] And while she had heard 'many dismaying accounts of the past ferocious conduct of the natives', she felt no cause for her future safety. Her greatest concern was for the young Maori women, whose condition was 'degraded indeed', for '[m]any are the evils, besides the rage for muskets and powder, which arise from the frequent arrival of European vessels'.[41] Another local practice that gained her disapproval was polygamy, and when a young chief called at the Williams residence with a second partner they refused to receive her, inflexibly 'acknowledging but one wife'.[42]

With the arrival of Henry Williams, a third mission station was established at Paihia, on the western shoreline of the Bay of Islands, across the bay from Kororareka. One of Williams' early tasks here was the construction of the mission ship *Herald*, the launch taking place on 24 January 1826 and attracting more than fifty war canoes and an estimated 1000 Maori. The completion of this vessel enabled the missionaries to overcome their previous 'humiliating dependence' on the carrying services provided by the loose-living whalers.[43] When Dumont d'Urville visited the Bay the following year he observed a dramatic contrast between the English missionaries' small and frail *Herald*, with its peaceful and pious passengers, and the war canoes of the Maori, with their bloodthirsty crews seemingly intent on death and destruction.[44] On one return visit from Port Jackson on the mission ship, Henry Williams described the welcoming appearance of his 'little cottage': the 'moon shone bright . . . the bay was calm . . . and the natives were rejoicing on all sides'. Inside, his wife had a fire going, and supper was ready.[45]

But things were not so settled outside. There was increasing intertribal tension, fuelled by firearms, which had now become the most desirable article of trade with Europeans. In 1825 missionary George Clarke arrived at Kerikeri and opened a school for Maori children, and soon became aware of this new challenge. He wrote: 'The great and grand cry of the natives is who will supply us with muskets, lead and powder . . . For a musket a New Zealander will make great sacrifices, he will labour hard and fare hard for many months to obtain his musket, in fact it is his idol he values it above all he possesses, he will not only part with his slaves for one, but even prostitute his children to diseased sailor [sic] for one of those instruments of destruction.'[46] Following one incident involving firearms, Henry Williams went to Waitangi and found Waikato showing off his weapon to another chief. Observing that it was loaded, Williams attempted to half-cock it but managed instead to touch the wrong trigger. It discharged, just missing the head of the admirer. The startled missionary realised that had the man been shot, his own earthly duties would surely have ended right there. But as he put it: 'Thus does the Lord shew us ever to commit our way to him, and he will sustain us; for we are unable to help ourselves, or to tell what an hour may bring forth.'[47]

In March 1826 the Williams family in the Bay of Islands was extended further by the arrival of Henry's younger brother William, to take charge of the boys' school at Paihia. His wife Jane acknowledged the Lord's help in guiding them 'across the mighty deep' to their new land, and preserving them when they got there: 'Those who go down to the sea in ships do indeed see the wonders of the Lord.'[48] As for the Bay itself, William saw barren hills covered 'only with fern' but did concede that parts were 'picturesque and beautiful'. A rare bright spot was the arrival of a ship with the prospect of mail from 'dear old England', and in September 1826 the patiently waiting Jane Williams was disappointed to find that a new arrival was 'only from Port Jackson'. Another turned up the following day, and hoping this one might 'bring glad tidings from a far country' she was mortified to find that it was the *Emily*, under the command of one Captain Brind, and neither from nor bound for England. It wasn't just the lack of mail that upset Jane Williams, but the presence of Captain William Darby Brind.[49] He had 'enjoyed' a lengthy association with the Bay of Islands, and the missionaries would no doubt consider it appropriate that his surname rhymed with 'sinned'. They had a somewhat ambivalent attitude towards him, regarding him as both a help and a hindrance, for while they took a very dim view of the whalers' way of life, they were largely dependent on this contact. On occasions whaling ships were the missionaries' only link with the outside world, and so carried letters and reports – which regularly condemned the messengers – back to the

Church Missionary Society in London, along with their usual cargoes of whalebone and oil.

Brind had been born in Birmingham, England, in 1794. He went to sea on whaling ships at an early age, and came to the Bay of Islands as master on the *Cumberland* in March 1820. During frequent return visits he took a fancy to some of the district's more attractive features, one of which was Matauwhi Bay, immediately to the south of Kororareka. It lay in the domain of the chief Pomare, who welcomed Brind to the district and offered him one of his daughters as a wife.[50] Such liaisons between men of rank – chiefs and whaling masters – were not uncommon, and this particular one continued for at least six years. Another relationship associated with Matauwhi Bay, and one that was at least blessed with missionary approval, was the first Christian marriage in New Zealand, solemnised here in 1823 between Danish seaman Philip Tapsell and Nga Puhi mission girl Maria Ringa. The ceremony was conducted by Thomas Kendall, but not before he insisted on baptising the bride-to-be. It was the first baptism of a Maori, but it offered no firm foundation for marriage for she deserted the groom soon after the service.[51]

During his second visit to the Bay of Islands in 1827, Dumont d'Urville detected changes at the Maori village in Matauwhi Bay. Huts had previously been scattered widely about the slope of the promontory, but they were now grouped together at the foot of the hill near the shore and surrounded by a strongly fortified palisade. D'Urville put this down to recent disturbances, and the need to be able to resist surprise attacks. The chief Pomare had been killed in battle the previous year, and was succeeded by his nephew, Pomare II, who d'Urville saw holding his double-barrelled gun, this weapon having taken over from muskets, axes and knives as the most highly prized trade item.[52]

The challenges facing missionaries in the Bay of Islands steadily increased during the late 1820s. By now they suspected that the main motive for Hongi Hika's visit to Britain had been to increase his means of conquest over his fellow countrymen. Back at the Bay there were reports that Maori were now treating settlers with contempt, stripping ships' boats, breaking down garden fences and stealing tools for repairing their guns.[53] Another setback was an outbreak of whooping cough which caused deaths among local children, both European and Maori. In reporting a great mortality rate among Maori, missionary James Hamlin at the Waimate station regretted that many of the victims had 'rushed into eternity without any hope whatsoever'. There were also declining roles at the school, blamed both on the unsettled state of the local tribes and the European ships anchored off their settlement.[54]

By November 1826 Henry Williams began holding church services at Kororareka, openly acknowledging the sailors there as 'a bad set'. As he put it: 'It is with pain we see them coming near us.' Another irritation was that only a small number bothered attending, and those that did mostly arrived late. He hoped to counter the 'most deplorable' influence from the ships, which were 'wholly given up to iniquity from the captain to the cabin boy'.[55] Shipboard activities were a concern for the Williams household for another reason. In December 1826 Marianne lost the services of a useful domestic assistant, who had been taken away to go on to the ships. 'As soon as the girls become useful they are carried off', and the reward for this 'iniquity' was greater than the mission could afford to pay for their services.[56]

Earlier that year the Bay of Islands was visited by the *Rosanna* under Captain James Herd, sent by the first New Zealand Company to bring settlers. The expedition then called at Hokianga where land was purchased, but the intending settlers were sufficiently deterred by the activities of the local Maori to stay on board and cross to Sydney. One of them, Scots blacksmith Alexander Gray, decided to stay on at Kororareka, and was later joined by others, all tradesmen or 'mechanics'. As opposed to the itinerant types who had passed through during the previous twenty years or so, Gray may qualify as Kororareka's first permanent resident, settling there in 1827.[57]

In January that year Henry and William Williams went to investigate the arrival of a suspicious ship and found it was the brig *Wellington* from Port Jackson. Originally bound for Norfolk Island, it carried convicts who had risen up and imprisoned the crew, and the missionaries were now dismayed at finding a 'nest of pirates' on their doorstep. In Marianne Williams' view the native New Zealanders were 'quite amiable beings by comparison'. But when the pirate 'captain' confronted two other ships in the Bay – the whalers *Harriet* and *The Sisters* – they fired shots into the *Wellington* and law and order was soon restored. As Marianne Williams wrote: 'these wretches [were] checked in their career of mischief'.[58]

With the shift of their headquarters from Rangihoua to Paihia in 1827 the missionaries were uncomfortably close to the whalers' preferred anchorage. One morning Henry Williams was disgusted to observe a girl who had recently been living at the mission station now returning to shore from Captain Dillon's ship, and carrying a musket for services rendered. To make matters worse, that afternoon the same girl was seen resorting to the annoying Captain Brind's vessel.[59] Much as Williams found Brind acting 'with all civility', and grateful as he was for the carrying service he provided – in 1834 he took a cracked church bell back to England for repairs[60] – Williams maintained a dim view of the captain's 'infamous conduct'.[61] The missionaries conveniently overlooked the fact that whalers spent lengthy periods at sea, and looked forward to enjoying female company on shore. The married missionaries, at least, were not required to endure such lengthy periods of abstinence, as suggested by the number of their own offspring. In this regard, the growing mission families would soon be faced with having to decide where to send their children for their education. If they thought Kororareka was a haunt of wickedness and immorality, they conceded it had little on Port Jackson. William Williams had an 'utmost horror of that place', where the best class of society was 'degraded in the extreme with very few exceptions'. What's more, he would not entrust a child to any of the families there – even those who professed religion.[62] Samuel Marsden probably agreed, for upon his return to Port Jackson after one of his visits to New Zealand he described this country as 'the land of Goshen' and likened the one on the other side of the Tasman to 'the darkest part of the land of Egypt'.[63]

In all, Samuel Marsden made seven visits to his missions in New Zealand from his base at Parramatta. On the sixth of these, in 1830, he offered a spiritual comparison between the two settlements of Paihia and Kororareka, symbolically opposing one another across the western arm of the Bay of Islands. He reported: 'The contrast between the east and the west side of the Bay was very striking, though only two miles distant: the east shore was crowded with different Tribes of fighting men, in a wild, savage state, many of them nearly naked, and, when exercising, entirely so: nothing was to be heard but the firing of muskets, and the din and confusion of a savage military camp; some mourning the death of their friends, others suffering from their wounds; and not one but whose mind was involved in Heathen Darkness, without one ray of Divine Knowledge. On the West Side, there was the pleasing sound of the "Church-going bell"; the natives assembling together for Divine Worship, clean, orderly, and decently dressed, most of them in European clothing: they were carrying in their hands, the Litany, and the greater part of the Church Service, with the Hymns, written in their own language . . . Their whole conduct, and the general appearance of the Settlement, reminded me of a well-regulated English Country Parish. In the Chapel, the Natives behaved with the greatest propriety, and joined in the Church Service. Here might be viewed, at one glance, the blessings of the Christian Religion, and the miseries of Heathenism, with respect to the present life: but when we direct our thoughts into the Eternal World, how infinite is the difference!'[64]

Musket shots regularly rang out across the bay and the dutiful missionaries would row over from Paihia and attempt to ascertain what was going on. In March 1830 William Williams and Captain King of the *Royal Sovereign* investigated the latest disturbance at Kororareka and encountered two opposing tribal groups intent on war. Williams tried in vain to distract the sides from fighting, and fortunately hostilities did soon cease. He spoke to the combatants, who – he claimed – acknowledged 'the correctness of his arguments' and admitted they had been 'urged to this madness by Satan', but not before some thirty people had been killed and another seventy wounded. The casualties were now brought on board the *Royal Sovereign* and lay about 'in a mangled state' while the surgeon attended to them. Hostilities continued the next day, when Williams was awoken at dawn by more musket shots at Kororareka. That afternoon he saw houses on fire in the settlement, and canoes departing in all directions. Shortly, Samuel Marsden arrived, discovering his missionaries in 'considerable agitation' and large numbers of Maori 'up in arms against one another'. In an early form of shuttle diplomacy, Marsden and Williams were well received by both sides, finding war canoes ready for action at one camp and managing to persuade their owners against proceeding.[65]

That particular conflict was quickly blamed on Captain Brind, who had sailed into the Bay on the *Toward Castle* in February 1830. A quarrel had broken out on board between young Maori women of rank from different local tribes, and the decision to settle the matter on land led to all-out warfare on Kororareka Beach. The incident that sparked the conflict involved two young Ngai Taweke women, Pehi and Moewaka, the daughters of Hongi and Rewa respectively. The pair were having a playful fight in the water off Kororareka Beach with other young women from Ngati Manu – who now controlled the prized trading port – when things turned nasty. The wife of local chief Kiwikiwi supported the Ngati Manu women and cursed those from Ngai Taweke. This came to the attention of Nga Puhi chief Ururoa, who raised a war party to attack Kororareka pa on 5 March, and was joined by Titore of Ngati Rehia. The important Ngati Rehia chief Hengi was shot and killed in the fighting, and the situation remained tense until 17 March when the missionaries managed to get the two warring sides to discuss peace terms. An agreement was reached whereby Titore took Kororareka as utu for the death of Hengi, dividing up the land between himself and other chiefs, including Rewa, Moka and Ururoa. Kiwikiwi and his allies gave up possession of Kororareka, and he and Pomare II took their people to Pomare's pa at Otuihu. Not surprisingly, the conflict became known as 'The Girls' War', and was the last serious war in the Bay of Islands for a decade and a half.[66] The fighting had been 'all within hearing and in view' of the missionary settlement across the bay at Paihia and, in the words of Henry Williams, it all began with 'two ship-girls fighting on Kororareka beach. Behold how great a matter a little fire kindleth!'[67]

Another and less quarrelsome passenger on the *Toward Castle* during that fateful visit to Kororareka was sailing master Peter Bays. After surviving the wreck of the whaler *Minerva* on a reef in the Tonga group the previous September, he had been picked up by Brind and brought to the Bay of Islands, where he stayed for nearly two months. Immediately upon his arrival, his ship – and all others then at anchor – were so 'full of girls' to the extent that they were 'a continual pest'. He at least admired their aquatic skills, for they appeared not to be hindered in the slightest by their woven flax skirts, which he estimated would weigh no less than twenty pounds when wet. Every evening these 'Venuses' were to be seen swimming around the ships 'like so many seals', and washing themselves 'preparatory to going to bed'. The main point of this was to remove their anointments of fish oil, which was favoured by Maori men but detested by their European paramours.[68]

Bays was aware of the battle that had taken place earlier, and his own account was the 'united testimony of different persons'. It was his understanding that it had been fought between chiefs Kiwikwi and Pomare 'of the beach tribe' and Ururoa, while chiefs Rewa and Titore were present and remained neutral. Although it had been reported by an 'enemy of Captain —' (Bays omitted the name, but it was no doubt Brind) that the said

'Captain —' had offered muskets and powder to Rewa so he might avenge the insult given to his daughter, Bays felt it was an internal quarrel, and that Brind, whom he described as 'a brother and a companion', could not be blamed. Bays reviewed the battle with the comment, 'Behold how great a fire a small spark has kindled', which suggests he had been sharing notes with Henry Williams.[69] But he also provided the most appalling descriptions of the carnage on the beach, where some victims were still to be seen. He saw one who had been disinterred and burned, as though he had been 'a dead dog dragged out of a ditch'.[70]

As for Kororareka itself, Bays found it 'wretched and filthy' and with 'little form or regularity'. Each chief had an allotment of ground fenced in with 'eight or ten feet paling' which enclosed his own and other lesser huts.[71] Bays may have been the first to record the description for which that settlement would soon become famous, a result of a Maori girl wishing to quit the Paihia mission school so she could cross to Kororareka and join others on board the ships. The missionaries vainly attempted to dissuade her, and told her that if she was determined to go to 'hell' – in the after-life sense – then that was her business. When she duly turned up on the ships she advised that the missionaries called Kororareka 'hell', whereupon the sailors responded in kind and likened Paihia to 'heaven'. Bays also referred to that resort of sailors and ship-girls as 'hell-side'.[72]

Captain Brind had left Kororareka on the *Toward Castle* on 20 February, and Bays sailed for England five weeks later on the *Royal Sovereign*. But such was the unsettled state of things that for reasons of safety all the other ships departed at the same time: the *Anne* for the whaling ground, the *India* for New Brunswick, and the *Elizabeth* and the *Woodford* to other parts of the Bay to complete taking on water.[73]

It was from chief Rewa and his relatives that the missionaries were able to acquire land for their new church at Kororareka in 1834. And while they did not approve of Brind they were presumably happy to accept his two donations to the building fund for £2 and £4. In that same year Brind also acquired the land at Matauwhi Bay he had been living on by arrangement, obtaining some 600 acres in exchange for four double-barrelled guns and a substantial supply of gunpowder. In keeping with current practice, the extent of Brind's land purchase – from Rewa – was largely defined by natural features. The northern boundary was prescribed by lining up Mr Williams' house across at Paihia with Mill Island, the small island just offshore from the southern end of Kororareka. Brind's existing house on his Matauwhi Bay property was replaced in 1836 by a grander residence, built by trader Gilbert Mair, perhaps using the timber d'Urville had seen there nine years earlier.[74]

Back at sea, profits from cargoes taken to England enabled Brind to buy his own ship, the barque *Narwhal*. He also took a wife and continued his whaling voyages, but he posed another problem for the missionaries when he had a relationship with Rewa's daughter Moewaka. She had sailed with the captain, and in the late 1830s gave birth to a child. But this branch of the Brind family tree came to a tragic end, with Moewaka dying and the daughter being murdered in 1841 during the brutal attack on the Roberton household at Motuarohia Island by the young Bay of Islands chief Maketu.[75]

Crowds gathered on Kororareka Beach in October 1831 when Cyrille-Pierre-Théodore Laplace arrived in the corvette *La Favorite*. British officials were especially interested in this visitor, wondering if France was planning to take possession of the Bay of Islands – or perhaps the whole of the country. Laplace was advised that the region was already 'enjoying' a modest degree of protection by Britain, but his presence did at least hasten its colonisation by that country. Maori swarmed over the quarterdeck of *La Favorite*, insisting on bartering for such sought-after supplies as musket balls and powder.[76] The French captain accused local Maori of being robbers and thieves, and preoccupied with the acquisition of firearms.[77]

He also observed the behaviour of the local women, and how his men succumbed to the seductions of the 'attractive ladies of Kororareka'.[78] Those who were unmarried he compared to the Sirens of antiquity, enticing the sailors with lurid dances on the beaches.[79] Weather permitting, and 'bereft of all superfluous clothing', they would swim out to the ships and happily sell their favours in exchange for muskets and powder. After dinner the Frenchmen would make for the beach, ostensibly to fish, but in fact in eager anticipation of the local maidens. The Sirens appeared, again mostly undressed, whereupon all thoughts of fishing were abandoned. Much mingling ensued, with men and women disappearing behind the bushes. Higher-born women were said to be able to claim better-class sailors, whom they lured to the shady banks of a stream, a spot 'perfectly suited for any amorous tryst'.[80] But some trysts went unrequited, for sailors encountered women who pocketed their expected presents and offered nothing in return.

Laplace detected that these women tended to be distinguished by their superior beauty, and were already committed to whaling captains or officers who would later return to continue the arrangement. The French captain wistfully wished that such a system whereby women were sworn to remain faithful operated in his own country.[81]

Laplace visited Pomare at his pa at Otuihu, finding the chief an impressive figure with his lofty stature, long unkempt hair, and an eighteen-inch greenstone club. The Frenchman also considered the conditions here repulsive – far worse than Kororareka – and was pleased to leave.[82] When *La Favorite* left the Bay of Islands on 11 October, it carried a parting gift of potatoes and two pigs from chief Rewa. Despite the ship grazing a sandbank and rocks off Tapeka Point, Laplace felt that ships' captains would enjoy greater security at Kororareka than anywhere else, thanks mainly to the missionaries. This was a surprising admission given his criticism of some of their practices, such as their land dealings and apparent unwillingness to come to the assistance of his own sick sailors. In Laplace's opinion, the main concern for visiting ships was the consequence of the charms of its beautiful women. Some of his men took away painful memories in the form of an earlier European import, venereal disease. Once safely out into the open sea, *La Favorite* turned towards Valparaiso, 3000 leagues to the east, and no doubt more of the same.[83]

Samuel Marsden's plan to establish his mission at Rangihoua had been able to proceed with Ruatara's promise of protection. Tara had also been keen that his site at Kororareka be chosen, and we might now speculate on the outcome had Marsden preferred that option. Such a decision would have brought the missionaries into direct and daily contact with habits and practices that ran counter to their aims. For their own sake, it was probably better that they were at some slight remove from the main seat of the 'crime'. Their separate enclave at Rangihoua, and later at Paihia, could offer an alternative way of life and example, for those who cared to notice. Had they been based at Kororareka they would have been even more aware of the enormity, perhaps hopelessness, of their task. Even so, there could be no escape, for on a calm night they would have gained a very good idea of what went on in that alleged hell-hole across the water.

In 1819, while baptising nine children born in New Zealand, Marsden acknowledged the young mission's debt to 'His over-riding Providence which led the British nation to establish a colony in New South Wales'. Building on this transportation of those lost souls, He had now 'sent His Gospel to the very ends of the earth; and the Trumpet of the Jubilee has been sounded from pole to pole'.[84] The indefatigable Henry Williams was also quick to see the hand of God in their successes. We might wonder if either missionary suspected divine intervention in another earthly challenge that lay ahead: the arrival of agents of a competing faith.

3

ART AND SCIENCE

WITH CHRONOMETERS AND WATERCOLOURS

The whole view is any thing but picturesque, and there is little to meet the eye except bare hills and extensive sheets of water.[1]

From the early 1800s ships called at the Bay of Islands in steadily increasing numbers. Most were attracted by the refreshments on offer, while others came more out of necessity – which might have entailed evading the law. James Cook, the first known European visitor to this part of New Zealand, came in the name of science and exploration. Others followed with similar intentions, and even if this area was of no particular interest to them they might make some general – and mostly unfavourable – observations. Among them was one of the most famous scientists of all, on an expedition which also included two artists who left their impressions of the Bay.

Between its rediscovery and 'civilising' by Europe, New Zealand went through what was described as an 'anarchic' phase.[2] One who was here during this colourful period was 'wandering artist' Augustus Earle, distinguished as the first independent, professionally trained artist to visit each of the five continents and record his experiences. Born in London in 1793, he had begun exhibiting by the age of twenty-one, and in 1818 left England for six years in the Americas. From Rio de Janeiro he sailed for the Cape of Good Hope, intending to proceed to Calcutta, but he ended up instead on the island of Tristan da Cunha. He was rescued from there by a ship bound for Van Diemen's Land, and after reaching Australia he continued his wanderings eastwards, arriving in New Zealand in late 1827.

He crossed the Tasman on the *Governor Macquarie*, which also carried Wesleyan missionaries to the Hokianga. The ship negotiated the treacherous harbour bar and the party landed at Horeke, which Earle recorded phonetically as 'E.O. Racky'.[3] From there he paddled a canoe some nine miles, probably up the Waihou River which drains into the upper reaches of the Hokianga Harbour, before beginning the 'pedestrian' leg of his journey, across to the Bay of Islands on the east coast. He trudged through forests so thick 'that the light of heaven could not penetrate the trees', and over an extensive fern-covered plain.

At sunset Earle's party reached the Church Missionary Society settlement of Kerikeri where he found a 'complete little English village' with such cheering sights as smoking chimneys and fattened cattle in the fields. But so much for memories of home: he pushed on in a borrowed boat and reached Kororareka around midnight.[4]

Earle found Koroareka Beach a 'most delightful' spot situated between two picturesque promontories, consisting of a collection of huts and houses of both Maori and English construction. In his view the residents themselves fell into three distinct categories, the most respectable being the 'Scotch mechanics', the men from the *Rosanna* who had settled here a few months earlier. They included blacksmith Alexander Gray in his 'sooty mansion', and sawyers at their pitsaw producing neat piles of planks on the beach. Then there were those Earle termed 'Beach Rangers', both useless and dangerous and mostly from whaleships, having either deserted or been forcibly expelled for crimes that would otherwise attract the death penalty. Completing this sociological survey, Kororareka's third group consisted of runaway convicts from New South Wales, distinguished by their 'downcast and sneaking looks' and vicious natures – especially when in possession of liquor.[5]

In complete contrast was the scene Earle encountered on the opposite shore, at the Church Missionary Society settlement at Paihia. Here, with a view of the beach and the 'clear and blue expanse of water speckled over with fertile islands', lived the 'comfortable teachers of the Gospel'. Earle had little enthusiasm for the resident reverends, who allegedly gave him a frosty reception.[6] He also took a whaleboat to Rangihoua, finding a 'complete picture of English comfort, content, and prosperity'. He had looked forward to a hearty welcome and Christmas greetings from his 'secluded countrymen' in these distant regions, but claims he was offered nothing. Even as his party approached the shore, the missionaries withdrew to their houses, closing their gates and doors behind them. Earle claims they gazed at him through their windows, and for the three days he was at their settlement they didn't speak a word to him.[7]

Earle believed the missionaries despised all who pursued 'worldly wealth' and saw whalers as the enemy interfering with the spiritual interests of 'their flock'. Not surprisingly, there was little sympathy between missionaries and whalers, for 'the cold formality of one excite[d] the contempt and disgust of the other'. The artist could see little good resulting from the missionaries' efforts, and didn't know of anyone who had been converted by them.[8] Further, he was of the opinion that the local Maori were not rigorous observers of the Sabbath as was presumed: they merely got up and did several hours work before the Europeans emerged from their traditional Sunday lie-ins.[9]

As an artist Earle may have had grounds for accusing the missionaries of having no taste for the picturesque, as in their insistence on putting Maori pupils into bulky and 'uncouth' garments.[10] But those gentlemen had similarly uncomplimentary views of Earle and his friendly relations with the whaling crews. William Williams accused him of 'living in connection with a native woman', and no less a colleague than the charitable Charles Darwin felt that the missionaries had actually treated Earle with 'far more civility than his open licentiousness could have reason to suspect'.[11]

Earle's visit to Kororareka was at a time of increasing intertribal hostilities. In March 1827 Dumont d'Urville observed a war party from Kororareka heading south for Hauraki to seek utu for the dead Pomare. Earle now saw a fleet of victorious war canoes returning with grisly 'quantities of plunder', including human flesh, and saw victims' heads skewered on poles for public display.[12] The artist was in the thick of several dramatic events, as when the house he was staying in caught fire. The situation was not helped by the wind fanning the flames, which spread to a seventy-gallon cask of rum. Some of Earle's personal property was pillaged by Maori, and after the fire had subsided a missionary made him 'a cold offer of assistance'.[13] Near Kororareka, Earle saw the body of a female slave being prepared for the 'native oven'. Later, he and Captain Duke of *The Sisters* returned to the spot with spades and removed it for a decent burial elsewhere.[14]

When Earle arrived at Kororareka there were two ships at anchor near the beach, and he understood there were sometimes as many as twelve or thirteen.[15] Five whaleships turned up during his stay, and he believed that many more would have done so but for the lack of regulations and the likelihood of trouble. Some held out until Port Jackson, despite the higher costs of supplies at that port.[16] The importance of shipping to local Maori was made apparent when upwards of sixty armed and exasperated Maori pursued an individual who took shelter in Earle's house. He advised the chief Te Whareumu, also known as 'King George', that if this man was killed the Europeans and their ships would leave Kororareka and not return. The men began to make good this threat by loading goods on to a whaler in the harbour, causing the chiefs to relent and promise that if the Europeans remained the fugitive would go unmolested.[17]

The highly opinionated painter produced a number of views in and around Kororareka, the best known is *The Meeting of the Artist with the Wounded Chief Hongi, Bay of Islands*, November 1827.[18] In this romanticised scene the wounded Nga Puhi chief Hongi Hika is attended by his wife and daughter against a background of dramatic rock formations and war canoes drawn up on the beach. However, the focus of this painting was not the wounded chief, but the artist himself, sitting and regaling Hongi and his entourage. Another itinerant, Captain Peter Dillon, was in the Bay at the time, and he recorded that Hongi's wound was 'singular', the result of a bullet through the lungs. It had produced a hole in both his breast and back, through which the wind issued 'with a noise resembling in some degree that from the safety valve of a steam engine'. Dillon also added that Hongi himself derived some 'merriment' from these sound effects.[19] While he maintained his warlike carriage it was obvious the chief could not last for long, and he died the following year.

Although he was well aware of the potential for lawlessness, Earle considered New Zealand a most desirable spot for a colony. The climate was 'infinitely superior' to Sydney's, without the 'feverish heats' and 'long pestilential winds' he had endured across the Tasman.[20] Nevertheless, after leaving New Zealand, Earle spent several months in Sydney before returning to England, his wanderings then taking in the Caroline Islands, Guam, Manila, Singapore, Madras, Mauritius and St Helena. In late 1829 he arranged the publication of his views of Sydney, Tristan da Cunha and New Zealand,

and two years later was on the move again, as draughtsman on a ship bound for the South Atlantic.

The HMS *Beagle* left England on 31 December 1831 to circumnavigate the globe and survey the southern coast of South America. Augustus Earle was now thirty-eight years old and relatively aged when compared to others on board, especially naturalist Charles Darwin (twenty-two) and Captain Robert FitzRoy (twenty-six). Fourteen years later FitzRoy would play a pivotal role in the fate of Kororareka, but he was now preparing for a historic voyage, packing no fewer than twenty-two chronometers in the hope of clarifying some of the conflicting measurements of longitude.[21]

When the expedition reached South America, Earle was forced to resign through ill health. He returned to London, where he died in 1838, and was replaced by another accomplished artist. Conrad Martens was born in London in 1801 and left England in 1833, and while in Rio de Janeiro he heard that the *Beagle* needed a replacement artist. He travelled to Montevideo to meet the ship and was duly appointed. But FitzRoy, who had earlier bought an additional ship for survey work at his own expense, was soon running short of funds. He was forced to sell the vessel and dismiss the crew, and Martens was among those signed off at Valparaiso. In early December 1834 he went to Tahiti and then on to Sydney, spending five days at the Bay of Islands on the way. His first impressions on arrival there on 4 April 1835 were hardly promising, likening the 'grey, dull, and sombre' landscape to what he'd seen earlier at Tierra del Fuego. He described Kororareka as 'an assemblage of some 50 or 60 huts' made of wattled reeds, and saw their gloominess reflected in the character of the local Maori population, as compared with the cheerful Tahitians he had met. He reckoned there were some 1000 Europeans scattered about this 'out of the way place', most operating grog-shops or stores to supply the shipping. The Bay was frequented by sailors who were 'subject to no kind of restraint' when ashore, but Martens did encounter a few 'respectable' types. Among them was British Resident James Busby, who he felt did little to justify his salary of £500 per annum.[22] Conrad Martens' pictorial record of Kororareka included a watercolour view from offshore, with Maori canoes in the foreground. On 9 April the artist sailed for Sydney, where he settled and later painted a more ambitious interpretation of the Bay of Islands, this time in oils. This view looked out across the harbour, its focus a small group of Maori on a foreground hill above a picturesque tree trunk. It included a number of distant ships and reflected Martens' increasing interest in capturing luminous and atmospheric effects.[23]

The *Beagle* entered the Bay of Islands on the morning of 21 December 1835 to find three whaling ships at anchor and the occasional canoe crossing the harbour. Charles Darwin detected an air of 'extreme quietness', and made another unfavourable comparison with the 'joyful and boisterous' welcome the ship had received some five weeks earlier in Tahiti. The naturalist noted the surrounding country was 'clothed with coarse pasture' that gave it a 'desolate' appearance that reminded him too of parts of South America. He also found it difficult terrain for traversing on foot, and an alternative route around the beach was not much easier.[24]

Darwin estimated a population of 200–300 English people in the vicinity of the Bay of Islands, their mostly neat and white-washed cottages were in stark contrast to the small and 'filthy hovels' of the Maori.[25] He was comforted by signs that English civilisation had taken hold, such as gardens of roses, honeysuckle and jasmine, and sweetbriar hedges in front of houses at Paihia. He visited Waimate with William Williams and saw other familiar plants, including asparagus, currants, hops, gorse and oak trees, in what appeared to be a model English village, where servant girls reminded him of dairy maids.[26] But at Kororareka he concluded that while the Maori residents appeared 'superior in energy', they were of a 'much lower order' than the Tahitians.[27] On another outing Darwin ventured southwards up the Kawakawa River to Waiomio where he saw limestone outcrops resembling 'ruined castles'. He was unable to inspect these formations on account of their use as sacred Maori burial places, but twelve years later curiosity got the better of him and he wrote to Governor George Grey suggesting that excavation would reveal bones of animals contemporary with the moa, the recently discovered extinct flightless bird.[28] Darwin did not take much in the way of either scientific material or favourable impressions from New Zealand when the *Beagle* slipped out of the Bay on 30 December. He was pleased to leave this country whose English residents were mostly 'the very refuse of society'.[29] One redeeming feature had been Waimate and its Christian community: he had enjoyed a pre-Christmas family gathering at the house of William Williams. Darwin had never seen a 'nicer or more merry group', despite its location in the centre of 'the land of cannibalism, murder, and all atrocious crimes'.[30] While in Kororareka, Darwin, FitzRoy and officers of the *Beagle* donated a total of £15 to the fund for building a new church. There was a certain irony in this generosity, for with the publication of his landmark book *The Origin of Species* a quarter of a century later, Darwin offered a theory that would rock the very foundations of Christianity.

Two weeks after leaving the Bay of Islands Darwin was once again proud to be an Englishman. In Sydney he saw a 'magnificent testimony to the power of the British nation' with its broad streets, large houses and well-stocked shops. But what impressed him most was the settlement's rapid growth – it then had a population of 23,000 – and the opportunities it offered for great personal wealth. He heard of a 'convict auctioneer' who was planning to return 'home' with his recently acquired fortune of £100,000. That was probably Abraham Polack, brother of a well-known Kororareka resident.[31] But as impressive as Sydney's rapid development was, Darwin was not sad to leave Australia either. On 14 March 1836 the *Beagle* sailed from King George Sound, in West Australia, and he wrote: 'Farewell, Australia! You are a rising child, and doubtless some day will reign a great princess in the South: but you are too great and ambitious for affection, yet not great enough for respect.'[32] To put things in perspective, Darwin's negative remarks regarding Australia and New Zealand were probably coloured by his keenness to get back to England after more than four years at sea.[33]

Four years after the *Beagle's* visit, another scientific mission made its way towards New Zealand from the south-east corner of the Pacific. Lieutenant Charles C Wilkes, in charge of the United States Exploring Expedition, encountered the whaleship *America*, which was thirty-five days out from New Zealand and bound for New York with a full cargo of 3500 barrels of oil. Although the ship was 'very leaky' the captain claimed his crew were in good spirits, but Wilkes had rarely seen such an uncombed and dirty set of mariners, and was not surprised that scurvy was still known to afflict crews of whaling ships.[34] Going via Samoa and Sydney, Wilkes' expedition headed south and, after demonstrating the existence of an Antarctic continent, visited the Bay of Islands.[35] The lieutenant was disappointed to find it wasn't the place of 'unsurpassed beauty' he had expected, but he did concede that some 'fine views' were to be had from the elevated ridges. And like several who had already passed this way, he saw a resemblance in its black islets and worn rocks to the landscape at Tierra del Fuego.[36]

Wilkes described Kororareka as a collection of shanties and tents, and learned that it was known as 'Blackguard Beach' on account of its resident vagabonds, runaway sailors and convicts.[37] His arrival there in early 1840 coincided with a ceremony preliminary to the signing of the Treaty of Waitangi, a document which he suggested was understood by few of the Maori chiefs. He saw it as a 'disastrous circumstance', and one that would also greatly disadvantage American interests. Recently introduced laws now prevented non-British subjects from holding property in New Zealand, while duties and charges discouraged American whalers from using the country's ports. Another undesirable effect of the new British authority that came to the American's attention was rising prices. One of his own crewmen was Maori, originally from the Bay of Islands, and he now sought a canoe to go ashore at Kororareka. His fellow countrymen charged him $3 for the service; Wilkes considered that even half a dollar would have been 'exorbitant'.[38]

Other scientists who came to the Bay of Islands included Ernst Dieffenbach, members of the *Erebus* and *Terror* expeditions under the command of Captain James Clark Ross, and – much later – Thomas Henry Huxley, who became a close friend and ardent supporter of Charles Darwin. In addition to these visitors it was estimated that in the spring of 1840 there were 100 American whalers on the New Zealand coast.[39] Charles Wilkes conceded that the arrival of these ships might be seen as 'a blight upon a dawning civilisation' and was aware that his country's 'tars' were frequently considered 'worthless reprobates'. But he looked forward to the day when American ships might carry, 'on every breeze, to the ports and islands of the Pacific', examples that would promote the three great causes of 'morality, religion and temperance'.[40] With the possible exception of the second, there had not yet been much evidence of these at Kororareka.

4

INTEMPERATE TIMES

ON THE TIDE OF DELETERIOUS SPIRITS

Now, the tall ships, tossed up to heaven,
High on the mountain-wave appear;
Then down the steep abyss are driven,
While every heart dissolves in fear.

The seamen seem like drunken men;
They reel and stagger to and fro;
And all their wonted skill is vain,
To save them from the depths below.[1]

When the New Zealand Company was promoting its first settlements in 1839, it conceded that the country was already 'partially colonised' by a certain type of Englishman. Among the 2000 or so such settlers, there were 'several hundred' of a 'most worthless class', made up of runaway sailors, escaped convicts, keepers of grog-shops and 'other vagabonds of dissolute habits'. Less permanent, by definition, were the 'temporary sojourners', the crews of whaling and trading ships, and their behaviour also left much to be desired. New Zealand Company secretary John Ward claimed that there was scarcely a harbour not 'infested with lawless Englishmen of one class or another'. These arrivals not only encouraged the natural vices of the Maori but taught them new ones, introducing suspect business practices, diseases and a taste for alcohol. For this reason he labelled them the 'Devil's missionaries'.[2]

According to one account, by 1825 a few Europeans had 'peaceably' settled in the inlets around the Maori village of Kororareka, attracted by the trade that followed the shipping to its deep-water beach.[3] But the settlement would become somewhat less 'peaceable' with the opening of its first grog-shop in the early 1830s. That event did not, of course, represent Kororareka's first taste of the beverage with which it would soon become synonymous. While the settlement probably led the country in consumption, in 1835 it could also claim another first – for production – when local resident and trader Joel Polack built a brewery. He used hops from Sydney to produce what he styled as the country's 'first foreign manufacture', which was intended not just to slake thirsts but to stem the tide of 'deleterious spirits'.[4]

The liquor industry was the stimulus behind some early citizens' organisations at Kororareka. In 1833, when there were some 300 adult Europeans settled in the Bay of Islands, a number of the more civic-minded – or perhaps self-interested – inhabitants drew up rules that might encourage some sort of law and order. Those who sold liquor, and therefore had a vested interest in the excesses of the visiting sailors, realised that there could be too much of a good thing. If Kororareka's already colourful reputation were to extend further, whaling captains might prefer to call elsewhere, and trade generally would suffer. Local grog-sellers also agreed not to undercut one another – averting what might have been New Zealand's first price war – for such a practice would only promote excessive drinking. This organisation was short-lived, and the next one formed in Kororareka had a much narrower aim when it came to alcohol – attempting to stamp it out altogether.[5]

Back in 1815 missionary Thomas Kendall had claimed that Maori were 'averse to drinking spirits', which was not something he could say of himself.[6] But within a decade or so, any resistance to alcohol at Kororareka was under threat, with on-shore grog-shops now supplementing the alcohol available on board ships. The *Missionary Register* of 1833 reported that in Britain some four-fifths of all 'CRIMES' were committed 'under the excitement of liquor' and more than one half of the country's 'MADNESS' was 'occasioned by drinking', so there could be little hope for this corner of the antipodes.[7] The Rev. William Yate now observed that the 'poor unhappy natives connected with that dreadful place, Kororarika' had not only taken to drinking ardent spirits, but were also acting as national distributors. The Europeans were hardly setting a good example, and none less so than the local blacksmith.

Henry Williams was disgusted that two years earlier this man who had 'made a great profession of religion' was now seen carried through the town 'insensible from intoxication'. Flags fluttered outside grog-shops on Kororareka Beach 'bidding welcome to all who would enter therein'. Local Maori referred to these places as the 'ware karakia' of Satan, where his followers assembled to do him honour. Alcohol was now found uncomfortably close to the very people the missionaries were attempting to rescue from such evils. Chief Rewa's house was next to a public house kept by an Englishman, where Williams reported there were 'generally 20 or 30 drunken sailors rolling about'. And while this behaviour was ridiculed by Maori, he lamented that they too were now acquiring a 'relish' for the practice.[8] He also knew of large numbers of 'poor deluded females' who had been taken by their parents and masters on board ships at both Kororareka and Otuihu 'for the sake of sordid gain'.[9] But at least Williams had the satisfaction in 1832 of observing a Maori boy praying to be 'preserved from the evil communication of the shipping', and would soon be able to report that several young women who had previously 'congregated at Kororarika for the worst purposes' had been taken in by the mission.[10]

Some visitors to Kororareka were more convinced of the missionaries' effectiveness than Augustus Earle had been, and their morale-boosting testimonials were published in the *Missionary Register*. American sealing captain Benjamin Morrell, who had been operating in the Sub-Antarctic Islands south of New Zealand, came to the Bay in the early 1830s and claimed there had been significant changes. The place had once been inhabited by 'wild and ferocious cannibals' but, thanks to the labours of the missionaries, that element had been tamed, and they were now 'civilized, friendly, hospitable, and anxious to do good to others'. Among other improvements Morrell claimed that filthiness had given way to personal cleanliness, while idolatry had been replaced by 'the pure and undefiled religion of the Gospel'.[11] Another mariner with a similarly positive outlook was Captain Jacob of the East India Company, who arrived at Paihia on 9 February 1833. The next day being Sunday, he awoke to one of the most 'delightful Sabbaths' he had ever spent. The church was completely filled with Maori, and he never saw a 'more attentive, orderly and devout Congregation, even in a Christian country': the organ was almost drowned out by the 'full burst' of native worshippers uniting in the praises of God. But it was a very different story across at Kororareka. There, within hearing and sight of a church service, were scenes of 'immorality and vice', including two boatloads of European whalers in a state of 'brutal intoxication'.[12]

Muskets and gunpowder were now in growing demand among local tribes, and Henry Williams warned that any whaling captains who engaged in this trade would 'certainly stand charged with murder . . . in the Great Day of Account'. Compliance with this missionary request could be problematic, for while some captains claimed they would gladly not deal in such goods, such a stand might prevent them from being able to obtain other essential supplies.[13] But by 1834 Williams suggested that the musket was falling into 'disuse' and people were adopting 'more peaceable habits'. He alleged that men were now choosing to carry the Scripture in place of cartridge belts, and instead of polishing guns they could be seen 'under the shade of a tree, reading the Gospel'.[14]

As bad as Kororareka was, or was alleged to be, it might claim that it was never able to realise its full potential for lawlessness or wickedness. As Augustus Earle had noted in 1827, some captains mindful of its reputation preferred to avoid the place altogether and hold out for Port Jackson. Three years later, Captain Cattlin – whose name is immortalised by the Catlins (sic) district in South Otago – elected not to bring the whaler *Australian* into Kororareka and face any complications his men might cause. Instead, he traded for provisions at sea with the *Thetis*, which had been gone twelve months from London and had 600 barrels of oil on board, and had conveniently just stocked up at the Bay of Islands.[15]

From the early 1830s the Paihia-based missionaries had come across and preached in Kororareka, holding services in both Maori and English, and in the open air and local houses. It was now decided that the town should have a church of its own, and in late November 1834 Henry Williams inspected a suitable piece of land at the south-east corner of the settlement. He duly arranged the purchase of four and a half acres from several local chiefs, including Rewa, on behalf of the Church Missionary Society.[16] Donations were then called for, the initial plan was for a chapel measuring forty by twenty feet, but before long it was referred to as a church and its dimensions had increased to fifty by thirty feet.[17] The list of donors included local residents and visitors with such familiar names as James Busby, Joel Polack, Captain Brind, Benjamin Turner, Gilbert Mair and family, and Captain James

Clendon. The missionaries were included, along with the 'Children of W. Williams' and seven members of the Fairburn family, while some benefactors, such as 'a Friend to the Cause', 'A Little Girl' and 'A Friend', preferred anonymity. A number of donors were visitors from ships, among them Jas Brown on the brig *Harmony*, Captain Crozier and the officers of HMS *Victor*, and, as we have seen, Captain FitzRoy and men from HMS *Beagle*.

The church was located on an existing burial ground. First to be interred here was local grog-seller John Poyner: when he died in 1835 the fee for his burial went into the building fund, and while his earthly trade was considered counterproductive to the missionaries' cause, his posthumous contribution was much appreciated, even if he now lies in an unmarked grave. Construction of the church began in 1835, undertaken by Gilbert Mair and supervised by Henry Williams and catechist Charles Baker, and it was in use by the end of that year. In Low Church style, without a steeple and topped by a hipped roof, the structure was surely a visible sign of progress.[18] But irregular attendances were a problem, the result of what Henry Williams identified as a conflict of interests, for many locals felt that their craft was 'endangered by the preaching of the Gospel'.[19] Apart from religious duties the new facility also served as a local community hall, hosting the first meeting of the Temperance Society on 11 March 1836. That organisation aimed to promote 'peace, order, and sobriety', but history does not appear to have recorded how many abstemious citizens turned up to support what was surely a lost cause.[20]

In 1834 Kororareka was visited by 'Regency buck' Edward Markham.[21] Born in Yorkshire in 1801, he received little in the way of education, which was probably the reason his exploits in New Zealand remained unpublished – and unpublishable – until 1963, nearly a century after his death. He wrote in an ungrammatical manner with a highly original approach to punctuation and spelling, while the content was equally colourful. The missionaries might have been eternally grateful that Markham's book did not appear during their lifetimes, for circulation of his amorous adventures with Maori women may have induced others and even less desirable types to try their hand in New Zealand.

Markham sailed from England in 1833 for Van Diemen's Land, and the following February took the *Brazil Packet* across to New Zealand. Like Augustus Earle before him he came to the Hokianga on the west coast, then

Temperance Society.

On WEDNESDAY, the 11th day of MAY, inst.,

A

Public Meeting

WILL BE HELD, IN THE

CHURCH at KORORARIKA,

FOR THE PURPOSE OF ESTABLISHING A

TEMPERANCE
SOCIETY.

The attendance of all Persons desirous of promoting
Peace, Order, and Sobriety, is most earnestly requested.

THE *BRITISH RESIDENT* WILL TAKE THE CHAIR AT 12 o'CLOCK.

Dated, May 4th, 1836.

PAIHIA: Printed at the Press of the Church Missionary Society.

The first poster printed in New Zealand, by William Colenso, gave
Kororareka residents one week's notice of a meeting to establish a
temperance society in the town. *Courtesy of Russell Museum*

took the well-worn path to Kerikeri and a canoe to Kororareka. Although the
northern part of the country was now embroiled in tribal hostilities, things
were relatively calm at the Bay following The Girls' War of 1830. According to
Markham there were probably now about 200 permanent European settlers
there – not counting the floating body of vagrants and deserted sailors – while
the Maori population was some ten times that figure.[22]

In another early reference to its now established reputation, Markham
recorded that Kororareka was known to the missionaries as 'Hell', and he
personally admitted it certainly was 'a loose place' when the ships were in.

When upwards of thirty-five whaleships, which had been at sea for a year, came into the bay for three weeks, some 400 to 500 sailors might require 'as many Women'. He knew of some ships that had been out for all of thirty-two months and 'of course the Ladies were in great request'. Young Maori women living within the missionary establishment at Paihia were, 'in spite of their prayer-lessons', brought across to Kororareka. Their three weeks on board ship was spent 'much to their satisfaction', their material gains likely to include a musket, blankets and clothing. Canoes brought the women alongside ships as they came to anchor, and they went aboard 'to see old Friends'.

Markham was circumspect about the business, agreeing with the missionaries that many of the women engaged in this trade were too young. Many were also barren, which he suggested was a reason for the decrease in population, quite apart from the effects of any diseases they were likely to contract. But he did see some positive spin-offs from the contact with whalers, feeling that as a result of many ships taking on 'eight or ten New Zealanders' there was now evidence of increased 'familiarity' between the races in other respects. Also, chiefs had recently married women who had been 'civilized' by previous contact with whaling crews. Markham even made the suggestion that sailors may have had a more beneficial effect in this regard than the missionaries, which would not have gone down well in certain quarters at Paihia.[23]

This 'buck' was in his element on the subject of Maori women, describing some as 'very fine Creatures and even beautiful'. He noted that breasts were uncovered in warm weather, and unmarried women took it as a compliment for admirers 'to put [their] hands on them'. But he warned potential fondlers to be careful about taking liberties with a married woman, and especially with a chief's wife. He commented on the frequency with which European men cohabited with Maori women, and personally recommended having a chief's daughter as a form of protection. Parents, it seems, encouraged such liaisons, exchanging a daughter for a musket and a blanket or, in one case he was aware of, twenty pounds of tobacco.[24] When asked by a chief if he would like a 'wahine', Markham replied, 'Certainly' and availed himself of the daughter on offer, 'New Zealand style'.[25] He also enjoyed the spectacle of a troupe of eighty female dancers, wearing 'only mats around their middles', having never seen a finer set of women in an 'Opera Ballet'.[26] On another occasion he watched the women's action song known as the ruriruri, recording it as the 'Roody Doody'.[27]

As well as womanising, Markham had opportunities for hard drinking. He described a two-day session with sawyers – all of whom lived with Maori women – when 'eighteen Irish devils' broke out a cask of spirits. He observed that a taste for liquor among Americans was not confined to the Bay of Islands when he encountered a gin-drinking Yankee carpenter named 'Juniper Jack' at Mangungu, in the north-eastern reaches of the Hokianga Harbour.[28] Markham was also aware of the effect that European arrivals were having on the landscape. The Bay of Islands had once been covered by trees, but with an estimated '80 sail' calling each year and requiring timber to fire the furnaces for 'trying out' the whale blubber, they were now scarce.[29] He also offered one of the more original descriptions of the local geology, likening a rocky ridge near Mr Busby's house at Waitangi to 'Black Laver full of holes like a Gruyere Cheese'.[30]

One of Markham's more unusual contacts with whalers at Kororareka occurred when one of them stole two cured hams that were in his possession. He rowed out to a ship and recovered one of his lost items, and stayed on board long enough to enjoy part of the other for dinner. He later made off with the remnants, now reduced to cold ham.[31] But in spite of such distractions, Markham found the Bay monotonous. After a stay of four months he returned to England where he compiled his *New Zealand or Recollections Of It*, and died in 1865.

Other visitors to the Bay of Islands in the early 1830s offered their perspectives on the local populace. In 1833 John B Knights of Salem, master of the trading vessel *Spy*, pigeon-holed the European population here as either missionaries and adventurers, or 'bare-faced villains'. He didn't think much of either category, but preferred the latter, whom he feared less because they 'act[ed] in character'.[32] The following year an unidentified 'Gentleman' passed this way, and while he described the Bay as 'one of the noblest and safest harbours in the world' – and one in which the British navy could ride at anchor in complete safety – he was less complimentary about other aspects. He was of the view that the Maori here had acquired nothing from their contact with Europeans apart from vices, diseases and, recently, a strong taste for rum.[33]

According to Joel Polack, the Bay of Islands had been the port favoured by whaleships working on the middle ground, the 'fishery' between Australia and New Zealand, for the previous thirty years. Upwards of thirty vessels were in port at one time, averaging about 150 per year, and they were able to get all they wanted in the way of supplies, in particular pigs and potatoes. The average cargo of the latter, grown by local Maori, was put at five tons, and Polack made the significant point that these growers not only supplied all the ships' requirements, but also had sufficient for exports to Sydney.[34] While these ships took away local produce, Polack was aware that they invariably brought trouble. But he wondered whether Kororareka was any different from overseas ports, suspecting that the 'jack-tar of Portsmouth', 'the French *matélot* [of] Nantes or Bordeaux' and the 'Yankee sailor of Massachusetts' behaved much the same wherever they went.[35]

Polack did at least give the missionaries credit for their efforts in countering the downside of the shipping, describing Henry and William Williams and others as gentlemen with 'enlarged and scientific minds' which they had turned to the service of the country.[36] He also acknowledged their intervention and effective damage control during The Girls' War of 1830, prompted by the conduct of the 'disgraceful' Captain Brind.[37] But the reverends' progress among the Maori community had been paralysed by 'the reckless and immoral conduct' of runaway prisoners from Australia and casual European visitors, some of whom Polack likened to 'wild beasts', being 'vicious, untameable and roaming at will'.[38]

Another serious threat to morality and respectability lay some six kilometres south of Kororareka, on a bluff above the fork of the Kawakawa and Waikare estuaries. This was the fortified pa of Otuihu, built by chiefs Kiwikiwi and Pomare II after their retreat from Kororareka following the war of 1830. Known as Pomare's pa, it quickly attracted grog-sellers and a reputation as an even worse sailor's haunt than Kororareka. In 1837 Samuel Marsden reported that it housed 131 residents, who were generally men 'of the most infamous character; runaway convicts, and sailors, and publicans, who have opened grog-shops in the pas, where riot, drunkenness and prostitution are carried on daily'.[39] Four years after Marsden listed the evils lurking at Otuihu, Henry Williams described it as 'a place of extreme wretchedness'. Even so, the ever-hopeful missionaries handed out tracts to seamen and other types who gathered here, and so 'the seed of eternal life was continuously scattered'.[40]

Many of the whalers who arrived at Kororareka were already familiar with alcohol, particularly those on British and French ships, where it was often part of the ration. But it might be a different matter on American ships, most of which were either dry or – in theory, at least – committed to temperance.[41] That movement had sprung up near New Bedford in the mid-1820s, and remained particularly strong in Massachusetts. Before long there were large numbers of societies committed to the cause, and anti-liquor sentiment spread to ships, where the only alcohol carried was in the medicine chest or captain's trunk. Hard drinking had been an important part of American tavern life before the temperance movement, but this recreation was at least still available in the south-west Pacific. For those sailors who also hankered after female company, any connections were likely to be well earned on the part of the women, despite the price of a musket or its equivalent for services rendered. The men's workplace at sea was notoriously filthy, resulting in clothes becoming so stiffened by dirt and grime that they might need to be softened by being steeped in the urine bucket.[42] While there are detailed accounts of the whorehouses of San Francisco in the roaring 1850s, no sailor appears to have left a first-hand account of the trade's workings at Kororareka in the 1830s.

Whether to guarantee a sexual partner for the duration or to give the arrangement a veneer of respectability, sailors would enter into temporary marriages at the Bay of Islands. Such practices were no doubt on the mind of the Bishop of Australia when he visited New Zealand in the late 1830s and gave Henry and William Williams authority to grant official marriage licences. As the bishop put it, the current lack of these only encouraged the 'irregular celebration of marriage-rites'.[43] In February 1838 the whaler *Colombus* from Fairhaven, Massachusetts, called in at Kororareka and within a day of anchoring there were 'about 8 young ladies on board to do the washing kitchen work etc'. Shortly, two 'marriages' took place between crew members and '2 beautys of this country', and on Sunday the crew exhibited their usual disregard for the Sabbath by taking on board barrels of water (sixty) and sperm oil. By the time the *Colombus* had left harbour, all the men who had got 'married' on arrival were now 'divorced by mutual consent', their former spouses, along with their children and others, either going ashore or boarding other ships in search of 'new employment'.[44]

The consequences of prostitution in New Zealand at this time would soon be part of a much bigger issue, the apparent changes to the Maori population. Missionary William Wade, who arrived at the Bay of Islands in 1834, spent eight years working and travelling around the country before leaving for Australia, where his book *A Journey in the North Island of New Zealand* was published in 1842. While he acknowledged that there were widely ranging estimates of the Maori population at that time – from a million down to little more than 100,000 (he was inclined to go for 150,000) – there was no doubt there had been a rapid decline during the previous half century.[45] There were now 'immense' numbers of vacated hilltop pa sites, including five near Waimate, although Wade was careful not to interpret these as necessarily evidence of a population loss, for some were simply the result of migrations.[46] One likely cause for a decrease was introduced diseases, while malnourishment and the heavy physical demands made on Maori women would also cause a reduction in the natural birth rate. Wade also believed that infanticide was to blame, having heard that a fellow missionary's wife in the Bay of Islands had prevented many instances of this 'horrible' practice by promising mothers-to-be a garment for the new-born baby. He was also aware of the 'reservation' of female children for future profits from prostitution, and the great extent to which 'illicit intercourse' took place between Maori women and both seamen and white settlers. There was, for example, a 'disgusting spectacle' on a vessel in the Bay of Islands when every sailor appeared to 'lay claim to more girls than one'. Wade also learned that at Tauranga, in the Bay of Plenty, girls as young as ten or eleven visited ships for the purposes of prostitution. He was aware that, perversely, the oldest profession could be a deterrent to infanticide, when 'unnatural mothers refrain from one crime to rear their female offspring for the habitual practice of another'.[47]

Another, and later, perspective on contact between European shipping and Maori was made by physician and ethnologist Alfred Newman. He subscribed to Charles Darwin's new ideas on the survival of the fittest and was convinced that Maori – like other indigenous peoples throughout the Pacific – were dying out, their demise hastened by contact with a 'newer and a fresher race'. In 1881 Newman itemised some of the causes of death among Maori as consumption (the main one) and scrofula, and then in descending order, infanticide, suicide and murder. He added that slaves were known to have died from 'nostalgia' while chiefs could expire from 'excessive excitement'. Of the imported diseases, Newman had heard much talk of that 'awful scourge' syphilis but he had enquired of doctors ('the only class of men whose opinion is worth taking') and concluded that while Maori were affected by it, the symptoms were rarely severe. In fact, several doctors reported that they had never seen syphilis in a Maori. Newman believed that reports of its frightful ravages were unfounded, but he did suspect that a 'mild' form had existed here earlier and that Europeans had since introduced a more severe strain.[48] (In 1980, almost a century after Newman, anatomist Philip Houghton concluded that there was no skeletal evidence that the disease existed in New Zealand before the arrival of Europeans.[49])

Alfred Newman's systematic list of imported causes for the decline in the Maori population extended even to the horse, which not only caused fatal falls, but also was a convenient form of transport that assisted in the spread of diseases, and may have also unwittingly induced abortions.[50] European clothing was also identified as a source of disease, particularly when worn damp and improperly. Of course, the new arrivals had introduced alcohol, and that drunk by Maori was 'usually . . . the most adulterated', while the incessant smoking of certain 'fiery' brands of tobacco allegedly resulted in a lowered vitality. The result might be an 'enfeebled' progeny, which would then be vulnerable to further evil influences.[51] Newman touched on another effect of visiting seamen in New Zealand, for despite the frequency of 'promiscuous unions' between Maori and Europeans, the number of offspring was 'surprisingly small'. Short of any accurate census he estimated the number of half-castes of all ages and sexes to be well under 1000. And while such offspring were often 'handsome and well-made', he claimed they all died young – mostly of consumption.[52] Newman believed that the only imported vice that had in any way hastened the disappearance of the Maori race was alcoholism.[53] But despite the alleged and imminent departure of its indigenous people, this physician regarded New Zealand as the healthiest country on earth, its isolation making it less vulnerable to catching its neighbour's diseases.[54]

As to which Europeans were due the ignominious distinction of introducing venereal disease to New Zealand, obvious candidates were the crew of Cook's *Endeavour*. The claim that during a visit to the Bay of Islands in June 1772 by the French ship *Le Mascarin* several sailors contracted such diseases from Maori women does suggest that Cook's men were implicated. Lieutenant Roux reported that the effects of venereal disease were apparent the day after the men had mingled with Maori women. He insisted that the Frenchmen were not the carriers; besides, they would have been cured of it during their five months' privation at sea.[55] Half a century later when Major Richard Cruise visited the Bay of Islands on the British naval supply ship HMS *Dromedary*, he observed that 'illicit intercourse' had brought diseases to local Maori women and there were some 'truly melancholy cases of its fatal ravages'.[56] Europeans also introduced the concept of prostitution to Maori, for pre-marital intercourse and sexual freedom were accepted among most groups in their society. This new practice could have serious effects on fertility through women electing not to bear children, or resorting to infanticide or abortion, and through exposure to sterility-causing diseases.[57]

The surprisingly small number of offspring resulting from the 'extensive intercourse' between the crews of European ships and Maori women led Richard Cruise to suspect that infanticide was widespread. He saw just two results of such unions in New Zealand – the son of a whaler, and the daughter of a person 'residing in New South Wales' – and heard of only two others. He was told that women denied that they carried out infanticide, avoiding the need to do so by causing premature birth. Even so, Cruise noted that 'many' Maori women left the *Dromedary* in a very advanced stage of pregnancy, which was presumably the result of earlier connections with other ships.[58]

Early grog-sellers in Kororareka were not subject to any official control or interference, or the need to observe closing hours. But 1840 saw the arrival of the concept of licensed premises, and New Zealand's first was, naturally, at Kororareka. What had been John Johnson's grog-shop now became the Duke of Marlborough Hotel, standing on the waterfront at one corner of Sydney Square. But like almost all the other buildings in the town at that time it was short-lived, being burned to the ground in 1845. It rose again, before suffering a similar fate in 1875. The third Duke was more durable, surviving until 1931 when it too was consumed by flames spreading from The Gables next door. The current hotel, on the site of its three predecessors, was built from an accommodation block that was at the old cable station at Cable Bay and floated down from Doubtless Bay on a barge, and it still holds the oldest licence in the country.[59]

In 1837, seven years after The Girls' War, the Bay of Islands was again the scene of tribal warfare, the latest outbreak was between Titore at Kororareka and Pomare at Otuihu. This conflict was less serious than that of 1830 and lasted some three months, ending with the death of Titore on 2 June.[60] Joel Polack witnessed the hostilties, and estimated that upwards of 3000 men were involved and at least 20,000 rounds of ball cartridge were expended during the campaign. He put the cause down to another quarrel involving a Maori woman cohabiting with a European on a whaleship, and such was the fury of the combatants that their haka 'resounded for miles afar'.[61]

It was into this scene of conflict that the whaler *Australian* sailed in April. Captain William B Rhodes observed some thirty-five large canoes manned by warriors armed with muskets, and so set about getting stores on board as quickly as possible. But he had difficulty enlisting a crew; as fast as he could get two or three men signed on, others deserted. No doubt the local grog-shops – which Rhodes described as 'detestable' – played a major part in this, for his crew and officers were 'constantly in a state of drunkenness'. On top of that, five men ran away while another was turned out of the ship for attempting to kill both a seaman and the captain. Finally, with a crew of twenty-nine, which included large numbers of boys and 'New Zealanders', Rhodes was able to leave the Bay for the sperm-whaling grounds.[62] Two years later he returned to settle in New Zealand, establishing the first cattle station in the South Island. He also encouraged three of his younger brothers to try their luck in New Zealand; perhaps mindful of his own experiences, he advised them above all else to 'avoid *Public Houses* and *whores*'.[63]

5

ROUGH JUSTICE

AN INCUBUS ON THE PEOPLE

There are but two spots about the bay where towns could
be built – one, the site of the village of Kororarika,
notorious at present for containing, I should think, a
greater number of rogues than any other spot of equal
size in the universe, and the other on the opposite
side of the bay, near the missionary establishment,
Paihia (Pyhea).[1]

While Kororareka's growing reputation in the 1830s was shaped largely by itinerants, there were two individuals who settled and contributed much to the colour and character of the place. They arrived about the same time, with personalities destined to clash – and with historic results. The younger of the pair was Joel Polack, born in London in 1807. The son of an artist, he also took up the brush, and one of his paintings, a miniature of a young man, survives in the collection of London's Victoria and Albert Museum. But he gave up art to go abroad and become, in his own words, a 'servant to the British Government (Commissariat and Ordnance) in Africa, and a traveller for personal gratification in America'.[2] In 1830 his travels took him to Australia, perhaps following his brother Abraham who had been transported ten years earlier for allegedly stealing a lady's watch.[3] Abraham did well after his release, his spectacular material success impressing Charles Darwin in 1836, as we have seen. Joel joined his brother in business as a merchant and chandler in Sydney, before moving on again and reaching New Zealand in 1831. He initially spent twelve months at Hokianga, and after a period of exploration in the Kaipara, Poverty Bay and East Cape districts he settled at Kororareka, anticipating its potential as a commercial centre for shipping.

Joel Polack was New Zealand's first Jewish settler and also one of its early European property owners.[4] In August 1833 he acquired some nine and a half acres at the north end of Kororareka Beach bounded by a hill known as Parramatta, a name which was carried over from New South Wales and which Polack adopted for his own property. He bought the land from a number of chiefs, including one who he described as an 'old cannibal', for merchandise to the value of £48, and some two years later he acquired an adjoining section, with boundaries defined by a rock on the beach and the stump of a tree. He thought he had concluded the deal until one of the vendors, chief Titore, demanded further payment. The would-be purchaser then sought the mediation of Henry Williams, who pointed out that it was he who actually owned the land, having secured it earlier by the 'native law' of planting on it and reaping the produce. But the missionary now generously gave up his claim in recognition of the trouble and expense Polack had gone to. Another payment was mutually agreed to, whereupon Polack finally had closure.[5]

In addition to property dealing and establishing a trading store and brewery, Polack wrote two books. His observations and experiences were the basis of *New Zealand: Being a Narrative of Travels and Adventures* and *Manners and Customs of the New Zealanders*, both published when he returned to London in 1838. Thanks largely to these volumes Polack had the distinction of being included in the British *Dictionary of National Biography*, which acknowledged his second book as providing one of the earliest accounts of Maori, along with displaying 'considerable erudition and capacity for observation'.[6] While in London, Polack also arranged an auction of some of his land, and this may have qualified as New Zealand's first subdivision into quarter-acre sections, soon to become the national standard.[7]

Polack described New Zealand before the arrival of Europeans as a land of secluded wilds, broken only by 'the chirping cricket, the feathered tribes of the forest, or their croaking neighbours in the adjacent marshes'. But already such picturesque spots had been invaded by the 'busy hum of British mechanics', whose dawning villages and settlements were 'the early germs of rising towns and cities'.[8] Polack had a high opinion of Britons as colonials, believing that their commercial and settling habits rendered them the only people able to readily amalgamate with Maori. They alone could bring the 'blessing of morality, religion, and good example' to these 'hitherto benighted people'.[9]

As a trader Polack's regular contact with American whalers enabled him to pick up such nautical terms as 'It's a master big crittur' and 'tarnal', the latter being an eighteenth-century sailor's contraction of 'eternal damnation'.[10] Perhaps the same individuals gave him the benefit of their opinions on the local Maori women, for he recorded that, contrary to belief, their favours could not be bought for a 'paltry trinket'. Those of unmarried female chiefs of the highest class were even more difficult to obtain, and it was love, not money, that 'generally render[ed] them propitious'. These women also had an effective 'artillery of charms', while their dances were 'lascivious exhibitions' of suggestive smiles and gestures.[11]

As well as his books Polack wrote letters that give an insight into the trader's life at Kororareka. In December 1834 he thanked his brother Abraham for sending goods he had requested, but also complained about the arrival of some he hadn't. These included casks of tar (which leaked en route) and soldiers' coats (which were moth-eaten). Joel appears to have had an old debt to his brother, and hoped he might be able to clear it by selling goods in New Zealand. In particular he needed wine, rum and porter, while the requested two crates of beer and wine bottles and five gross of corks were probably for his brewery operation. He was also after blankets, shirts, various types of guns, and such 'trifles for the natives' as mirrors, scissors, flints and steels, teapots and packs of cards. But an early delivery was essential, for the whaling season was about to begin, and he expected five ships to arrive in the bay to 'fit out' for England and another thirty to prepare 'for the Fishing'.

Joel was also in need of an assistant and asked his brother if he could recommend a steady and sober young man who would forgo the luxuries of Sydney for 'plain pork & potatoes'. He was after someone who was 'neither a dandy or a sloven' but 'sober – industrious & moral'; he was prepared to pay £20 for the first year, and more as business improved. A good temper was also a prerequisite, for the Kororareka trader admitted to having a 'rascally bad one' himself. He had a further request, in the form of a 'good wife', and hoped his brother might also be able to help in this department. He had heard that the Solomon family in Hobart had a 'fine' daughter, aged about seventeen, and were in need of a son-in-law who was of their 'persuasion'.

In a later letter Joel reported that despite some extremely inferior rum Abraham had sent him – 'the worst in this bay' – his business was improving. But there were now six other dealers competing, so he needed more goods. He didn't repeat his request for a wife, but he still sought an assistant to mind the house while he visited the ships. He requested puncheons (casks, usually of eighty-four or 120 gallons) of rum, casks of wine and hogsheads of porter, along with further quantities of bottles and corks. He also wanted soap, tumblers, bales of shirts, duck trousers and blankets, white lead, linseed oil, green paint, turpentine, sheet lead, nails and window glass, along with spades and hoes. He had the locals' leisure pursuits in mind, requesting twenty-four gross of large bowl pipes, twelve packs of cards and twenty-four violin strings. But potentially much less peaceable was his order for kegs of powder, double-barrelled guns and 500 pounds of duck shot.[12]

Parramatta was not Polack's first land purchase in the Bay of Islands, for he had earlier bought a house on the site of the massacre in 1772 of Marion du Fresne.[13] He made numerous land deals, and at times appeared confused by the extent of his own holdings, admitting that some transactions were complex and troublesome and involved 'no end to claimants'. The 'requisite method' of purchasing began with the drawing up and signing of title deeds with the name or facsimile of moko of the chiefs concerned. Payment was then made to the principal chief, who distributed it to each claimant. The thoughtful Polack 'invariably' added a quantity of trinkets so that the slaves of the various claimants might also benefit. Once, when he was passing a beach in his boat, he became the beneficiary of someone else's transaction. Hailed by a group of Maori who were negotiating a deal with an Englishman, Polack went ashore and accidentally received 'a trifling portion of the payment', as did his four boatmen.[14] But he strongly resented any accusation that his properties had been bought cheaply from Maori. Far from offering the 'merest trifle', he had bought some portions at the rate of £6 10s per acre – an 'equitable, fair and just price' – and claimed that in some instances what he paid seven years earlier was twenty-six times the value now being asked by the New Zealand Company. As to the size of his portfolio, the 'utmost extent' of his several waterfront sections in the Bay did not exceed 1100 acres which, he pointed out, paled in comparison with the holdings of many landed proprietors in Canada, the United States and New South Wales.[15] At one stage Polack also had three properties at Waitangi, purchased from Maori chiefs and others in 1835 and 1836. One, of an unspecified size, encompassed half a waterfall and part of a river and had a 'remarkable Puridi' (puriri) tree as a boundary marker.[16] His plot back at Parramatta was also distinguished by trees, numbering nearly 100 and including olives, pomegranates, nectarines and exceptionally flavoursome peaches, brought over from the Sydney Botanical Gardens.[17]

Another of Polack's claims to national as well as local fame was his participation in New Zealand's first duel. This historic event on Kororareka Beach in 1837 was described as a 'running gun battle' in which his opponent, innkeeper Benjamin Turner, was wounded. The mutual animosity between these two early settlers continued and a second duel took place in 1842. On this occasion Polack was shot in the elbow and Turner took a bullet in the cheek.[18] Their long-standing feud would not have been helped by Polack's claims in 1837 that the other was a runaway convict and the leader of a gang of desperadoes, and had acquired his wealth by trading in drunken sailors, grog-selling and dealing in stolen property.[19]

Surprisingly, perhaps, Polack did not mention this landmark duel in either of his books. While his accounts and descriptions were subject to a certain amount of elaboration, his liberties with the truth did not match those of his rival. Unlike Polack, Turner was not given to writing at an early age, and when his version of events did appear much later it was subject to much forgetfulness and exaggeration. It was provoked by a lecture given by Thomas Gillies, Superintendent of Auckland, to the Young Men's Christian Association in 1871, and Turner's astonishing response may have had something to do with his own (brief) political career, as Bay of Islands representative on the Auckland Provincial Council from 1861–62.[20] But in the first instance this lecture was of interest for what it revealed about the superintendent's own attitudes. Gillies began by advising that the choice of topic – 'Our Province' – was not his own, and proceeded to suggest that it was not in fact 'Our' Province, for at least two-thirds was in the possession of Maori, whose 'supposed rights . . . we have foolishly recognised'. Gillies then described the 'celebrated so-called "Treaty of Waitangi"' of 1840 as 'one of the most disastrous pages in the history of the colony'. And while the 'native difficulty' stood in the way of the province's progress, he conceded it was 'gradually and surely solving itself by the inevitable extinction of the race'.

Having dealt with the Maori land issue, Gillies then moved to the business of the Bay of Islands. It was here, he claimed, that the first grog-shop was opened around 1830 'by an old colonist, still resident amongst us'. He put the European population of Kororareka in 1838 at 1000, served by 'a church, five hotels, numberless grog-shops, a theatre, several billiard tables, skittle-alleys, finishes and hells', and acknowledged that the source of his information was the 1859 book *New Zealand: Past and Present – Savage and Civilized* by Arthur S Thomson, surgeon-major to the 58th Regiment, who had arrived in this country in 1847. The superintendent's talk was subsequently published in the *Daily Southern Cross*, and Benjamin Turner quickly took exception.[21] He pointed out that if he was the 'old colonist' referred to, then he was away from the Bay from 1826 until 'about 1836 or 1837'. He also claimed the European population of Kororareka at that time was more like 100 than 1000, before disputing most other details of the speech. Turner also used his lengthy letter as an excuse to attack Gillies, suggesting it would be a day of rejoicing throughout the whole province if the superintendent were to give up his office – and the sooner the better.[22]

A second correspondent, 'Crepitans' (making a crackling sound), rallied to Gillies' support, assuring him that he was 'substantially correct' on the state of Kororareka. He referred to evidence given at the Select Committee of the House of Lords in 1838 by the Rev. F Wilkinson, who stated he never saw 'such a bad community' as Kororareka, where there was 'drunkenness and profligacy of all kinds'.[23] Turner struck back, and while now admitting that 'there was a deal of drunkenness amongst the sailors', he insisted he never knew of any robberies, swindlers, bankrupts or even bad debts in the town. And if Kororeraka had as many 'hells' as was claimed, when there weren't even fifty inhabitants there, he wondered how many might now be found down in Auckland. As for Thomson's book, 'There never was [one] published containing more inaccuracies.' But if the superintendent – or anyone, for that matter – wished to know the 'true history' of New Zealand during the last forty-five years then there was no one better equipped to provide a 'correct epitome' than himself. Turner then recounted his own history, from ship-building and sealing on Stewart Island, flax-trading in the Wellington region and moving north, arriving in 'that wicked place' Kororareka in 1837. Most improbably, he claimed there were only six white inhabitants in the town at that stage, and he knew all of them. One he mentioned by name was 'John Poiner [sic]', 'who sold grog when he could get it'. On the subject of bad characters, Turner wrote that there was one 'well-known scoundrel' whom he personally made 'fly for his life'. The newspaper chose not to print the name, so we can only wonder if that individual was Joel Polack, following the famous duel. If so, he certainly used his time away to write an account that would prove a lot more useful than his adversary's hazy recollections.

In his second letter to the editor, Turner – who signed himself as 'a true lover of the truth' – wrote that he never knew of one runaway convict living at Kororareka. But most extraordinary of all was his claim that governors Hobson, FitzRoy and Sir George Grey had all asked him to write his 'life and history of New Zealand'. At least he was honest, declining to take up their flattering suggestions on the sole ground that he had a problem remembering dates.[24]

Five years after this exchange Turner died at his residence, Retreat Cottage, near Newmarket, Auckland, and the *Daily Southern Cross* printed an extensive obituary, consisting mostly of material the subject had thoughtfully provided some time earlier. As a boy in England he had read books about the 'savages and cannibals' of New Zealand, and first arrived in this country at Chalky Island, Fiordland, 'on or about October, 1823 or 1824'. His subsequent adventures included a Maori wife, 'a great chief's daughter', a narrow escape from Te Rauparaha (two of his European mates were not so lucky, allegedly ending up in the oven), and travels to Nelson, 'Wangarei [sic]' and Tauranga. According to this account he first settled at Kororareka in 1832 as a trader, and owner of sawmills and trading vessels. When a 'Committee of Public Order' – otherwise known as the Kororareka Association – was established, Turner was elected chairman, thereby qualifying him in his opinion as 'the first Governor of New Zealand', and in which capacity he thus made the country's 'first laws'.

The *Daily Southern Cross* described Benjamin Turner as 'one of the most remarkable men of New Zealand' and suggested that he would have a 'permanent place' in the history of the country.[25] As it happened, he did gain a modest entry in the 1940 *Dictionary of New Zealand Biography*, which recorded yet another of his claims, that he was the first European to engage in the trade of dried human heads.[26] But sixty years later this 'remarkable' man would no longer warrant his own section in the *Dictionary of New Zealand Biography*, and would be unimpressed by the fact that his only mention was in a generous entry on old rival Joel Polack.[27]

Benjamin Evans Turner was born at Worcester, England, in 1796. The fact is that his claimed year of arrival in New Zealand – 1823 or 1824 – conflicts with something he chose not to divulge, that in 1821 he received a seven-year sentence for some unknown offence and was transported to New South Wales. At the same time he was described unflatteringly as a 'pockmarked' waterman.[28] It therefore seems likely that he first appeared in New Zealand around 1831 and reached the Bay of Islands the following year. In more recent years his colourful past has been exposed: in 1959 he was described as an 'escaped convict who acquired property and respectability' and whose grog-shop had been the scene of so much 'hilarity and misery'.[29] In 1993 another historian summed up the old Kororareka identity rather more succinctly as a 'transported felon, violent ruffian, notorious grog-seller and natural businessman'.[30]

It is now impossible to establish how many grog-sellers were operating in Kororareka in the unregulated days of the late 1830s. But in stark contrast to Turner's sanitised recollections was a letter published in 1837 in the *Sydney Herald* from a correspondent identified only as 'M'. Because he had spent eighteen months at the Bay of Islands he felt his remarks 'may be relied upon as a true picture'. He claimed there were 'about 17' grog-sellers there. One of these 'notorious men' was a 'well-known runaway convict . . . who went to the bay about four or five years ago, without anything to his pockets, [and] now boasts of being worth from one thousand to twelve hundred pounds, made by sailors and grog-selling, and the purchase of stolen property!' That description sounds remarkably similar to the one of Turner offered by Joel Polack. Correspondent 'M' described the scenes of 'immorality and drunkenness' during 'the shipping season', when it was 'not an uncommon sight to see near one hundred sailors roving about Kororarika beach, most of whom are drunk, and about ten or twelve pitched battles are the inseparable consequences'.[31]

According to Turner's selective – or defective – memory, Kororareka was not such a bad place around the time of his arrival. But others disagreed, and the decision was made to appoint a resident British authority in the Bay of Islands. James Busby was born in Edinburgh in 1802, and emigrated to New

South Wales with his parents at the age of twenty-two. His passion was viticulture, and he had hoped to found a wine industry in the new settlement. His dream was that every small farmer might have an acre of grapes and be able to drink wholesome home-made wine as an alternative to evil imported rums and spirits. But things did not turn out as planned, and in 1831 he was back in England. He went on a wine tour of France and Spain, but after impressing authorities in England with his grasp of colonial matters he was dispatched to the new post of British Resident in New Zealand.

Busby was responsible for protecting the Maori population against the outrages of recent arrivals, looking after the interests of law-abiding settlers and traders, and apprehending escaped convicts. But lack of means of enforcing his authority led to him being famously labelled a 'man-of-war without guns'. Six days after landing at the Bay of Islands in May 1833 he read out a message from King William IV, bringing hope to the assembled Maori chiefs. The following March he assisted northern chiefs in the selection of a national flag, to be recognised by the Admiralty and to provide protection for New Zealand-built ships overseas. Then in October 1835, in response to French immigrant Baron de Thierry's plan to establish a government in New Zealand, Busby persuaded the chiefs to sign a Declaration of Independence in the name of the Confederation of Chiefs and Tribes of New Zealand. Although nothing came of it, this document was a step towards the treaty between the British Crown and Maori that would be signed five years later.

The perceived threat of a French takeover also provoked a large number of self-confessed 'faithful, obedient, and loyal subjects' to petition King William IV. In 1837 these European settlers craved His Majesty's 'condescending attention' to the 'present crisis of the threatened usurpation of power over New Zealand'. They wished to alert him to the 'serious evils and perplexing grievances', mostly due to some of his own subjects, individuals who 'fearlessly commit all kinds of depredations'. British property was exposed 'to every imaginable risk and plunder' and the 'humble petitioners' therefore suggested that if His Majesty was thinking of extending the colonies of Great Britain, here was one for the taking. They emphasised the importance of the Bay of Islands to shipping, with thirty-six vessels at anchor there at one period, and no less than 101 entering the Bay in the six months to June 1836. This traffic brought huge problems, with robberies, on both ship and shore, frequently involving firearms.[32] In the words of Joel Polack, the reprobates responsible were 'lawless runaway' prisoners and seamen, who had either escaped from their employers or been ejected from ships for guilty conduct. They were an 'incubus on the people', bringing 'crimes hitherto unknown'.[33]

Among the 190 petitioners to William IV were two listed as 'John Wright'. At least one of these was a storekeeper at Pipiroa, a small bay between Te Wahapu and Okiato.[34] One evening in June 1837 he went to investigate dogs barking outside his house and saw three men approaching from a boat. When he asked what they wanted, one of them – later identified as Edward Doyle – replied they were after tobacco, before grabbing hold of Wright and threatening him with a pistol. Wright managed to discharge the weapon in the struggle, while his stepdaughter, Miss Featherstone, begged for Doyle's mercy, and another of the intruders urged him to 'knock his brains out'. Miss Featherstone was dragged away by the hair, screaming, when Mrs Wright came out of the house and was struck with a blow that removed four teeth and loosened several others. It may have been significant that her attacker was later described as a 'shoemaker', for along with tailoring this was a trade which commonly engaged prisoners in jails at that time. Meanwhile, Mr Wright continued the struggle with Doyle on the verandah of the house, while the two women managed to get back inside. But Doyle then forced an entry, and the intruders went into the store and plundered property worth £120, later itemised as twenty yards of calico, ten shirts, twenty pounds of gunpowder and sundry other articles. While one remained sentry on the door, the others took the booty to the boat and made their getaway.

Next morning the victims sought the assistance of Henry Williams, who visited a nearby pa and located the robbers, along with a quantity of tobacco. A few days later Doyle was taken into custody, but managed to escape. He was later given up by Maori and sent to Sydney. In the Supreme Court of New South Wales he denied all knowledge of the robbery. He also stated that he was a native of New Bedford, America, who had been left at one of the South Sea Islands and from there had made his way to Sydney. But he could not shake the testimony of Miss Featherstone, who claimed that because it had been a clear night and there were three lamps on the kitchen table she had been able to obtain a good view of Doyle when he stood on the verandah. The jury had to determine whether the accused was a British subject, and then quickly found him guilty of stealing and putting a person in bodily fear. The judge described the crime as a great outrage and assured Doyle that the remoteness of the Bay of Islands would not exempt him from 'the penal visitation' of the law. An example would be made to show 'lawless ruffians' that they could not escape justice, and so he passed the death sentence.[35]

Following Doyle's execution in 1837 the colonial secretary in Sydney ordered notices to be carried on vessels bound for New Zealand and the South Sea Islands as salutary warnings to any prowling European 'ruffians'. Although one of these had been effectively eliminated, law and order – or the apparent lack of it – remained a concern at the Bay of Islands. That the British Resident would not or could not act was the stimulus for the establishment in May 1838 of what could claim to be New Zealand's first form of government, the Kororareka Association. Its aims and methods largely reflected the personal and business interests of its founding members, a group of local settlers. While certain misdemeanours, such as robbery and the receiving of stolen goods, would see the accused handed over to James Busby, this association gave itself the right to take appropriate action if the British Resident chose not to do so. Operating somewhat outside officialdom, such as it was, it was hardly surprising that it dispensed some highly unconventional forms of justice.

The Kororareka Association elected a president, vice-president, secretary, treasurer and a committee. All members had to live within its chosen area of jurisdiction, defined as the northern end of the Kororareka Peninsula and consisting of all the land bounded by the coast and a straight line from Matauwhi Bay across to Long Beach at Oneroa Bay. It drew up fifteen resolutions, prescribing procedures and its modus operandi. In the first instance, each member was to equip himself with a good musket and bayonet, a brace of pistols, a cutlass, and at least thirty rounds of ball cartridge. Constant preparedness was expected, for these arms could be inspected at any time by a specially appointed officer.

Members met monthly in one another's houses, and were bound to offer mutual support. If one was threatened by 'natives of New Zealand, or others', suitably armed members were required to assemble at the house of the person attacked, and any who refused to do so would face a £5 fine. In general, the association anticipated that many of its activities would be connected with shipping. Members risked a £10 fine if they aided or secreted runaway mariners, and £5 if they did not assist commanders of vessels in the recovery of the same at Kororareka. One resolution shone some light on the definition of such escapees, for if the captain or officers of a ship had made no application to the association within four clear days of a mariner absenting himself then he was not considered a runaway.[36]

Anyone accused of robbing an inhabitant of Kororareka was obliged to appear before at least seven members of the association, and if considered guilty would be forwarded to the British Resident. But if Busby declined to take action, the 'guilty' person could be punished by the association 'according to the local laws which necessity may compel [it] to frame'. Approved methods included horse-whipping for tardy debtors, with the creditor permitted to continue such treatment every time he saw the miscreant until the required funds were forthcoming. Then there was a local version of tarring and feathering, in which the offender was stripped of his clothing, smothered with tar and then covered with the feather-like fluff of the raupo. To add to the humiliation, the victim was then publicly exposed by being marched down the beach to the accompaniment of a drum and pipe band. Benjamin Turner noted that this procedure involved no less than three coats of tar, but claimed it was only used on three or four occasions. Even so, one wonders how victims managed to remove their sticky coatings, but if proof alcohol was a suitable solvent it was likely to be readily available in Kororareka. For want of a suitably secure gaol, victims of the Kororareka Association could also be detained for the night in a sea chest, thoughtfully ventilated by means of 'gimlet holes'.[37]

The interests of members who were landlords – such as Benjamin Turner – were well looked after, with a subcommittee to arbitrate on tenants who didn't pay their rent. There was also a resolution which made any inhabitant of Kororareka who was not a member and who transgressed liable to a £10 fine. As with the earlier organisation, Busby steered clear of the association's activities, but was probably grateful for any positive effect it had on reducing general disorder and protecting personal property. But if the organisation was of some unofficial assistance to the British Resident, the missionaries felt that its rugged methods of enforcement only encouraged further violence. Eventually the existence of the association became a concern to the British government, and in December 1838 it was suggested that a British consul be appointed for that country. Even allowing for the difficulties and lack of support, Busby's performance had been less than impressive, although Joel Polack accepted the soon-to-be-sidelined British Resident's word for it that he had 'in vain' made representations to colonial authorities in Sydney regarding 'the deplorable state of anarchy and confusion' in New Zealand.[38]

The Kororareka Association and its novel approach to the dispensing of justice became redundant with the arrival of Captain William Hobson in early 1840. Turner and his fellow law-enforcers disbanded on a socially responsible note, applying their surplus funds to the establishment of a local hospital. One visitor at that time considered the Bay of Islands unique, in fact harbouring a 'greater number of rogues than any other spot of equal size in the universe'. Botanist and explorer John Carne Bidwill was born in Exeter in 1815, and made the first of three visits to New Zealand in February 1839. He conceded that the environs of the Bay of Islands were 'very pretty', but were less impressive than they appeared in a panorama recently exhibited in London. In view of the imminent arrival of organised British settlement it was appropriate that many of Bidwill's comments looked to the future. He described the surrounding countryside, for example, as 'nothing but a succession of gullies', which would make wheeled traffic 'almost impracticable'. He saw only two spots there where towns could be built, at Kororareka and Paihia, and while the first provided the best shelter for shipping, it was situated on a narrow neck of land and so was cut off from the rest of the country. The forward-looking Bidwill also noted that it was confined, and the land available for building purposes could not support more than a couple of thousand inhabitants. Bidwill did not favour the prospects of the Bay of Islands, believing that settlement would be better south of the Thames district, where large areas of land were still available and consisted of rich plains rather than barren hills and ravines.[39]

Some eighteen months before Bidwill's first visit, the Bay of Islands gained a doctor, who was also the first resident surgeon in New Zealand. Born in 1811, Samuel Hayward Ford became a member of the Royal College of Surgeons in 1833 and decided to become a medical missionary so that he might combine the healing of the sick with the bringing of glad tidings of salvation to those 'now sitting in darkness in the regions of the shadow of death'. He and his wife had a dramatic departure from England in November 1836 when the *City of Edinburgh* was struck by a hurricane off Plymouth. They finally reached New Zealand after a nine-month voyage, passing through Sydney, which the surgeon described as a sad and wicked place ruled by Mammon. In New Zealand he encountered much sickness, with influenza, skin affections and consumption being particularly prevalent among Maori. Ford suggested, controversially, that some of the sick in the Maori settlements had been visited by the missionaries only on Sundays. After six months in the country he reported that of the 600 patients he had seen, four-fifths had scrofula and nineteen had died. In general he blamed the cold, scarcity of food, limited diet, and contact with Europeans. He also attended to the health of his colleagues, including William Colenso who caught influenza and suffered temporary 'irritation around the head'. Another of Ford's patients was Henry Williams, whose lumbago and hepatitis he treated with suitably spirituous brandy and water.

Ford was described in 1838 by a whaler's wife as a 'distinguished' individual, who was somewhat out of place on Kororareka Beach in his black suit, bow-tie and fine white pleated shirt. He also carried a scrimshawed walking stick, presented by a grateful whaling patient. There was further gratitude the following year when the surgeon amputated a seamen's leg that had been badly fractured after being crushed by a whale. This unfortunate sailor had been at sea for five weeks without medical attention, and for want of anywhere else to go – apart from the grog-shops – after the operation, he convalesced at the home of the hospitable Fords.

From the outset the Church Missionary Society wanted Ford to be stationed in the southern district of the North Island rather than at the Bay of Islands. He objected on the grounds that warfare was now prevalent there, and medicines and hospitals were likely to have little beneficial effect. But in February 1840 he was forced to resign from the society's employment because of his own ill-health, and two years later he and his wife moved to a house at Te Wahapu, where he continued to practise.[40]

As New Zealand awaited the arrival of British authority in the form of William Hobson, it received a passing visit from another surgeon, a Mr Jameson, who came via South Australia. He described Kororareka as consisting of about 300 European inhabitants, not counting large numbers of sailors whose 'nightly revels constituted the only interruption to the peace and harmony which generally prevailed'. He was aware of the lucrative grog-selling trade as well as another of a 'still more discreditable kind' carried on nearby at Pomare's village. Here was the 'curious spectacle' of a 'still savage chief' enriching himself at the expense of supposedly civilised types now availing themselves of 'unbridled licentiousness'. Jameson wrote that 'crimes, misdemeanours and larcenies' were remarkably rare here, which may suggest that the Kororareka Association was an effective deterrent. He went so far as to suggest there was no place in the world where people and property were more secure than this small settlement. If so, it was not for want of incentive for the criminally inclined, for the local stores and grog-shops were stocked with at least £20,000 and perhaps £30,000 worth of merchandise. Even more remarkable was Jameson's claim that there was no truth in the statement that the Bay of Islands was 'a nest of outlaws and criminals'.[41]

6

HERESIES AND INFIDELS

THE IMPENETRABLE DESIGNS OF GOD

I arrived at Kororareka, and stopped at a sort of inn, kept
by a white man for the accommodation of travellers,
and inhabited by savages.[1]

Irish-born Peter Dillon went to sea at an early age, and is known to have been in the Friendly Islands (Tonga) by 1809. In 1814 he was commissioned by Samuel Marsden to command the *Active* and take the first band of missionaries from Sydney across to the Bay of Islands.[2] Back in Sydney in 1825 he embarked on a trading voyage across the full expanse of the Pacific, but at Valparaiso his ship, the *Calder*, was driven ashore by a gale and wrecked. Dillon then bought the *St Patrick*, a Paraguay-built vessel, and set out for Calcutta. He called in at Tahiti and arrived at Cape Colville, at the northern-most point on New Zealand's Coromandel Peninsula, on 31 December 1825.[3] Trading took place, with second-hand muskets, gunpowder, old lead (to be recycled as bullets) and other items being traded for timber, and one particular day's business saw 166 spars exchanged for fifty pounds of gunpowder and fifteen hatchets. Dillon also took aboard two sons of the Ngati Maru chief Takurua, from Thames, giving them the names Brian Boru (after the tenth-century Irish king) and Morgan McMurragh. These young chiefs were taken on to Calcutta, where they planned to further their trading interests. After taking on water and potatoes and filling the on-board sties with pigs, the ship left for the Bay of Islands.

When the *St Patrick* anchored off Kororareka on the evening of 7 April 1826 there were three other ships in the harbour, including a South Seas whaler and a barque bound for the Marquesas Islands in search of pearls. Those on the *St Patrick* noticed that there were several Englishmen living ashore, some of whom had been discharged from ships and others who were runaways. The ship was visited by a number of chiefs, most receiving a present from Dillon, and on one occasion a large war canoe approached with its warriors brandishing their paddles and acting defiantly, but no clash ensued. The carpenter had gone ashore to make a pump and two new topmasts, and as soon as those were done the ship put to sea, not requiring any further provisioning in the Bay on account of having stocked up earlier while in the Thames district.[4]

Continuing to Calcutta as planned, Dillon had hoped to take the *St Patrick* via Fiji but stormy weather forced him to sail further to the north-west to Tikopia. Here he was shown relics believed to be from the expedition of the French navigator Jean François La Pérouse, who had gone missing after leaving Sydney for the New Hebrides in 1788. The whereabouts of these French ships had been a mystery for nearly forty years, and Dillon now realised that the discovery might bring him recognition, as well as material benefits. After reaching Calcutta in the now badly leaking *St Patrick*, Dillon was given command of another vessel to investigate further the fate of La Pérouse. During the course of this voyage he again visited New Zealand before going on to Vanikoro where he obtained conclusive evidence of the French expedition. He returned to Calcutta and in 1829 went to Paris, where he was liberally rewarded for his efforts, among other things receiving the Chevalier of the Legion of Honour.[5] He was also made consul for the Islands in the South Seas – resigning in 1838 – an appointment which he saw as reflecting the French government's interest in establishing settlements in New Zealand.[6]

If Peter Dillon had provided vital early assistance for the Church Missionary Society in New Zealand, he would later become extremely critical of that organisation. He accused its members of having a proprietorial attitude towards the country, by right of being the first Europeans established there. In his opinion they wished to keep the country for themselves, and feared any influx of European immigrants which might reduce their own influence over the Maori. To deter others they suggested that the 'fatal oven' might await those who did not first get permission from the Church Missionary Society in London before establishing a settlement.[7] In return, the missionaries may not have thought too highly of Dillon, for apart from his French sympathies he was a most unusual character. He was certainly colourful, at six feet four inches (1.93 metres) tall and topped with a 'flaming mop of red hair'. We might also wonder how he managed consular duties in view of the fact that he could neither read nor write.[8] A fellow seaman considered Dillon 'the most passionate man' he'd ever known, harbouring feelings that could be expressed in fits of rage or by throwing things at the crew. He was said to frequently thrash his wife, who lived on board, and on one occasion broke a telescope over her head. He was also suspected of insanity, as when he was seen eating woodchips in the carpenter's workshop.[9] But whatever else he was, Dillon was a man of action, and something else he achieved in Paris had serious consequences for Protestant missionaries back in New Zealand. He suggested to Catholic Church authorities that they also establish a mission in the Pacific, one that could take advantage of the regular French naval ship service to Valparaiso.[10] The idea was considered and approved, and in 1830 two vicariates were created in the region. While the early death of the first priest responsible for this post delayed progress, the project began in earnest in late 1835 with the appointment of Jean Baptiste François Pompallier. He had been consecrated bishop in Rome, and given responsibility for the mission territory of Western Oceania, a vast expanse of the Pacific that straddled the Equator, taking in New Zealand to the south and extending to the north of the Caroline Islands.

On Christmas Eve 1836 Pompallier and his small band of priests of the Marist Order, or Society of Mary, sailed from Hâvre de Grâce in northern France. They hardly got off to an auspicious start, for the *Delphine* damaged its rudder while leaving the harbour and was forced to make for Tenerife for repairs. From there the expedition set out for Valparaiso, but nineteen days later, when the ship was about to cross the Equator, one of the party died of a brain fever. On this further misfortune a philosophical Pompallier commented, 'How impenetrable are the designs of God.'[11]

From Valparaiso they took the American ship *Europa* to Gambier and then on to Tahiti, whose inhabitants Pompallier was disappointed to find had already 'exchanged infidelity for Protestantism, with its commerce, politics, corruption, and intolerance'. But twenty days later, when they came in sight of Vavau, Tonga, a fearful electrical storm blew up and a strong current began to sweep them on to nearby rocks. They saw themselves going 'into the jaws of death' and their only hope was for a breeze to spring up and enable them to make headway against the current. They prayed, and just when they expected to strike the rocks, their sails filled and they were carried back in to the open sea and out of danger. Pompallier acknowledged their miraculous deliverance and noted that the captain – a Protestant – had fallen on his knees, joining his hands and lifting his eyes heavenward in gratitude.[12]

On 10 January 1838, after a twelve-day sail from Sydney, Pompallier and his party arrived at the entrance to the Hokianga Harbour. Guided by a European pilot, they ventured into the interior of the country and quickly discovered that Protestant missions were already established there as well. Pompallier claimed that these Methodists were alarmed at his arrival, and had told the Maori population that this new religion would bring wicked doctrines, along with wooden gods and plans to seize the country. Although he recognised the 'infidel New Zealanders' as warriors and cannibals, Pompallier believed they paid no attention to the claims of the opposition. And despite the rumours of impending 'pillage, death, exile, or incendiarism' that were being spread across the country by those 'ministers of heresy', he and his followers remained 'calm and unshaken'.[13]

Despite his faith, Pompallier's position in New Zealand was decidedly uncomfortable and came to the attention of Captain Cécile of the French corvette *Héroine* when it arrived in Sydney. Cécile now sailed for the Bay of Islands, where he learned that Pompallier was at Hokianga, some two days' journey across country. The bishop accepted the captain's invitation to visit him and so travelled to Kororareka, where he found accommodation in what he described as 'a sort of inn' inhabited by 'savages'. Cécile arrived and invited Pompallier on board, and when he later returned to shore in the captain's boat with the French flag flying at the stern, the *Héroine* fired a nine-gun salute in honour of his self-styled 'episcopal dignity'. Pompallier noted with satisfaction that the 'whole country, far and wide' resounded to the sound of those cannons, which he believed was the first military salute to be heard in the Bay.

While he was at the 'sort of' inn, Pompallier was approached by crew members from the *Héroine* requesting that he administer them their first communion. The bishop agreed, and so Low Mass was celebrated on the deck, which was suitably decorated with awnings and flags. Among the 300 or so in attendance were the commander and officers in full uniform, local residents – including 'Protestant ladies and gentlemen' – and Maori. That those bearded sailors had chosen to share in the 'sweetness and modesty of that lamb without stain' was a great consolation to the bishop. Thanks to the intervention of Captain Cécile he had been able introduce them to a god who had already been revealed to 'numberless infidels and cannibals'. Pompallier now felt that heresy had been pushed into the background, and his Catholic ministry would be able to flourish.[14] With the encouragement of local chiefs, he set about establishing his headquarters in the Bay of Islands before returning to continue his work at Hokianga. But he now suspected a 'last attempt' by Protestant ministers to resist the advances of the 'Mother Church', and a force of supportive Maori kept guard around his house in case any hostile attempt was made on him, although no such attack eventuated.[15]

It was appropriate that in the heavily forested Hokianga district Pompallier would resort to the analogy of the tree. He spoke of Catholicism in terms of the 'trunk of the true Church' and the 'living-tree Church' while Protestant sects were nothing more than 'cut-off branches'. But his struggle was not yet over, for the 'enemy' had the advantage of a printing press at Paihia, and was able to scatter its pamphlets, tracts and booklets across the country. While Pompallier conceded that these publications might teach 'the first truths of salvation', they were filled with all the usual anti-Catholic calumnies, in particular the one entitled *The Anti-Christ (Ko Te Anatikaraiti)*. For the present, Pompallier had only his voice and pen to combat the power of the competition's press.[16] But his plans for converting the Maori population were not made any easier by the recent spate of intertribal warfare. He suspected that no other race had carried cannibalism to such a ferocious extent, and recorded post-battle scenes reminiscent of a butcher's shop in which human limbs hung from victors' fences. On the other hand, he believed Maori had strict observance of temperance and sobriety: they were seldom seen drunk and despised those who 'fuddled' themselves with alcohol. He described Kororareka as consisting of fifteen or twenty European houses, a local Maori population of about 400, and a reputation for being a place of 'thieves [and] drunkards and given to licentiousness'.[17]

If Pompallier and his colleagues believed that the Protestants' Sunday services were 'filled with their prejudices, their dislike, their errors and their intolerance' and exhortations that the Catholic priests be driven from the country, the Church Missionary Society took a similarly opposing stand.[18] The decision by the Catholic bishop from Hokianga to establish his head-quarters in Kororareka was seen as part of a plan by the See of Rome to undermine the Protestants' efforts.[19] Apart from the dissemination of 'Popish Superstition', equally disturbing to the Protestants was Pompallier's claim that more than 450 Maori had chosen to follow his path to religion. If true, this large number of recent conversions may have been due to certain events, the most spectacular of which concerned Hoki, the niece of Kororareka chief Rewa. She had fallen dangerously ill and was given up on by the doctor, but thanks to prayer was quickly restored to full health. The grateful Hoki then asked Pompallier to baptise her, and as Péata she would later play a central role in a dramatic incident on the beach at Kororareka.[20]

In July 1839 Pompallier received sufficient funds to enable him to buy land for his mission. His chosen section at the southern end of Kororareka had been sold by Ngati Manu chief Kiwikiwi to local trader John Johnson in exchange for two muskets in 1827. It was bounded along the beach at low-water mark by a length of 168 feet, its extremities were a certain post and a saw pit, and it extended from the low-water mark up the hill for 600 feet. Ten years later Johnson sold the property to Gilbert Mair for £40, by which time Kiwikiwi and the Ngati Manu had been forced from Kororareka, which was now occupied by the Nga Puhi chiefs Rewa, Moka and others. Before long Mair had also capitalised on this waterfront property, selling it at a profit to Benjamin Turner. He built a string of rentable cottages on the property, which became known as Turner's Row. It was one of these that Pompallier bought, having decided to relocate the headquarters of his mission from the backwaters of Hokianga to the growing port of Kororareka. The bishop's narrow twenty-one-metre wide section was at the southern end of Turner's development and cost him a hefty £370. A humble three-roomed weather-board cottage stood on the beach frontage; Pompallier had this subdivided into small rooms to accommodate the presbytery and headquarters for his mission. Construction shortly began on a modest chapel for the use of the resident brothers and priests, and this was in use by May 1840.[21]

As Pompallier established his new base in the Bay he also ministered to individuals who were on the point of dying, and some appeared to make miraculous recoveries. Success bred success; and these 'providential occurrences' produced further conversions. In January 1840 a group of Maori chiefs from the Bay of Plenty asked Pompallier to visit them, sending their invitations to the Bay of Islands by ship. The bishop sent an assistant with written authority to uplift the expected letters, but the captain – who happened to be Protestant – was so enraged by the request that he threw it 'from the poop into the water'. Fearing for his life, the hapless messenger then cast himself into the tide and swam for shore. Hearing of this, Pompallier prayed that God might pardon the truculent captain, but there was no such happy outcome – he was later lost at sea. But before that he repented his resistance to the Catholic mission, and on a later visit north he bought more letters from the patient chiefs. In a face-saving ploy he had them rewrite their previous efforts under the pretext that they had not been tidy enough to present to a bishop.[22]

With the arrival of William Hobson in early 1840 Pompallier heard rumours that he might be forcibly removed from the new Crown Colony. But he soon had the satisfaction of the lieutenant-governor agreeing to guarantee free and equal protection to Catholicism and every other religion in the country. The new British administration included surveyor-general Felton Mathew who, while most unimpressed by Kororareka, was extremely positive about Pompallier, describing him as a 'very fine, handsome, intelligent man' and 'perfectly the gentleman'.[23] In contrast, the surveyor-general found 'old [Henry] Williams' to be 'a tiresome old fellow in the pulpit' who replaced the 'proper service' with 'his own extempore rubbish'. Matters of style aside, Mathew did concede that the Anglican missionary was a man of 'superior birth' and had a countenance that suggested 'shrewdness and intelligence'.[24] But if the Catholic bishop made the better impression, the Anglicans were holding their own, with Henry Williams enjoying increased attendances at the Sunday services at Paihia, 'notwithstanding the efforts of the Papists to mar the good work'.[25] In November 1841 competition between the two went head to head when Williams and missionary printer William Colenso took part in a public discussion on the Maori language with four Catholic priests at Kororareka. Despite their initial reservations, Colenso trumpeted that the Anglican team were 'more than conquerors', and he could scarcely believe that professing members of a Christian church could be 'so very ignorant of Scripture'.[26] The following year Kororareka received a visit from another bishop, the Anglican Augustus Selwyn, recently arrived in the country. He acknowledged the efforts of the town's first resident Church of England clergyman, the Reverend Robert Burrows, for thanks to him 'little progress has been made by the French Missionaries'.[27] But when the staff at the Catholic mission was increased, services at the church were stepped up to four on Sundays. In April 1844 a relieved Burrows could assure his colleagues that popery was not on the increase, and while its priests did have their adherents, they were mostly 'worthless characters, who continue[d] in all their Heathen practices'.[28]

From his new base at Kororareka, Pompallier travelled extensively around New Zealand and the Pacific. He was frequently absent for long periods, such as the fourteen months when he visited outposts at Wallis and Futuna and the Friendly Islands. In August 1842 he returned to the Bay of Islands to find his mission in a state of financial difficulty. Fortunately an English bank – ironically, one with Protestant directors – favoured the bishop with their confidence and furnished the necessary funds, thereby rescuing him from bankruptcy and his mission from ruin. Work could continue, but many souls had been lost in the meantime. Pompallier rued that upwards of 18,000 souls had been deprived of missionaries from the 'true Faith and Mother Church' and had 'passed over' to Protestantism.[29]

In June 1841 the *Earl of Durham* arrived at Kororareka, bringing eleven French missionaries, church bells and other ecclesiastical essentials, including the much-needed printing press. With the arrival three months later of Lyonnais architect and lay missionary volunteer Louis Perret, work could now begin on the printery, to be situated at the rear of the mission complex. While Perret would have preferred to build the new facility out of timber, a shortage of funds forced him to design it in a traditional French form, with a masonry lower section and a half-timbered upper storey. The missionaries used a familiar medium, the pisé de terre or rammed-earth construction of their native Rhône valley, and the structure was surmounted by a French hipped roof, shingled in kauri and pierced by two small dormer windows. The new building would function as a printery and storehouse until 1850 when the Bay of Islands mission station effectively ceased to operate, and the Marists and (later) the printing equipment were sent south to Auckland. The old building then endured a succession of owners, uses (including a tannery), alterations and a 'restoration' based on misconception. In 1990 its owners, the New Zealand Historic Places Trust, undertook to return Pompallier, as it was now known, to the appearance it had when it operated as the Marist printery.[30] The old building now had several claims to its name: the oldest French building, the oldest Catholic building, the oldest standing printery, the oldest standing tannery, the only example of Lyonnais pisé construction and one of the few half-timbered buildings in the country.[31]

In his own recollections Bishop Pompallier listed the several advantages those 'ministers of error', the Protestants, had enjoyed over his own mission in New Zealand: they had preceded his band by some twenty years; there were more of them; and they had more widely spread stations and greater financial resources. One apparent benefit of the latter was that their clothing was 'black and of a fashionable cut'. But on the other hand, because they were also mostly married and 'burdened with families', the Protestants' energies were – in the Catholic bishop's opinion – directed mainly towards accumulating personal property.[32] But perhaps the most serious advantage they enjoyed was their ability to disseminate their literature. To compete with books printed in Maori by both the Anglican Church Missionary Society and the Methodist missions, the French at first had to make do with handwritten prayer books, along with some items managed on a primitive press or produced commercially at Kororareka. By June 1841 the Catholic mission also had a priest able to prepare manuscripts in Maori. He was Father Claude Baty, who had already encountered the opposition's printer, William Colenso, when the two had followed a similar route across the East Coast, competing for the allegiance of local Maori. Baty was recalled from mission work at Mahia to take charge of the printery at Kororareka, and in October 1842 the press was ready to roll. Pompallier and his colleagues were at last equipped to counter the forces of those pesky Protestants.

THE ROARING 40s

SAILORS, WHALERS AND SURVEYORS

Of all the vile holes I ever visited this is certainly
the vilest . . .[1]

In 1850 HMS *Rattlesnake* came to the Bay of Islands carrying naturalist Thomas Henry Huxley, then trawling the southern oceans for new creatures. Shortly after his return to England, Huxley met Charles Darwin and became a strong advocate for his theory of evolution, most famously at a meeting of the British Association for the Advancement of Science at Oxford in 1860, when theologians mocked the heretical suggestion that humankind shared an ancestry with the ape. Huxley took up the challenge on his friend's behalf, systematically dealing with the specious arguments and working up to a well-measured climax that caused members of the audience to leap to their feet. Among the anti-Darwinians in attendance was the head of the government's meteorological department, Robert FitzRoy, who raised a large Bible above his head and implored the meeting to put faith in God rather than man.[2] Ironically, FitzRoy had been present when raw material for this revolutionary theory was first being gathered, as commander of HMS *Beagle* during Darwin's voyage of 1831–36. A decade later he would be appointed Governor of the Crown Colony of New Zealand.

Governor FitzRoy's predecessor was William Hobson, who first came to New Zealand on an earlier visit of HMS *Rattlesnake*. He was born in Ireland in 1793, and was at sea by the age of ten. A decade later, as a lieutenant on a sloop, he saw extensive service ranging from the West Indies to the Mediterranean and was promoted to commander. In 1828, after suffering from yellow fever, he temporarily retired from the Navy, but six years later, now married and with a daughter, he was posted to the *Rattlesnake*. He sailed for the East Indies, and then on to Australia to assist in survey work. But there were now troubling developments in New Zealand, and New South Wales Governor Sir Richard Bourke dispatched him to report on the situation across the Tasman.

After his first visit to New Zealand Hobson saw further service in the East Indies, before returning to England and being paid off. He appeared to have few further prospects in the Navy, but in 1838 the British government took positive action and appointed him British Consul to New Zealand. The following August he sailed with his wife and family for Sydney and took the *Herald* across to the Bay of Islands, arriving on 29 January 1840. Along with Hobson the party on board included Lieutenant Willoughby Shortland (police magistrate), George Cooper (colonial treasurer), Felton Mathew (surveyor-general) and James Freeman (private secretary), all supported by a sergeant and four men of the New South Wales mounted police. The latter were actually of the 'dismounted mounted' type, having preceded the arrival of their horses.[3] Nonetheless they qualified as the first official police force in New Zealand, eighteen months after the formation of the Kororareka Association, although it would be another twelve years before there were any rules and regulations regarding the colony's constabulary.[4]

Not unexpectedly, it was surveyor-general Felton Mathew who offered the most detailed description of the situation at this pivotal time in Kororareka's and New Zealand's development. He was not impressed, and his dismissal of the place as a 'vile hole' – and the worst he'd seen – was in a sense complementing earlier opinions of the place as a 'Hell'.[5] Surveying the settlement he counted about twenty cottages ('some tolerably good ones'), apart from the Maori dwellings which stood on a narrow shingle bank above the beach. But if he didn't think much of Kororareka itself, there was worse behind it in the form of the 'nasty, fetid morass' of a swamp, five times as large as the town. And beyond that rose steep hills, covered with 'coarse fern and dwarf cypress' and looking 'as barren and inhospitable as can be conceived'. The local residents hardly fared better in Mathew's estimation, as he noted the 'half-drunken, devil-may-care sort of look' of the Europeans and the 'squalid, debased appearance' of the Maori. His opinion of this place, 'against which [he was] most vehemently prejudiced', was hardly improved by the standard of his initial accommodation. With nowhere else available, he and Freeman were quartered with Shortland in a 'dog-kennel of a cock-loft', which he did at least concede was 'snug'.[6] Mathew did find other redeeming features among all that vileness, such as the pleasant 'gentle murmuring' of the sea lapping the shingled beach. He anticipated taking a 'glorious dip' in the bay before breakfast, and that such a regime, combined with the congenial climate, would enable him and his wife to enjoy better health in this country.[7]

Another view of Kororareka at the time of Hobson's arrival was offered by the Rev. Burrows. Towards the front of the town stood two Maori pa with about 100 permanent occupants, while the total 'mixed population' was somewhere between 600 and 1000. The place 'had its own laws', which were neither well defined nor rigidly carried out, and as for the moral character of many of the inhabitants, Burrows wrote, 'the least said . . . the better', with most 'absent from Sydney and other penal settlements without leave'. With the arrival of Hobson's police force, most of these individuals allegedly 'made themselves scarce'. While they only had to find their way to a native settlement to be safe from these authorities, they did need to be wary of who offered them refuge. Whaling captains were known to pay £2 or £3 per head for each man returned to the ship, and it was not uncommon to see a Maori canoe returning such culprits, their hands bound with flax. Sailors as well as settlers were frequently involved in drunken quarrels that further enlivened Kororareka Beach, and in Burrows' view the local magistrate 'very wisely' discouraged the interference of the police in all such incidents. Instead, the combatants were likely to be left to slug it out, or perhaps some game or public-spirited citizen might manage to put a stop to the brawl.[8]

Notwithstanding the state of surroundings or the inhabitants, there was important business to attend to. On 30 January 1840, the day after his arrival at the Bay of Islands and despite the short notice, Hobson invited Maori and Europeans to attend a meeting at Kororareka. He came ashore, and read out various official documents to a crowded 'congregation' in the local church. Among them was the proclamation extending the boundaries of New South Wales to include New Zealand, and the commission appointing him lieutenant-governor. Later, with the assistance of British Resident James Busby and members of the Church Missionary Society, Hobson summoned the northern chiefs to a meeting at Waitangi. Discussions began there on 5 February, and after explanations of its terms the Treaty was signed the following day. But in March Hobson collapsed from a paralytic stroke, and New South Wales Governor George Gipps ordered Major Thomas Bunbury and a detachment of troops to New Zealand, to take control if necessary. A camp was established at Okiato, some four miles up the harbour from Kororareka, but by the time Bunbury's force had arrived Hobson's health had greatly improved.

A little over two months after the signing of the Treaty of Waitangi, New Zealand received its third visit from Dumont d'Urville. After stocking up on pigs at Poverty Bay, the French navigator brought the corvettes *Astrolabe* and *Zélée* into the Bay of Islands on 26 April to find a dozen whaling ships, among others, at anchor. He also learned that Britain had formally taken possession of the country. But his surprise may have been matched by consternation among the British settlers, for there were suggestions that these new arrivals were about to plant the French flag, despite Hobson's proclamation. D'Urville's views on the recent developments would hardly be without bias, for he suggested that Kororareka was now in a state of turmoil and its prospects would be dire, not only for French settlers but for whaling operations. As for the original Maori inhabitants, he thought that all they had gained from European contact was a thirst for strong alcohol and tobacco. Their warlike demeanour had given way to moral degradation, and they were now reduced to watching new settlers establish homes on what had once been their land.

D'Urville described Kororareka as a scruffy assortment of small houses, less salubrious huts for Maori, and tents for new arrivals. He took a dim view of the Protestant missionaries, suspecting that they were engaged in land speculation, while – predictably – praising the Catholic missionaries for their efforts among the Maori. Nevertheless, while visiting the Anglican missionary establishment at Paihia, he was delighted to be presented with a kiwi, a bird he had heard about but not yet seen. Another highlight was the opportunity to sample wine grown on Busby's estate. D'Urville was most impressed with this drop, predicting a bright future for a local viticultural industry. But the low point of his visit occurred when two sailors from the *Astrolabe* were severely punished, presumably flogged, for what was probably the rape of a Maori woman.[9]

As the population of Kororareka increased with the arrival of officials and bureaucrats, its old habits and trades persisted, as did the missionaries' efforts to save the place from itself. While the settlement continued to receive mostly bad press, any such judgement needs to be considered in the light of similar situations elsewhere. The American Lieutenant Charles Wilkes, who came to the Bay of Islands in early 1840, had recently visited Sydney and inspected a newly arrived convict ship. Despite the conditions on board, he was impressed by the 'ruddy, healthy, and athletic looks' of the main cargo and saw little about them to suggest they had been perpetrators of heinous crimes. But it didn't take long for these new colonists to slide down the slippery slope. On arrival, many were assigned to persons who exposed them to 'contaminations and temptations', while hardened criminals took it upon themselves to complete the 'education' of novice convicts. Such influence removed all hope of reform, and ensured a constant supply of recruits for the criminal class of New South Wales – and beyond.[10]

Wilkes also observed a local convict chain-gang, a 'rough-looking set, with bad countenances', and heard about the crimes committed by these hardenened types in New Zealand and the Pacific.[11] He believed that intoxicating liquor lay at the root of Sydney's problem, for rum, a generic name for hard spirits of all kinds, had assumed the importance of money itself and became both the 'delight and despair' of the town.[12] One anecdote tells of elderly women patrons of the Black Dog hotel in The Rocks being so rum-soaked that when they lit their pipes, blue flames flickered flambé-like from their lips.[13] It didn't help that many of the keepers of drinking holes were notorious drunkards themselves, and their premises were a human zoo of thieves, cut-throats and receivers of stolen goods, along with 'slatternly women' and 'raddled old harpies' who paraded their 'charms' for women-hungry sailors.[14]

The Rocks was a complex of narrow, twisted and blind alleys and passages with such colourful names as Black Dog Lane and Cockroach Run.[15] Whalers and sealers ruled the taverns, where unwary visitors were said to be likely to be entrapped and shanghaied off to sea. Some of these places were alleged to have special basements equipped to hold drunk and drugged sailors until they could be on-sold to a captain short of a full complement. Those involved in this human traffic were known as crimps, and might also slip a corpse among the supposedly drunk and comatose sailors; the disposal of dead bodies was a lucrative sideline.[16] Charles Wilkes became only too familiar with the workings of the Sydney waterfront when wily crimps managed to entice away some of his own crew.[17]

The Rocks was, of course, merely one of a string of sailors' haunts throughout the Pacific, along with the Bay of Islands and Tahiti. Valparaiso in Chile was an especially popular haven for sailors who had recently rounded the notorious Cape Horn. Wilkes had called here in 1840 and observed certain of its attractions, in particular the dark-eyed local women with their red bayettas (garments), who were a great source of annoyance for ships' captains, their men invariably leaving this port with empty pockets and 'injured health'. But Wilkes did note a great improvement in matters of the locals' habits and civil obedience since his previous visit to Valparaiso in 1821–22. At that time robbery, murder and various vices, including smuggling and bribery, were openly committed under the eyes of the authorities. Wilkes also saw several dead bodies lying about in the public squares, victims of knife wounds sustained during one night's 'debauch'.[18]

While in Sydney Wilkes had observed individuals whose most immediate aspiration may have been escape to New Zealand. Correspondingly, at Kororareka he was able to comment on the effectiveness of Hobson's imported police force in dealing with such vagabonds.[19] He deplored the 'infamous practice of traffic in women', which may have been one of the reasons his own men visited Pomare's pa, an attraction which he estimated consisted of about 300 huts.[20]

Lawlessness and immorality were not confined to Kororareka. The residents of Wellington had problems on their own doorstep in 1842 when the beach alongside Lambton Quay was considered unsafe to walk on because of the broken bottles. Of this 'wicked' place it was said: 'O how sin does here abound. The Swearing, Sabbath breaking, Drunkenness and Whoremongering is most awful.' But the situation may not have been as bad as it sounded, for that was the view of a temperance lecturer.[21] Much worse were certain of this country's shore-whaling establishments, in particular Waikouaiti in Otago and Cloudy Bay and other places in the Marlborough Sounds – outposts which, man for man, might claim to rival the Bay of Islands in misbehaviour.

In the first instance, sealing had attracted some rugged and lawless types to New Zealand. When their source of skins died out, many of these individuals looked for opportunities in the new business of shore whaling and so continued to exist under conditions of hardship and danger, in lonely and inhospitable places. Although whaling could be a lucrative business, those involved tended to be an improvident lot, dissipating their earnings. They were encouraged to do so by the Sydney-based owners of the stations, who supplied stores and liquor in lieu of wages, thereby keeping the men in a constant state of both debt and drunkenness. Nor was there any physical escape, for they lived in a state of perpetual exile, and mostly at the mercy of the infrequent visits of their employers' vessels.[22]

Shore-whaling bases were said to be places where men practised 'every species of iniquity without restraint', 'the very soil [was] polluted' and the 'atmosphere tainted'.[23] A sense of the conditions at New Zealand stations can be gleaned from surviving records, some of which were written as the result of those communities being considered in desperate need of salvation. The missionaries who took the Gospel to such places anticipated that their biggest challenge would be the depravity and bloodthirstiness of the Maori community, but in fact it was likely to be the gross and 'unblushing wickedness' of many of their own fellow countrymen.[24] These improving efforts began when enterprising businessman John Jones decided to plant 'the wholesome leaven of Christian morality in the minds, if not the hearts' of workers at his whaling station at Waikouaiti. The Wesleyan Methodist Missionary Board in Sydney appointed the Rev. James Watkin to the task, and so he established what would be the first missionary station in the South Island. He had earlier served in the Friendly Islands and was rather hoping to be given a post in England. Instead he got Waikouaiti, and had no idea what he was in for.[25]

Watkin would later admit that had he known something of the state of Waikouaiti he would never have gone there. He began his 'labours' in June 1840, and came to regard the place as his 'Purgatory'. Disgusted and repelled by the vices of his fellow Europeans, he also came to loathe the already corrupted local Maori. As far as they were concerned, he felt he was ten years too late, for he saw the race as 'fast decreasing' and those remaining 'almost . . . beyond redemption'. Watkin also had other challenges, for in a repeat of events at the Bay of Islands he had to deal with the inroads of other religions. He had been at Waikouaiti only some six months when Bishop Pompallier came to preach in the district, 'seducing the natives into a system not much less idolatrous than their own'. Watkin needed to reclaim souls and prevent others from falling into that 'corrupt system', but the Catholic competition had the advantage of 'dazzling vestments and superstitious forms', which Watkin confessed made a greater impression on the Maori mind than his own plain dress and mode of worship. Watkin had a further challenge when the Anglicans extended their range to the South Island, leading to disputes between 'The Children of Wesley' and 'The Church of Pahia [sic]'.[26]

To add to his difficulties, Watkin was a sick man and at Waikouaiti was forced to live with his wife and four children in a hut barely large enough for two people.[27] His despondency and feeling that he had been abandoned by his Sydney employers was well founded according to Edward Shortland, government interpreter and younger brother of Willoughby, who visited the station during an exploration of the South Island in 1843 and 1844.[28] Whatever else the men got up to at Waikouaiti, Shortland's records show that theirs had been one of the most productive of the twelve or so whaling stations in the lower half of the South Island. The 1838 catch, for example, was forty-one whales, yielding about 145 tons of oil and one and a half tons of bone, with a total value of about £1500 in New Zealand, or £4500 on the London market. He heard how a ship would turn up near the end of the season to collect these whale by-products and bring supplies. All hands would then give themselves up to rum, or 'arrack', for as long as their credit lasted. In the following off-season, having exhausted their rum and food, they went in search of more at another whaling station. If supplies were available they would remain there until those too were consumed, and then this larger and hungry group would descend on the next likely station.[29]

It was recorded that 120 tons of liquor was landed on the beach at Waikouaiti at a time when there were only forty Europeans based at the whaling station. The massive booze-up that surely followed no doubt hardened Watkin's attitude towards this 'distilled damnation'.[30] Shortland did at least encounter one individual, Stephen Smith, who had resisted the temptation to squander his hard-won gains. Instead, he had bought several head of cattle and established a picturesque cottage and garden, while his Maori wife dressed 'like a European country girl, wore a white apron, and made excellent butter'. The whaler's village, Maori settlement and mission station were all within a short distance from each other, near the mouth of the Waikouaiti River, and Maori and Europeans appeared to be on good terms. Two local Maori women had married whalers, while nine had 'formed similar connexions without the solemnity of the marriage ceremony'. And, as Shortland put it, the 'fruit of these unions were fourteen half-caste children'.[31]

The effects of Europeans on the coasts of Otago became apparent to Dumont d'Urville when the *Astrolabe* and *Zélée* called in 1840. There were four whaling ships in port at the time, and the French captain found the local population much degraded by the types who arrived on such vessels. In his opinion the Maori had gained nothing from contact with these dregs of European society, with the men becoming undermined by alcohol which they purchased by coercing their wives and daughters into prostitution. The situation was hardly isolated, for d'Urville had observed similar deterioration of native cultures throughout the Pacific, while he was also critical of the missionaries, accusing them of creating further social problems by destroying traditional beliefs and customs.[32]

The harassed Rev. Watkin was of the opinion that shore whaling and the individuals involved had been 'a curse to this country'. Conflict between the men and the missionaries was inevitable, not least because the former – like their prey – did not observe the Sabbath and encouraged Maori to do likewise. But their drinking and whoring aside, these whalers were credited with possessing 'unselfish courage and manly endurance', although any finer characteristics were likely to be stifled by the privations of their calling.[33] To deal with the situation at another of the South Island's blighted settlements, the Methodist mission sent the appropriately named Rev. Samuel Ironside to Port Underwood, Cloudy Bay. This part of the coast was described as a 'Pandemonium on earth', compared to which the Bay of Islands looked like paradise.[34] Ironside arrived on 20 December 1840 and quickly confirmed his suspicions, finding the local Maori – Ngati Toa – to be in great need of the Gospel. The whaling station here attracted 'the scum of all nations': men who hired Maori women for the season for half a keg of tobacco or rum. At least the reverend began his ministry on what he would regard as a positive note, for on Christmas Day he was able to join five Europeans and their Maori wives in holy matrimony.[35]

In 1839 New Zealand Company naturalist Ernst Dieffenbach visited Te Awaiti on the south coast of Arapawa Island in the Marlborough Sounds, the site of New Zealand's first bay-whaling station, established in 1827.

Dieffenbach found the beach littered with whale remains, and described the pervading stench and 'exhilarating' scene of blubber being rendered down in bubbling cauldrons. The community here consisted of a few substantial wooden houses, but most were of thatched vines and rushes and with clay floors, built by local Maori. There were some forty whalers here, all of whom had Maori wives, and Dieffenbach counted twenty-one offspring, many distinguished by the dark glossy hair of their mothers or the flaxen hair and blue eyes of their fathers.[36]

There were then three whaling establishments in Te Awaiti, and others nearby. Dieffenbach learned that employees lived here in a perpetual state of debt, which the owners only encouraged by the supply of alcohol. On the other hand, the workers here were mostly a 'reckless class' with little commitment to their employers. Although drunkenness was common, especially after the return of the whaleboats, Dieffenbach noted that Maori did not take part in these nightly revelries. And despite the nature and intemperate ways of these whalers, 'outrages' against persons and property were surprisingly infrequent. During the summer season the men were mostly idle, although some maintained vegetable gardens and livestock and so lived in relative comfort.[37] As well as the personal habits of the workers, Dieffenbach was critical of how the whaling industry was conducted, predicting that unless restrictions were imposed it would, like sealing before it, soon be annihilated.[38]

Thanks to shore whaling, for a time parts of Otago and the Marlborough Sounds were able to emulate Kororareka's notorious reputation. In the estimation of author Errol Brathwaite, Port Underwood qualified as 'Hell-hole Number Two'.[39] All these places' standings would soon be overtaken when human flotsam flooded across the Pacific to San Francisco, following the discovery of gold in California in 1849. But a decade earlier Kororareka could claim to be this country's largest centre of lawless and licentious behaviour and, in spite of that, now had good reason to expect that it might also be made its first capital.

8

CAPITAL TIMES

A PERFECT PICTURE OF DEPRAVITY

The village of Kororarika is inhabited by a set of lawless
fellows, the greater part of whom are convicts escaped
from New South Wales and get a livelihood by decoying
seamen from their ship – and shipping them at an
enormous advance – on board of any other vessel
that may have been in like manner distressed . . .[1]

Two of Hobson's immediate duties in New Zealand were the acquisition of
sovereignty and the invalidation of all titles to land that had not been derived
from the Crown. A third challenge was the selection of a suitable site for his
official government settlement.[2] If the new governor had originally considered the Bay of Islands a likely candidate, that was certainly the
impression gained by some local residents. When a select committee of the
House of Commons looked into the state of New Zealand in 1844, Walter
Brodie, an extensive world traveller, merchant, writer and, much later,
member of the House of Representatives, gave evidence that Hobson had
told a meeting of 200–300 people in the Bay that Kororareka was the best
location, but a fortnight later he had decided that a spot a few miles to the
south was more suitable. As far as Brodie was concerned, Hobson's word was
'not to be depended on'.[3]

Kororareka's expectation that it might get the official nod was based largely
on the very things that had stimulated its development in the first place: a

safe anchorage and deep water close in-shore. It was also, of course, already a fully functioning settlement in several respects. But Hobson ordered Felton Mathew to investigate other locations in the Bay. Not surprisingly, given his extremely negative first impressions, the surveyor-general found Kororareka wholly unsuitable, mainly because of its lack of available land. Other potential sites that were considered and rejected were Kerikeri (at the head of a tidal river), Te Puna (exposed anchorage), Paihia (no sheltered anchorage), Busby's planned town of Victoria at Waitangi (lacking a suitably sheltered anchorage) and the property of local trader Gilbert Mair at Te Wahapu, between Okiato and Kororareka (insufficient flat land). In the end Felton Mathew chose the site of another trader's property, Captain James Clendon, at Okiato, and began laying out a town to be known as Russell in honour of the British Colonial Secretary, Lord John Russell.[4] In its favour was a good anchorage, immediate possession and suitability for subdivision, but in the opinion of one historian there was 'more than a hint of jobbery' about this transaction.[5] The asking price was considered excessive, and when Governor Sir George Gipps in Sydney refused to approve the purchase it took years before Clendon received his payment.

Hemmed in by a swamp and hills on three sides and with little land available for sale, Kororareka appeared to have few prospects for future development. Ironically, as the colony's most established settlement, it could have absorbed the extra responsibilities of being capital for the brief period that Okiato operated as such. In hindsight it may have been a more economic option, avoiding the complications posed by the Clendon purchase. Although Governor Hobson was in residence at his new capital of Russell in May 1840, he had previously instructed Felton Mathew to investigate other sites even further afield at the Whangarei, Mahurangi and Waitemata harbours, for while the Bay of Islands offered excellent facilities for shipping, it did have some serious disadvantages. It was isolated in the far north of the country, was already heavily populated, and had insufficient land for future development.

Thoughts now turned southward, to the narrow isthmus straddling the Waitemata and Manukau harbours. As well as the essential anchorage, there was ample land available for purchase, a lack of population, and a location that enabled easier access to other parts of the North Island. It was here that Hobson decided he would locate his capital, Auckland, and so he moved south in March 1841. Despite his strong feelings about Kororareka being overlooked, Walter Brodie conceded that when it came to Auckland, the governor 'could not have pitched on a better situation'.[6]

In 1828 James Reddy Clendon, captain of the *City of Edinburgh* – a ship already known to Kororareka – had carried female prisoners from England to Port Jackson and later crossed to New Zealand for spars from Hokianga. In December 1830 he was at the Bay of Islands and met the Ngati Manu chiefs Pomare and Kiwikiwi, who had retired to their pa at Otuihu at the junction of the Kawakawa and Waikare rivers after being forced from Kororareka following The Girls' War. Clendon now arranged his first purchase of land at Okiato, settling there with his family and establishing a business supplying the lucrative shipping trade.

Because of his involvement in the local temperance society, Clendon's stock of provisions was not likely to include alcohol. In 1835 he publicly drained all his rum casks, a sacrifice intended to encourage sober habits in the Bay of Islands. He may not have been able to turn the locals away from drink, but he was nonetheless an influential figure through his regular contact with Europeans and Maori. As an indication of his standing in the community he was made president of the New Zealand Banking Company, which opened the country's first bank at Kororareka in September 1840, and whose first board of directors included Gilbert Mair and William Mayhew. Clendon's profile and shipping connections also led to his appointment as United States Consul, to protect American interests in this country. He carried out these duties from October 1838 until the end of 1841, during which period he dutifully recorded the arrivals, departures and details of 151 visiting American ships, along with other matters in that country's interest.[7]

Clendon's records indicate that the average stay of American ships in port was two to three weeks, although many lingered for much longer – the *Brilliant*, for example, was at the Bay for nearly two months. It was not uncommon for five or six ships to be in at the same time, while in early March 1839 there were some days when no fewer than twelve vessels coincided. Among other things they brought a colourful and cosmopolitan flavour to the Bay. There were geographical references, such as the *Ganges, Helvetia, France, Panama, Java* and *Caledonia*, and a veritable pantheon of classical themes: *Alpha, Omega, Hercules, Atlas, Chariot, Concordia, Corinthia* and *Pleides*. Another name that arrived was a self-fulfilling prophecy the *Harvest*, carrying a cargo of 1200 barrels of whale oil. Most of these American ships were from Rhode Island, New Bedford, Sag Harbour, Salem and Nantucket, with the last of these well represented by one of its old families, the Starbucks: in February 1839 a Captain Starbuck brought the *Dartmouth* to the Bay of Islands, while the following January saw the arrival of the ship *Levi Starbuck*. The Christian names of many of the ships' masters were straight out of the Old Testament: Seth, Obed, Ab, Isaac, Abner, Silas and Moses, while a particularly appropriate surname was borne by Fred Fish, captain of the *Columbus* from Fairhaven.[8]

Clendon advised the Secretary of State in Washington of such news as the loss of American ships and the welfare of their crews. One such casualty was the aforementioned *Brilliant*, which went down on 11 June 1839, just eleven days after quitting the Bay of Islands.[9] A different kind of loss was the demolition of the house of a British resident at Kororareka by the crew of an American whaler, which Clendon reported in August 1839. Three men from the *Hannibal* had absconded when it was in port, and one was later sighted in the house of a local grog-seller. The captain ordered the man back to the ship, but instead the reluctant whaler retreated into the loft of the house. Prevented from following, the captain was subjected to a barrage of obscene language, and so he returned to the harbour to muster a force from American ships in port. He came back with two boats and twelve men from his own ship, plus five boats with officers and men from other vessels, all armed with pistols, cutlasses and guns. The United States flag was unfurled in front of the house, and the captain demanded that the men be given up. There was no immediate response, so the order was given and the men began to peel weatherboards from the lower parts of the house. Before long evidence of the missing men was found, but Henry Williams turned up and recommended that the demolition stop. The occupier of the house then appeared, extremely drunk, and gave the captain a further round of abuse, whereupon the removal of boards was ordered to continue forthwith. The house was reduced to a skeleton, now minus its whole front and ends and with its roof supported only by some gable posts.[10] It was not recorded whether the three deserters were actually found in the remains of the house, but some of the locals were grateful for the captain's initiative, thanking him for eliminating one of the 'greatest sinks of iniquity' in the town.[11]

As if to paint the American sailors in a better light, Clendon prefaced his

'Report of Riot at Bay of Islands' with a description of the inhabitants of Kororareka. He warned the secretary of state that the locals here were 'lawless fellows', most of whom were escaped convicts from New South Wales who specialised in decoying (or crimping) crews from ships. Clendon also related the unfortunate case of Thomas H Jenkins of Maine, who had deserted from the whaler *Alpha* of Nantucket and was found distressed and in need of medical aid, food and clothing. The consul placed the sailor under the care of Church Missionary Society surgeon Dr Samuel Ford, based at Paihia, where he stayed until he had regained his health. But one evening in late September 1839 the recuperated Jenkins was crossing the harbour to Kororareka to seek employment when he drowned, presumably after falling overboard.[12]

In the months following Hobson's arrival, and with the delivery of their horses, mounted trooper units began to provide surveillance of the settlements in the north, showing the new administration's determination to maintain law and order. These men had been 'the shock troops of frontier expansion' in Australia, but their potential mobility in the Bay of Islands was impaired by the rugged and bush-covered terrain, as the important route linking the police camp at Okiato with the main trouble spot of Kororareka was an 'impassable swamp'. There was also the significant problem of insufficient fodder for their horses. These troopers were quartered at outlying mission stations, and while their personal behaviour might have been tolerated back in Australia when dealing with a largely convict population, they now managed to offend some of the missionaries.[13]

The capital of Russell consisted of Clendon's existing complex, which included an extensive four-bedroom house, stable, two wooden cottages, two sizeable storehouses of two and three storeys, a blacksmith's shop, and a 180-foot long wharf and jetty. Felton Mathew intended other improvements, among them a public quay around the waterfront, various streets and reserves, but it appears that the only new dedicated buildings were a gaol and barracks and others associated with the military camp.[14] A couple of months after Hobson abandoned the short-lived northern capital his old Government House burned down, and the police headquarters were relocated to Kororareka. But even the law-enforcers were not above suspicion in the Bay, for there was an element of scandal surrounding Police Magistrate

Thomas Beckham, the suggestion was that he chose to live in the relative isolation of Russell so he could indulge in immoral behaviour. His private life aside, his professional conduct would certainly come into question in 1845.[15]

In 1840 military authorities at Sydney employed a constable at Russell to track down escaped convicts in the Bay of Islands, the part of New Zealand to which they were most likely to be attracted. He may have been this country's first policeman to specialise in detection work, receiving £2 for every runaway recaptured, while he was also paid for performing more perfunctory policing duties. He may have had plenty of escapees to deal with, for such individuals tended not to follow the general drift south to the new capital at Auckland where they would stand a greater chance of being detected.[16] By at least July 1841 there were two prisons at the Bay of Islands, at Kororareka and Russell, both were 'common gaols' and each under the jurisdiction of a sheriff.[17] But the lock-up at the capital was not secure enough: four months later two prisoners broke out – William Chalks, aged about forty-one, stout, with sandy whiskers and a nose 'broken and near half flat', and John McKenny, aged about twenty-six, of slender build and with a 'long' face. The public were cautioned against harbouring these runaways, and a reward of 40 shillings each was offered for their recapture.[18]

Mrs Hobson followed her husband to New Zealand, travelling from Sydney with her governess and four children on the store ship *Buffalo* in April 1840. This ship had been to New Zealand before, to uplift kauri spars, and in July 1840 would be totally wrecked at Mercury Bay on the Coromandel Peninsula, in a cove now known as Buffalo Beach. One of Mrs Hobson's fellow passengers was a young army officer, Ensign Abel Dottin William Best, a member of a detachment of the 80th Regiment. He was much taken by his first sight of the Bay of Islands, and like John Bidwill before him had seen the painted panorama in London's Leicester Square, based on drawings by Augustus Earle. But Best was much less impressed with 'Kororarireka' itself, a 'wretched place' consisting of about fifty houses, most of them grog-shops. There were 'one or two' good stores and a club, whose members were mostly land speculators, where he was made welcome.[19]

Best was witness at a tense moment in local history. Following the murder of a European, Colonial Secretary Willoughby Shortland proceeded to lay charges against a Maori named Kihi, using the Kororareka church as a venue. During the formalities a large group of Maori, reportedly numbering between

150 and 300, arrived from Waitangi and demanded that the prisoner be handed over so they could dispense their own justice. Shortland sent for assistance from the military camp at Okiato, resulting in some eighty armed troops being landed at the upper end of Kororareka Beach. While some took a circular route through the scrub at the back of the town, others advanced along the beach to within fifty paces of the Maori party. Shortland stepped forward, and was informed that the Maori did not have hostile intentions, but merely wished to show their abhorrence for the crime that had been committed. The tense situation was defused, with both sides withdrawing and the troops returning to Okiato.[20] In the opinion of one historian: 'Had a trigger been pulled on this occasion, this would have been the beginning and the end of the Colony of New Zealand.'[21] It seems likely that the handing over of the prisoner to satisfy the apparent demands of the Maori group would have created a dangerous precedent, making the administering of any future (British) justice extremely fraught. As for the unwitting instigator of this testing incident, Kihi died in prison of dysentery before his trial.[22]

On 20 April 1841 Clendon tendered his resignation as United States Consul, citing his distance from 'the seat of commerce in New Zealand', now Auckland. Unable to give his full attention to such duties, he recommended the appointment of William Mayhew as vice consul.[23] Clendon had supported Hobson in his negotiations for British sovereignty, but the signing of the Treaty of Waitangi dealt a blow to his American business, and if selling his Okiato property was intended as some sort of compensation, administrative problems would result in his receiving only a small part of the purchase price and accepting in settlement a 10,000-acre block south of Auckland. After relinquishing his consular functions altogether, Clendon assumed minor government functions in the Bay of Islands. He then retired and became a merchant in Rawene and, in contrast to his earlier practices, was now licensed to sell beer, wine and spirits.[24] Mayhew, a merchant, was previously an American whaling captain who had operated in the Kapiti Island region near Wellington. As the new vice consul, on 21 February 1842, he advised his superiors in Washington that the British government had now enacted laws and levied imports that were 'particularly harrassing' to American citizens and 'most destructive' to their commercial pursuits.[25]

Hobson's arrival in New Zealand heralded what would be a major and continuing concern for the new colony – land. The new governor read out a land titles validation proclamation, which provided for the appointment of a commission to inquire into and report on all claims to lands purchased before January 1840. Those that had not been derived from or confirmed by Her Majesty would have to be proved, and would be limited to 2560 acres, except in special circumstances.[26] Land commissioners began their investigations in Auckland in July 1841, and the gazetting of these gives a sense of the scale of transactions over the previous decade or so.[27] Some were massive, such as that of Sydney merchant Alexander Brodie Spark, who alleged he bought 100,000 acres on the Thames River from six chiefs for £210. He also claimed another 2500 acres, a prime slice of real estate which included all of North Head, then known as Takapuna, at the entrance to the Auckland harbour.[28] It soon became apparent that some of the largest claims had been made by members of the Church Missionary Society. Topping one such list was the 50,000 acres claimed by the Rev. Richard Taylor at North Cape, of which he would be granted 2726 acres 'with certain exceptions', with William Fairburn's 40,000 acres (of which he was granted 3695) at Tamaki not far behind.[29] Another big loser was James Busby, whose services as British Resident were no longer required with Hobson's arrival. His own land holdings of some 10,000 acres in the Bay of Islands were also investigated: of those he was granted just 2090.[30]

Many of the land claims revealed a complex web of previous owners and property definitions, along with varying means of payment and rapid resales. One Donald McKay, for example, claimed that he bought an allotment at the south end of Kororareka's York Street, measuring 100 feet on all four sides, from chief Riva (Rewa) on 27 February 1827, for a double-barrelled gun valued at £12 and tobacco to the value of £6 16s 6d,[31] while Henry Day claimed twelve acres near Tapuna (Te Puna), bought from three chiefs in October 1834 for 200 pounds of tobacco valued at £12 10s.[32] American currency was also acceptable, with Henry Williams negotiating on behalf of the Church Missionary Society and claiming a portion of land 'bounded by an old path road close to the east side of the swamp, at the back of the pa' and other identified Kororareka landmarks, purchased from chief Rewa, in November 1834, for $25.[33]

An early claim relating to Kororareka was for 'about one acre' on the beach, with a frontage of 90 feet and depth of 198 feet, purchased by 'Alexander Grey' from chiefs Kiwa Kiwa (Kiwikiwi), Erika Erkeo, Emene and Ewariki in

July 1830.[34] Several of Joel Polack's land transactions have already been mentioned, while his rival Benjamin Turner was also active in local real estate. He bought a piece of land named Taumata Rahiro from chiefs Pakiria, Ewrie, Ehuru and Jack White in 1839, and resold it the following year.[35] He was involved in at least two lots which were 'part of Aputada' (also 'Apurada'), purchased from chiefs Ahongi, Ahoki and Atoko, the cost of one in 1838 being twenty-eight 'yards print' (presumably fabric) and £22.[36] Another property, adjoining one of Turner's, had been purchased from chief Mangonui and his wife Apere in 1839 for £10 and one horse.[37]

A number of properties enjoyed frontages on Kororareka Beach, among them William Baker's purchase from chiefs Uduroa (Ururoa, a cousin of Hongi) and Ehongi or Shongi (Hongi, not Hongi Hika who died eleven years earlier) in 1838,[38] and several acres on a hill near the 'watering place', known as Waipaia, bought by another claimant from two chiefs in 1839 for £5.[39] More affordable but much less desirable were sections further back, in the swamp. John Johnson, who had quite a portfolio of properties, claimed more or less two acres here in the 'Ripo, or swamp', for which he had paid chiefs Parangi, Amene, Tareha and Akeno two double-barrelled guns and two great coats valued at £31.[40] And in October 1839 the Kororareka Land Company claimed an elevated section that would later play a pivotal part in the town's history: two acres on Mt 'Mike' – Maiki, also Flagstaff Hill – purchased from chief Mahore Katookoo for merchandise to the value of £9 10s.[41]

In March 1842 William Mayhew was replaced as United States Consul at the Bay of Islands by John Brown Williams of Salem. He and his seven brothers had followed the local tradition and joined the maritime trade, with Williams making his first voyage to Australia and New Zealand in 1832 and 1833. A decade later, as consul, he noticed a number of changes at the Bay of Islands. American landowners and traders were unhappy with the recently introduced port and excise taxes and regulations regarding land titles, while prospects generally seemed to have been reduced since the capital had shifted to Auckland.[42]

Like many accounts left by early visitors to Kororareka, Williams' was a particularly rich collection of fact and opinion. Some of his more colourful comments were the result of him being a self-confessed 'chauvinistic Yankee' and particularly critical of the new British bureaucracy at the Bay. He believed that local Maori had been victims of 'English robbery' and 'wronged' out of their land, although he admitted that some of his own countrymen were also at fault in this regard.[43] Williams supported the missionaries, acknowledging their perseverance in the rescue of Maori from cannibalism and 'savage despotism', while the influence of Bishop Selwyn had resulted in military officers being required to dispense with 'their young miss's'.[44] In that vein the sin-obsessed Yankee consul was especially offended by the sub-collector of customs, John Guise Mitford, managing to malign him on three occasions in his journal. This functionary was accused of living licentiously with 'lewd Mauries' and being a seducer of 'innocent young native girls in their primitive simplicity'. What's more, he was 'an intolerable disgrace to the British name', 'about a 6th rate man' (which, in nautical terms, would rate him with a sloop) and a 'half educated upstart of a boy'.[45] For his part Mitford was also an amateur artist, painting landscapes throughout the northern and central parts of the North Island. He spent a year and a half in the Bay of Islands, complaining of his duties that required him to work on Sundays and being held responsible for the security of 'plunderable government funds'. He returned to Auckland in October 1844 after the abolition of customs duties had rendered him redundant, and for a period was able to concentrate on his painting. Despite what John Williams thought of him, this one-time customs collector has been rated 'one of the foremost among New Zealand painters of the mid-nineteenth century'.[46]

Williams also painted a grim picture of the goings-on at Wahapu Bay – now known as Te Wahapu Inlet – where Gilbert Mair established a trading post in 1824. There were gaming houses, possibly 'scores of them', where robbing and swindling took place, and other places that cast 'a dark shade over humanity, darker than hell!' – houses of 'ignominy and ill fame'. When the ships were in their decks they were 'alive with native women' – who also danced all day Sunday – and each was a 'floating castle of prostitution'. Intemperance raged here 'with all its fury', and Williams knew of nowhere that endured more 'anarchy, profligacy and prostitution' than this place. And although he was American, he conceded that his own countrymen could be just as bad, if not worse, than the English and French who revelled here. Behind it all, above Wahapu Bay, rose a hill which he suggested would be appropriately named 'Mt. Hell'.[47]

The combination of visiting sailors and European inhabitants had produced a 'sink of infamy and disgrace' in the Bay of Islands. The main trade here took place in the grog-shops, and Williams ranked 'grog vendors' along with spongers (finanacial hangers-on), finished sharpers (professional swindlers), thieves and gamblers, just above pimps and prostitutes, who were the absolute lowest of 'God's Creation'. He estimated that 'six eighths' of all the European houses in Kororareka were nothing more than grog-shops, and wondered how Her Majesty felt about giving her otherwise good name to the Victoria Hotel. That establishment, and the nearby Duke of Marlborough, were in his view 'incontestably worse than the most ignominious house in England'. Wherever Williams went he saw sin, which may not have been too difficult in Kororareka at that time, but his complaints bordered on both the excessive and obsessive, with suggestions of rampant corruption and complicity among the local constabulary and courts as well. To sum up, this place was a 'perfect picture of moral depravity combined with everything disorderly, vicious, illegal, unjust and impolitic'.[48]

John Williams believed that members of 'the aboriginal fair sex' had been reduced to 'fornicatrices', to be ravaged by brutish Europeans. Then there was the practice whereby 'vile . . . concupiscent and licentious' types were 'married', and within a week had separated and were free to repeat the process with someone else. These temporary nuptials were a 'burlesque, a mockery', and often noisy affairs, involving the banging of pots and pans and the throwing of rocks against the sides of houses.[49] Within 'wedlock' or without, Williams observed that visiting sailors had left offspring of mixed race, and this new generation of New Zealanders was 'more extraordinary than can be imagined', showing evidence of Maori, African, Jewish, Portuguese, Spanish, French, English, Irish and Scotch input. In his view, these young Kororarekans may have come in as many mixtures as were to be found in the dog world.[50]

In late 1840, as Kororareka adjusted to British sovereignty, a development in the eastern Mediterranean would anticipate certain events in the Bay of Islands. Along with its increasing commitment to New Zealand, Britain was also concerned with the growing influence of Egypt, which had conquered Turkish Syria in 1838. In September 1840, determined to restore Turkish rule, a fleet of British, Austrian and Turkish ships sailed for the enemy stronghold, the ancient coastal fortress of Acre (now in Israel). The twenty-two ships anchored close offshore in two lines, among them the eighteen-gun sloop

---

NOTICE.

—

Colonial Secretary's Office,
Auckland, 12th January, 1844.

HIS Excellency the Governor has been
pleased to direct that Kororareka be
henceforth included within the Township of
" Russell," and be officially designated by the
said name of " Russell," and be the Port of
Entry at the Bay of Islands.

By His Excellency's command,

ANDREW SINCLAIR.

HMS *Hazard*, nestled between the seventy-two-gun *Edinburgh* and forty-six-gun *Castor*. The fleet began a bombardment of Acre, which was rocked by a devastating explosion when its main magazine took a direct hit. The town was evacuated and troops and marines were landed and were able to occupy the fortress.[51] The *Hazard* involved in that mission had been the sixth Royal Navy sloop of that name, and its participation in a naval bombardment of a town whose fate was sealed by an exploding magazine would soon be resoundingly echoed at Kororareka.

On 12 January 1844, Hobson's successor, Governor FitzRoy, directed that Kororareka would henceforth be included within the (now virtually non-existent) township of Russell, and would officially be known as Russell. At the same time it was reinstated as Port of Entry at the Bay of Islands.[52] In view of the slight that Kororareka had already received from officialdom, it was hardly likely that its residents would be in any hurry to adopt this new name. In recognition of their resistance it seems appropriate for us to continue using the original name Kororareka, at least for a while yet. But if the residents of 'new Russell' derived some slight satisfaction from the passing of the settlement to the south, a similar fate now awaited their own.

THE POWER OF THE PRESS

A MIGHTY STIRRING OF THE PEOPLE

The Bay of Islands generally, and this spot in particular, has been we might say, celebrated in the neighbouring Colonies and even in England, for the lawlessness of its inhabitants.[1]

In 1830 missionary William Yate introduced a new form of technology to New Zealand. Initially intended to better spread the word of God, it would also shortly play a significant part in the secular development of the country. Yate was sent to Sydney from the Bay of Islands to arrange the printing of some mission texts in Maori, and on his return to Kerikeri he brought a press. With the assistance of a fifteen-year-old apprentice he managed to produce a few hymn sheets and a six-page catechism in Maori, but the venture was not considered a success. Little further use was made of this press, and it was later sold to a printer back in Sydney.

Fifteen years before Yate pulled the first faltering impressions from moveable type in New Zealand, Thomas Kendall compiled what has been identified as the first work devoted wholly to the Maori language. It too had been sent to Sydney for printing, but the 'Maori' used proved to be barely recognisable. At least it was a start, and when Kendall went to England in 1820 he was able to assist oriental linguist Professor Samuel Lee at Cambridge University in establishing New Zealand's first language on a more scientific footing.[2]

The real father of printing in New Zealand was another missionary,

Cornishman William Colenso. He described his arrival, along with his Stanhope handpress and boxes of type, at Paihia on 30 December 1834 as a 'memorable epoch in the annals of New Zealand'. As for his reception by the local Maori: 'They danced, shouted, and capered about in the water, giving vent to the wildest effusions of joy.'[3] But unfortunately the Church Missionary Society had forgotten to send certain vital printer's equipment, and the inventive Colenso was forced to improvise. Before long his press was rolling, and, on 17 February 1835, a large crowd of missionaries and their families and other curious locals witnessed the first impressions of the first book to be printed in New Zealand. In all he produced 2000 copies of the slim sixteen-page volume – which he also folded and stitched – of William Williams' translation in Maori of *Paul's Epistle to the Philippians and Ephesians*.[4] With his press operating successfully, Colenso detected a 'universal movement, a mighty stirring of the people', and they gladly brought him potatoes to exchange for one of these new books.[5]

The advantages of having a printing press were quickly appreciated by all the missionary societies established in New Zealand. Less than two years after the appearance of Colenso's landmark book, a press was also underway at the Wesleyan station at Mangungu, on the Hokianga Harbour. First to be printed here was a ticket, in Maori, which was followed over the next decade by some thirty items, including a 120-page book on the Gospels, prayer books and catechisms.[6]

Back at his Paihia printery, in the first half of 1835 Colenso had composed and printed 1000 copies of St Luke's Gospel, and 600 tables instructing in the arts of addition, multiplication and shillings-and-pence for the mission schools.[7] As the only printer in town he also undertook secular commissions, and it was a pertinent comment on the state of Kororareka at the time that in 1836 one of his clients was the New Zealand Temperance Society. Alcohol stimulated some of New Zealand's earliest printing, a report for the organisation was the country's first English book – all of eight pages – while a small poster was its first public notice.[8] This foolscap-sized item earnestly requested the attendance of all persons desirous of promoting 'Peace, Order, and Sobriety' at a meeting in the church at 'Kororarika [sic]', at midday 11 May 1836, with the British Resident James Busby in the chair. Colenso also did other jobs for Busby, reporting in 1836 that he had provided him with seventy-five circular letters printed in English and seventy in Maori.[9]

In the five years until January 1840 Colenso printed a total of 74,600 items, ranging from 27,000 copies of a thirty-six-page prayer book to 100 copies of the *Service for Consecration and Burial Grounds*. During the next year his output would include 10,000 twenty-eight-page catechisms and 11,000 126-page psalm books.[10] There was also a growing amount of work to be done for the new British administration, which began immediately upon the arrival of William Hobson. It included a circular inviting Maori chiefs to assemble at Waitangi and, subsequently, copies of the Treaty that would be signed there, and Hobson's proclamation of 21 May 1840 of the sovereignty of New Zealand. In this the governor asserted the sovereign rights of Her Majesty Queen Victoria over all of New Zealand, specifying the Northern Island, Middle Island and 'Stewart's [sic]' Island. While, in Hobson's view, the northern districts of the North Island had been ceded to the Queen with the signing of the Treaty of Waitangi on 5 February, the recent establishment of the New Zealand Company settlement and an independent form of government at Port Nicholson now stimulated the proclamation of the rest of the country as British. To make sure there was no confusion, the area covered was defined as 'extending from thirty-four Degrees thirty minutes North to forty-seven Degrees ten minutes South Latitude and between one hundred and sixty-six Degrees five minutes to one hundred and seventy-nine Degrees of East Longitude'. In fact, this published definition of the extent of New Zealand was in error, for the first latitude should have been thirty-four Degrees thirty minutes *South*. As *North* it accidentally extended New Zealand's claim some 2500 miles beyond the Equator in the North Pacific. It seems that the alert Colenso had noticed the error, but because of stormy conditions decided against travelling over from Paihia to the government office at Okiato to discuss the matter, and so stuck to the supplied copy. The proclamation was later reprinted correctly.[11] Perhaps there was little incentive for Colenso to concern himself with such details, for these official jobs were all in addition to his considerable mission duties, and he was given no extra remuneration, either by the Church Missionary Society or the government. He did, however, receive a 'very handsome' letter of thanks from Hobson himself, made all the more impressive by the fact that it was entirely handwritten by the governor during the period he was suffering from paralysis.[12]

Colenso's load was temporarily lightened from June 1840 when the *New Zealand Advertiser and Bay of Islands Gazette* began publication in

Kororareka, and took over responsibility for printing government notices and proclamations. The editor of this, New Zealand's second newspaper, was Barzillai Quaife, who was born in Kent in 1798. Shortly after emigrating to South Australia in 1839 he accepted the challenge of establishing a newspaper at Kororareka. His arrival there echoed Colenso's own of some five years earlier, for he discovered that the printing equipment he had been sent was inadequate, and had also been damaged during the voyage over. Overlooking those problems for the time being, Quaife described the hills around his new home as 'immense lumps of clay' clothed with fern and other plants 'of perpetual green', and found the climate 'pure and exhilarating'. He was also complimentary about the local European population, putting it at upwards of 400, and suggesting that they weren't altogether the 'set of thieves' he had expected.[13]

The *New Zealand Advertiser and Bay of Islands Gazette* was launched on 15 June 1840, and the very first item, top left of page one, advised that all communications from the government appearing in this newspaper were 'deemed to be official'. Then followed Hobson's proclamation, asserting the sovereign rights of Her Majesty Queen Victoria over all of New Zealand. It included the incorrect latitude but the error was quickly detected and rectified in the second issue four days later. Hobson also used the new medium to announce recent government appointments, among them Willoughby Shortland as acting colonial secretary, Felton Mathew as surveyor-general, and Major Thomas Bunbury, Thomas Beckham and James Clendon as magistrates of the territory.

Barzillai Quaife used the first issue to outline his own hopes for the newspaper. He was determined that the *Advertiser* would be dedicated to the public good and be strictly a 'paper of commercial utility', promoting the interests of the community and benefiting the population at large. And because he did not wish it to cause offence, or its columns to become the medium of 'personal attack and vituperation', correspondents were invited to adopt a 'temperate' style. Quaife anticipated New Zealand taking its place among the civilised nations, with the influx of European arrivals now reducing the fear of 'ferocious natives' and the perception of this as a 'nation of cannibals'. He hoped to advise those 'at home' of this country's advantages – 'natural and acquired' – and believed it now offered 'subsistence and even wealth'.

As if to demonstrate that things at the Bay of Islands were not as bad as was commonly believed, the first issue carried an account of recent events as supplied by one of Hobson's officials. There had been exaggerated reports of a disturbance at the 'Pah', or Pomare's village, during which several Europeans were allegedly murdered. According to this official version, two whaleboats belonging to American vessels had been attempting to capture a deserter who had sought refuge at the 'Pah', but residents there would only give up the sailor if an exorbitant reward was paid. In an ensuing scuffle, two men – a Maori and a European – were slightly injured. After the matter was settled, Pomare, Kawiti and other influential chiefs from the Kawakawa district called on Hobson, expressing gratitude at government intervention and suggesting that police be stationed at the troublesome 'Pah' to prevent any further such incidents. On a commercial note, elsewhere in the paper one William Wilson advertised that 'goods of every description' were carried at his store at the pa. And further to the policy of carrying good news stories, the *Advertiser* was gratified to report, under 'Domestic Intelligence', that when His Excellency attended a public meeting on 28 May to discuss the need for a local hospital he appeared to be in good health and spirits, despite his 'late severe indisposition'.[14]

It was a curious coincidence that both of New Zealand's pioneer printers got themselves into trouble with the Church Missionary Society: William Yate was dismissed for alleged homosexual activities, and William Colenso was temporarily relieved of duties for his relationship with a Maori woman. Thomas Kendall was not a printer, but as an orthographer he was a pioneer in the transcription of the Maori language, and he also got offside with the society for adulterous activity and left the country.

Barzillai Quaife, who was a minister as well as a pioneer editor, also managed to get into trouble with the authorities, but the cause was an entirely different type of organ. His newspaper became increasingly critical of Hobson's administration, in particular over the choice between Okiato (Russell) and Kororareka as the capital, pointing out that there already was a population and township at the latter location, 'ready for government to work upon'. But he was also able to suspend parochialism, as in response to the demand by the only other New Zealand newspaper at that time, the *New Zealand Gazette*, that the government be at Port Nicholson (Wellington). That aside, Quaife insisted that that there must be some sort of a government at the Bay of Islands.[15] He was also a strong advocate for Maori rights, and concerned that this 'noble, intelligent and ingenious race' should not be reduced to beggary. He admired their carved houses, canoes and finely woven mats, and felt that the Maori population was entitled to be 'masters of their own actions and property'.[16] Quaife used the pages of the paper to give vent to his feelings on such matters, and inevitably put himself on a collision course with the authorities.

Another controversial issue in the Bay of Islands was the matter of a general hospital. While most Kororareka residents felt there should be one in their town, Hobson was disposed to locate it at Russell. He told some forty locals at a public meeting that he anticipated that the planned government town would soon be prosperous and flourishing, and also trusted that Kororareka would keep pace with its new neighbour. But at his suggestion that a road be formed between the two townships, locals expressed a greater interest in improving the state of the existing 'road' that ran from one end of Kororareka Beach to the other. A week later, at another meeting – and without Hobson being present – it was moved and seconded that the hospital be located at Kororareka, and Bishop Pompallier was thanked for his offer of ten acres of land for the facility. A committee (which included Benjamin Turner) was formed, and the recently wound-up Kororareka Association was requested to apply its funds to this cause, while a public subscription was also announced. A letter was penned to Hobson advising him of developments. In reply, he reiterated that while he felt duty-bound to support Russell, he wished Kororareka 'continued prosperity'.[17] Before long there were some ninety-five names – including those of the Reverend and Mrs Quaife – on the list of subscribers for the hospital. The editor was gratified by such public support, but felt that the population of Kororareka and Russell was not yet large enough to allow for a division of energies, and was not likely to be for some time. In lieu of a suitable road between the two rivals, the *Advertiser* of 25 June reported that Felton Mathew had laid out the government settlement the previous week, and that a regular twice-a-day boat service to Kororareka was about to begin.[18]

The paper also reported some of the disturbances that continued to dog and distinguish Kororareka, such as an 'unusual derangement of public order' on various parts of the beach in mid-July 1840. Commodore Lavaud of the French frigate *Aub* and Captain Bernard of HMS *Britomart* both claimed that their men were not involved in the fracas, but the *Advertiser* insisted, 'there *was* a disturbance, and it is highly proper that the right parties should bear the blame'. Another mariner in the news at that time was Captain Brind of the *Narwhal*, charged with violent acts towards the surgeon of his ship, ostensibly to secure possession of the surgeon's chest and break it open.[19] Some months later there was happier news regarding the captain, the newspaper reporting that at 'Mrs Robertson's Island' (Roberton Island, or Motuarohia), the 'lady of Captain William Brind' had given birth to a son.[20] Around that time the masters of the ships *Alexander Henry* and the *Plough Boy* warned the public against giving their crew any credit while in port at Kororareka. Perhaps some of that credit might be spent at the store ship *Tuscan*, whose current stock included 240 half cases of gin, seventy-seven hogsheads of rum and forty-one bales of tobacco.[21]

In late August 1840 there was an auction of thirty-seven allotments in the town of Russell. For those who preferred a more established settlement there was 'an excellent allotment' of land fronting York Street, Kororareka, containing a good 'Rapoo House'. Kororareka was now reported to have revived itself from the depression which had followed the announcement of the government's intention to investigate all settlers' claims to land purchased from Maori. Changes to the original 1840 bill had improved the public's confidence to the extent that there was now a shortage of houses in the town, and several tents had appeared as temporary homes for newcomers.[22] In September 1840 houses and buildings continued to start up with 'singular rapidity'. About a dozen had appeared in the last few weeks, and several more were planned. Not surprisingly, Quaife's paper suggested that this 'boom' had nothing to do with any government promotion, for the town's recommendations as a seat of commerce were 'altogether natural'.[23] By December Kororareka had enjoyed several more positive developments, including the starting of work on a bridge at one end of York Street. At the same time the removal of scrub and rushes from a large part of the swamp would provide additional building sites, which would be improved by their 'exposure to the sun's rays'.[24]

But there was still a lawless element in Kororareka, along with an apparent inability to do much about it. The newspaper reported the stealing of several fowls and geese from a local roost, the resulting 'noise and fluttering' awaking residents. Even though the scattered feathers indicated the path of the robber, the lack of a magistrate stationed in the town meant that no search warrant could be taken out immediately. Quaife responded cynically, and presumably with no pun intended: 'Surely it will not be long before we have the protection of the laws, since the British Government has taken us under its wing.'[25]

Arguably more serious than the lost poultry was the escape by an alleged forger named O'Donnell from the local lock-up. It seems he made his getaway while the constable in charge was at a public house playing cards, although the constable protested that he had never left the premises.[26] Despite a £5 reward, O'Donnell remained at large, and was later suspected of breaking into Thomas Spicer's store on the beach and taking valuables and cash to the value of £800. Spicer claimed that O'Donnell had been seen drinking with a local policeman, with whom he was on extremely friendly terms. Spicer also reflected wistfully on past practices in the town, when thieves were flogged, tarred and feathered and paraded along the beach to the shipping in the harbour, while Quaife used the recent incident as an opportunity to stress the need for improved prisons. At the same time he acknowledged that the Bay of Islands was not as lawless as it once was, and there was more good news shortly when Spicer and a party of police apprehended the runaway O'Donnell.[27] There was a further development in late October when a large proportion of the bills stolen earlier from Spicer's store were found by a 'Native Boy' hidden under a tuft of grass in the Kororareka swamp.[28] Another sign that civilisation might be dawning at the Bay of Islands was the establishment of the New Zealand Banking Company at Kororareka. Quaife suggested that there would be astonishment in England at the news that there was a bank with a capital of £100,000 in this 'hitherto considered cannibal land'.[29]

In 1840, by all accounts, a large amount of alcohol flowed through Kororareka. One auction of £12,000 worth of merchandise included sixty hogsheads of rum, 1000 cases and half cases of gin, 250 dozen bottles of port wine, 250 dozen sherry, 350 dozen English bottled ale, and 200 dozen porter, while for smokers there were 56,000 'good cigars'.[30] Perhaps some of the above were responsible for the town's regular reversions to its old behaviour. When in October an uproar occurred at a public house at the back of the beach during Sunday evening divine service, the *Advertiser* asked accusingly: 'Of what use are Publican's Licenses, if they are not employed to prevent such riots as are an injury to all quiet and orderly people?' The local chief constable was also reported to have been seen 'with his wife . . . in such a shameful state of intoxication, as to excite disorder sufficient to alarm the whole neighbourhood'. This man also kept a public house, which was frequently open 'the greater part of the night'. Quaife added that the man alluded to had since been discharged, and that licenses could not be granted to any person holding any government office. Publicans were required to have their names legibly painted in letters 'three inches long' in front of their house with the words 'Licensed to retail wine, beer and fermented liquors', as the case may be, and such signs were to be legible by lamp at night.[31]

Locals continued to be frustrated by bureaucracy. One disgruntled resident bemoaned the difficulty of getting a satisfactory answer as to Hobson's intentions regarding Kororareka – or any other place in New Zealand for that matter. In his view His Excellency was 'as ignorant as any of us' and it was a waste of time sending deputations to him or even Sir George Gipps in Sydney; the only proper mode of redress was to the 'Home Government' in London.[32] But in what turned out to be the last issue of his newspaper, Quaife was in full flight, claiming that the local post office, 'like almost every other thing connected with Government, cries loudly and imperatively for reform'. Mail which arrived in Kororareka on Sunday was not delivered until Monday. Instead of coming ashore it went to Russell, presumably because it may have included government dispatches. Quaife reiterated that Kororareka was, for the present at least, the place of trade, and should have first consideration. A mailbag from Kororareka and Russell had recently been seen to spend a whole day in an open boat on the beach, without any protection. 'We will not hold our tongue until remedies are applied. Now is the time or never to save the Colony from the ruin that impends. Glad shall we be to hail the dawn of good Government.' Quaife noted the frequent suggestion that Kororareka's problems arose from Captain Hobson's hostility to it, but he had considered this to be so incredible that that he had avoided mentioning it until now. Quaife continued in like fashion: 'To be hostile to Kororareka is to be hostile to a very large portion of the trade of New Zealand.' What's more, Kororareka was governed by 'an idle and useless police', its custom house business – such as it was – being in the hands of a subordinate, and having no resident magistrate.[33]

Eventually, Quaife's mounting criticism of the government resulted in him being called before Colonial Secretary Willoughby Shortland. He learned that he was running foul of a long-forgotten 1827 New South Wales act designed to prevent the publication of material that would excite convicts. As a result he was ordered to post a substantial bond and pay a fine, which he could not afford; while if he continued to publish what were regarded as anti-government expressions, a second conviction could mean transportation to Van Diemen's Land.[34] On 15 December 1840 Eager & Co, publishers of the paper, sent a notice to subscribers and the public, explaining their predicament in the event that the government invoked the New South Wales act. There were several courses of action open to them, one being to pay a bond of £600 and then be subjected to the harrassing operation of the libel clause, and remain in perpetual fear of publishing material offensive to the government. Alternatively, if they continued to publish they would be liable to a weekly fine of £20, which needed to be seen in the light of the paper's average weekly income of £10–12 before expenses. A third option was simply to stop publishing. As far as they were concerned, it was a free press or none at all: 'We will not be fettered by any Law or any power as to what we write on political matters affecting the rights of every Colonist and of every Native. And when this privilege is denied us, we will altogether lay down our pen.' They did not believe that Hobson was obliged to invoke the act referred to, for he had discretionary power in matters relating directly to his own government. In fact, the publishers believed that Hobson's superiors in New South Wales would commend him for laying aside such an act, regarding it as 'worse than useless'. They also believed that the object of that legislation was to bring newspapers entirely under government control. It was already difficult enough for a newspaper in a country with insufficient advertisers and subscribers to meet the weekly expenses, and the *Advertiser* had the added problem of not yet managing to get over the cost of the damage sustained by its equipment on the voyage from Australia. Aware of their unique position, to be able to expose and correct public wrongs, the publishers concluded with the demand that the New Zealand press must remain 'unchained as air'.[35]

The *New Zealand Advertiser and Bay of Islands Gazette* had attacked officialdom with 'a libellous vigour' and paid the price.[36] The paper was suppressed, and its last issue – the twenty-seventh – appeared on 10 December 1840. Hobson now turned again to William Colenso to publish government notices, and so the *Gazette Extraordinary* No. 1 appeared on

24 December 1840. Just as its predecessor had begun life six months earlier with the advice that all government communications appearing therein were official, this one pointed out that the other had 'declined publishing' any such advertisements. Therefore, all government communications found in this *Gazette Extraordinary* were 'deemed Official'. But it was the only issue of the newspaper to be produced by Colenso, for its appearance stimulated his colleagues to remind him that the press had been sent to New Zealand for holier purposes, the production of books for the mission rather than publications for the government.[37]

Following the suppression of his *Advertiser*, publisher Geoffrey Eager carried on at Kororareka producing the *Gazette*, a small free publication concentrating on advertising and shipping reports. He produced nineteen issues, the last appearing on 15 July 1841, by which time the capital was well established in Auckland, as were the government's printing requirements.[38] The following year the citizens of Kororareka met to establish a new independent newspaper, with the aim of preserving trade in that part of the country, which was now suffering from a commercial crisis. The *Bay of Islands Observer* was to be free from any political control, and would exclude all religious matters and promote morality and the advancement of the Maori population. Quaife was given the job as editor, and in the new paper he reverted to his old habits, continuing his criticism of what he saw as government inefficiency and corruption. But he now committed an indiscretion, rashly printing gossip regarding the colonial treasurer, and so was once again relieved of his duties. The paper struggled on under other editors but it wasn't the same without Quaife. Business dropped off and in October 1842 the publishing company was dissolved.[39]

Without a newspaper to work on, Barzillai Quaife devoted himself to his other interest as minister of the Congregational church. On the first Sunday after his arrival at the Bay of Islands in May 1840 he had conducted a religious service in a tent on Kororareka Beach, later building a more permanent church on land behind the Victoria Hotel. The outspoken editor had another claim to local prominence, for it has been suggested that his position within his church gave him the equivalent position to a bishop. In which case he was occasionally part of a venerable trio, when bishops Pompallier and Selwyn also happened to be in town.[40]

10

EVE OF DESTRUCTION

CREATING ANARCHY AND CONFUSION

Where were the constables? – at home, not at the place
of mischief![1]

The short-lived *New Zealand Advertiser and Bay of Islands Gazette* was the country's second newspaper. This irritation to Hobson's government had been preceded by the New Zealand Company's *New Zealand Gazette*, printed in England before the departure of its first emigrant ship for the antipodes. The next issue came off the press at the company settlement of Port Nicholson, Wellington on 18 April 1840, and was the first newspaper printed in New Zealand. Company secretary Francis Dillon Bell had high expectations for this colonising scheme, and claimed an early success. When operations began in 1839 he estimated the European population of New Zealand to be about 2000, ranging from missionaries to runaway sailors, convicts and whaling parties, and including 'store-keepers, keepers of grog-shops, sailors, crimps and other vagabonds' at 'a sort of village' called Kororareka. In his view that settlement was largely accidental, resulting from the arrival of missionaries and British Resident James Busby. But by September 1841 Bell could report that both Kororareka's importance and its European population were greatly reduced, for the establishment of Port Nicholson was taking trade away from the Bay of Islands. And while he conceded the excellence of that northern harbour, for reasons of its isolation and the sterility of its soil, he did not hold out much hope for the future of Kororareka.[2]

Despite Bell's gloomy prediction, Kororareka was still in business – at least for the time being. But there was not much evidence of forward planning, for the port was still without a sizable jetty. Instead, boats from visiting ships needed to be hauled up on the beach alongside the Maori canoes. At the north end of the beach, around Kororareka Point at the watering place, casks filled from the Waipara spring were roped together and towed out to the thirsty ships. Above the beach, one- and two-storey weatherboard buildings, many of them trading stores and grog-shops, mingled with Maori whares of fern and raupo. When the whalers turned up, their cosmopolitan crews took over the bar-rooms and saloons. Chandlers and general traders could also anticipate increased business, while other locals lounged about awaiting opportunities.[3] Some sense of the sights around town can be gained from contemporary newspaper advertisements for the latest shipments of clothing. While seamen might wear what were termed 'slops' on board, shore-leave was likely to call for pants of woollen 'flushing' or cotton duck, or perhaps flannel canton trousers. There were red and blue serge and striped regatta shirts, vests and twilled cotton fustians, short closely-fitted monkey jackets, and woollen pea jackets for colder conditions. There were canvas and manila hats, while a more swashbuckling sailor might accessorise with a black silk or bandanna handkerchief. July 1840 saw the arrival of a surname that became synonymous with New Zealand retailing when David Nathan opened his Sydney store on Kororareka Beach. His clothing range catered for the better-dressed gent on the beach, offering frock and dress coats, moleskin shooting coats and 'trowsers [sic]', and white shirts with linen collars.[4]

In 1842 the English architect Edward Ashworth visited Kororareka and sketched a profile of the town as seen from out in the bay. The house of police magistrate Thomas Beckham enjoyed a superior position on the hill at the northern end of the beach, while the Catholic mission complex dominated the other end. The United States flag flew above that country's New Zealand consulate, and a schooner temporarily obscured the palisaded Maori village nearby. But the most telling evidence of local character seen here was a hulk moored offshore, serving as a floating grog-shop. In its previous life this improvised liquor outlet may have been the whaler *Richmond* of New Bedford, which in August 1839 had been surveyed, deemed unseaworthy and sold at auction. The ship itself went for $1670, while its cargo of 1250 barrels of sperm oil was sold by the master by private contract.[5]

There was a second hulk in the Bay around that time. In 1840 the ship *Sourabaya* – said to have been captured from the French at the Battle of Trafalgar and named after the port (now Surabaya) in Indonesia – arrived with a cargo of horses from Chile. When found to be leaking and unseaworthy, this ship was also sold at auction. Benjamin Turner got it for a bargain and employed three men to break it up, but when they found they had committed themselves to a bad deal they demanded more pay. Turner refused and they went on strike, so he took the matter to the local magistrate. Only one of Turner's reluctant employees appeared at court, where he was given a three-month sentence with hard labour – and then required to complete the demolition of the ship. Apart from whatever Turner felt about having to wait so long for the job to be completed, this was an extremely unpopular verdict with locals, who took their dissatisfaction directly to William Hobson. He sought out the magistrate in question, who claimed he had acted according to the law of New South Wales. But when pressed he was unable to show the specific legislation, so the governor ordered the prisoner to be released. This victory over injustice caused much rejoicing in Kororareka. Just as the local population had been swelled by undesirables from across the Tasman, it seems that Hobson had been sent some incompetent and corrupt functionaries from the same general 'talent' pool.[6]

After this incident Turner had what remained of the *Sourabaya* towed around to Matauwhi Bay. It was still there in 1843, lurching at a drunken angle, when Charles Pharazyn painted a view of Kororareka from the north. But whatever became of the hulk, a systematic underwater search of the bay in 1978 by Kelly Tarlton and a team of divers using metal probes failed to reveal anything but mud and rusted cans.[7] What did survive from the original ship was part of its ballast: three old cannons which had been dumped at Matauwhi Bay. They remained there until 1845 when they were incorporated into Kororareka's defences. One of the guns then lay abandoned until 1889 when it was included in the New Zealand and South Seas Exhibition in Dunedin. A few years after its return north it was put on permanent display on the Russell waterfront, where it remains today. Much less permanent was a selection of shot and cannon balls, for despite being embedded in concrete they fell prey to light-fingered souvenir hunters.[8]

Already weakened by ill-health, William Hobson was troubled by a growing number of administrative problems, mostly involving land and finances. The Colonial Office in London planned to recall the hapless governor, but he pre-empted that decision when he died at Auckland on 10 September 1842. Sixteen months later, the outspoken Barzillai Quaife also served one last public service in New Zealand. Shortly before leaving for New South Wales, financially exhausted after years of battling government and bureaucracy, he acted as chairman for a group of fifty-seven concerned Kororareka residents who sent a welcoming address to Hobson's replacement, Captain Robert FitzRoy. They had waited 'long and anxiously' for His Excellency's arrival, and now offered a 'fervant prayer for the blessing of heaven' upon him, his wife and family. The reasons for their eager anticipation were soon made apparent, for they blamed the previous government for 'the universal decay of trade, and of every department of industry of New Zealand'. In their view the country had become 'one general scene of anxiety, distress and ruin', where property had lost its value and 'happiness has almost ceased to exist'. The new governor's well-wishers were particularly concerned with the situation at the Bay of Islands, where the imposition of port duties had a detrimental effect on shipping and old land claims remained unresolved. The residents feared that New Zealand's oldest settlement and finest harbour might soon be deserted, and begged His Excellency to give his attention to their grievances. He responded promptly, promising to use every means in his power to bring about improvement in their 'immediate locality, as well as in New Zealand generally'.[9]

FitzRoy landed at Auckland on 26 December 1843 and took over from the unpopular Willoughby Shortland, who had assumed the post of administrator upon Hobson's death. But it was not just European settlers at the Bay of Islands who were disgruntled with the present state of things. Negative effects of the new British authority were also being felt by Maori, and the most vocal of these was Hone Heke Pokai. Born about 1810 at Pakaraka, south-west of Kororareka, he had attended the Church Missionary Society school at Kerikeri and come under the influence of Henry Williams. In 1840 he was the first of thirty-five influential northern chiefs to sign the Treaty of Waitangi, but quickly became disillusioned with the British presence. With revenue from shipping levies now going into government coffers, Heke was out of pocket, and also was annoyed that his land sales were under investigation. He determined to strike at the very thing that had eroded his own chiefly authority and disadvantaged his people: the British flag now fluttering from the flagstaff on the ninety-nine-metre high Maiki Hill, above the northern end of the town. There was another aspect to this prominent symbol of British sovereignty, for the flagstaff had been grown on Heke's own land and he and his people had donated it so that it could fly the first New Zealand flag at Waitangi. Its recent removal across the harbour to Kororareka had been done without his permission, and he now felt entitled to take appropriate action.[10]

Heke made his move on 4 July 1844, provoking a group of sixty local residents to convey their growing concerns to the new governor. They informed him of recent developments in the hope of obtaining sufficient military aid to prevent any recurrence. A party of Maori headed by the chief they identified as 'John Haki' had assembled at the mouth of the Waitangi River, intent on crossing to Kororareka to seek payment for a perceived insult. The Reverend William Williams and others had a long conversation with Heke on the beach, but to no avail. The chief and his group crossed the bay, and on Sunday evening the European residents could only watch helplessly as 'the honour of [their] country' was laid low on Maiki Hill. The defilers of the flag then performed a haka and discharged their muskets before returning to their canoes and departing for the opposite shore.

The writers hoped that FitzRoy would now approve the formation of an armed corps, which they were personally prepared to join, providing their own weapons. The recent Wairau affair in the South Island was uppermost in their minds, for it had 'much emboldened the more evil-disposed portion of the native population'. That category included Heke, who had been heard to ask: 'Is Rauparaha to have all the credit of killing the Pakehas; let us do so as well.'[11] Henry Tacy Kemp, who held the curiously titled post of Chief Protector of Aborigines, accused Heke and his party of 'rude young men' of having committed 'several depredations' on local inhabitants, although the Rev. Williams had managed to get them to remain in a 'peaceable state' during Sunday's divine service.[12] The local residents had gathered, believing they had sufficient numbers to repel Heke, but were advised against taking any action by Mr Beckham. He insisted that the situation was under control, but later admitted that the town's police force was in bed at the time a local pig was allegedly stolen and cooked. The townsfolk did at least manage to arrange for the church bell to be rung in an emergency, in which case they would gather at a gap between two stores on the beach.

Determined to put a stop to any further acts of violence and home invasions, they told the governor they would not put up with having their wives 'insulted by the natives wilfully exposing their persons to them' or their daughters' 'clothes pulled over their heads'. One of the more outspoken of the locals, Cornthwaite Hector, claimed that a force of at least 100 armed men could have been mustered to defend townsfolk and their property. He accused the police of standing by while plundering took place and Beckham of 'shrinking from his duty'. Appalled at the 'imbecility' of those in authority at the time of the outrages by 'Johnny Hackey', he asked rhetorically: 'Where was our police magistrate? – in bed. Where was Mr Kemp? – at Paihia. Where were the constables? – at home, not at the place of mischief!'[13]

In January 1845 James Busby offered his view of the recent disturbances. He considered that the actions of the Maori were 'not of an aggravated character' and were confined to one or two individuals. He understood it was their custom when engaged in war dances to 'throw off their upper garments', but did not feel this could be considered an 'outrage on modesty'. He claimed to have known 'John Heke' for the past eleven years, and had even been present at the baptism of the chief and his children. On that occasion, Heke's 'fast flowing tears' convinced Busby how keenly the chief felt 'the solemnity of that sacrament and the obligations it imposed'. He considered Heke a 'sincere and intelligent convert' and that his recent activities needed to be seen as the work of patriot, merely doing his duty to his country. While the cutting down of the flagstaff was 'a premeditated act of defiance and rebellion against the Government', Busby suspected that most, if not all, of the northern chiefs felt the same, as a result of the government's handling of the land question. He, along with the missionaries, had persuaded the chiefs to agree to sign the Treaty at Waitangi, but could not do so now in view of what he saw as the government profiting from Maori land.[14]

After being advised of events, FitzRoy concluded they had been 'unprovoked by any misconduct on the part of the settlers, but patiently borne by them with exemplary forbearance'. But he soon felt he had no alternative but to ask New South Wales Governor Sir George Gipps for military assistance to restore respect for the flag and 'ensure tranquillity in the colony'. FitzRoy had already chartered the barque *Sydney* to speed up the process, and hoped Gipps would send over at least two suitably equipped companies of soldiers, supported with field-guns, a howitzer, rockets and hand grenades.[15] The ship sailed for New Zealand in August, carrying one field officer, one captain, three subalterns, nine sergeants, three drummers and 154 rank and file of the 99th Regiment. Also on board were an acting assistant surgeon, two six-pounder brass guns, camp equipment for 300 men, 30,000 musket ball cartridges and 1000 flints.[16] At the time it was reported in Sydney that the recent outrage across the Tasman was an ill omen, for there was a large number of men of bad character, both English and American, who were living among the natives and keen to get rid of British rule, and were intentionally creating 'anarchy and confusion'.[17]

Not only had Heke cut the flagstaff down, but also a section had been burned and the signal-balls carried away. FitzRoy ordered Beckham to reinstate this symbol of British authority immediately, and the replacement would shortly be seen by the troops arriving on the *Sydney*. This ship was followed by another that would play a pivotal role in the looming conflict – HMS *Hazard*. After serving in the east Mediterranean it had returned to Portsmouth, and then left for Rio de Janeiro and on to Australia and New Zealand. A muster book, detailing crew and conduct, provides some idea of life on board at that time. Sailors were identified as either 'Pressed or Volunteer', with details of sickness and leave, whether they had been deserters or discharged with disgrace, and also for 'Dead men and Boys'. In 1845 the *Hazard* had a complement of 133, made up of ninety-five ship's company, sixteen marines and twenty-two boys. It carried other individuals as required, listed as 'supernumeraries', and male passengers who received two-thirds allowance 'of all species of provisions'.[18]

The *Hazard* made its first visit to Auckland about July 1844, and in later months took FitzRoy and troops north to Kororareka. On 2 September a number of Bay of Islands chiefs who did not approve of Heke's actions met with the governor, along with Colonel Hulme, Bishop Selwyn, Henry Williams and others, at Waimate. With regard to recent disturbing events, FitzRoy spoke of the flagstaff as a 'mere stick', but the British flag was another matter entirely, the 'signal of freedom, liberty and safety'. He proceeded to remind the assembly of its benefits, for only thirty years earlier they had been 'wild barbarians, utterly unlike Christians, utterly uncivilised'. He reassured them of the honourable intentions towards them, first of the missionaries and then of the British government, although he conceded that Busby's presence had been ineffectual. Queen Victoria was determined to protect the native inhabitants of New Zealand and FitzRoy reminded them how certain other countries had behaved in similar circumstances, in particular the French towards Tahitians and Marquesas Islanders.

FitzRoy advised that he had received a letter of apology from Heke, who had offered to put up another flagstaff. The governor now wanted only a sign of good faith on the part of the chiefs and requested that a number of guns be handed over as an 'atonement'. He suggested ten but about twenty were delivered, in addition to many tomahawks. They were all laid at the governor's feet and he was told he could have more, but he explained that as he only required an acknowledgment of Heke's error and not the guns as such, they would be returned to their owners. Other addresses and discussion continued over the next day, and there appeared to be a positive and satisfactory outcome. The local chiefs agreed to control Heke – or at least attempt to do so – and provide protection for European settlers in the district. Before FitzRoy left Waimate he received another note from Heke, in which he repeated his offer to effect a replacement flagstaff at Kororareka. At the same time he pointed out that the original pole had been his; it was not paid for by the Europeans and was intended for the native flag, not the Union Jack. With the business of the flagstaff apparently sorted out, FitzRoy dealt with a major Maori grievance by promising to introduce legislation to abolish customs duties and declare the Bay of Islands a free port. There now seemed to be no further need for a military presence in the far north, so he ordered the troops to be dispatched back to Sydney – as he had previously arranged with Governor Gipps – and Auckland.[19]

The New-Zealander newspaper reported that Heke had cut down the flagstaff because he believed it prevented American ships from entering the harbour. Around that time United States Consul John Williams had informed Washington that his fellow countrymen were now 'exceeding numerous' in this country, and their circumstances were not helped by the current 'depressed' state of things. He had detected that men from less affluent backgrounds were better suited to the conditions and challenges here, although many were dependent on 'charity of the natives for subsistence'. While the actual number was difficult to ascertain, Williams was sure that no country on earth had entertained as many whalemen on its coasts as New Zealand had for the previous forty to fifty years, and reckoned there were probably more American seamen here now than there had ever been. Many had deserted from ships, lured by attractive reports of this country, and at least 150 were eking out a 'scanty living' in the Bay of Islands.[20]

During this uneasy period Kororareka was visited by another itinerant artist, George French Angas. Born at Newcastle-on-Tyne in 1822, he had gone to South Australia, and while in Adelaide in July 1844 he saw some carved Maori weapons and decided to come to New Zealand. His arrival at Kororareka on 10 December prompted one of the most enthusiastic responses of any visitor to the Bay, his painter's eye appreciating the picturesque aspect of the local geography and botany. His timing was exquisite, as New Zealand's native Christmas tree, the pohutukawa, was in full bloom. 'Nothing can exceed the beauty of scenery surrounding this harbour,' exclaimed Angas, who took in the view from Maiki Hill, now sporting its replacement flagstaff. Angas wrote: 'The waters of the bay, indenting the rugged land, formed capes, promontories, and headlands innumerable; the distant hills appeared scattered over with cowdie [kauri] forest; the blue ocean broke beyond, against the tall dark rocks that flank the entrance to this sheltered harbour; and around, beneath a bright evening sky, appeared the vivid evergreen foliage, the tree fern glens, and here and there a lofty pohukatoa [sic], stretching out towards the sea its aged limbs, crowned with masses of crimson bloom.' He summed it up as 'a gay, glad scene'.

Angas considered Busby's house at Waitangi the prettiest spot in the Bay, while nearby Paihia was a 'little oasis', its dozen or so neat houses surrounded by gardens of banana and loquat trees. He described Kororareka itself – or 'Russell, as it was sometimes called' (suggesting the new name hadn't caught on) – as a settlement that 'smiled in peace and apparent serenity'. At that time there were few ships anchored in the harbour, for 'the days of its prosperity were already gone'. And because the whaling ships were now going elsewhere, the grog-shops on shore were not doing much business either. The old hulk and one-time floating grog-shop, which Ashworth had recorded earlier, was now lying stranded at high-water mark.

As well as the scenic aspects of Kororareka, Angas witnessed the downside of the contact between lower classes of Europeans – including whalers – and Maori. This was most apparent at the pa of that 'reckless and drunken character' Pomare, where all manner of bad types and scenes of 'low debauch' were to be found. Angas was also critical of the Catholic mission establishment, a 'conspicuous, ill-planned building', whose 'zealous Jesuits' he accused of paying their followers to attend services, although he was aware that Maori were not generally won over by such tactics.[21]

One month after Angas' visit, in the early morning of 10 January 1845, the flagstaff was cut down for a second time. Thomas Beckham now heard reports that Heke was planning to pull down the gaol and public offices at Russell as well.[22] Six days later the police magistrate reported that Heke and seven canoes of armed men had landed at a bay near to the capital and were deterred from their plan to destroy all the government buildings by the presence of some 200 followers of Nga Puhi chief Kawiti, and a force of armed locals.[23] His attempts at appeasement a failure, FitzRoy offered £100 for the chief's apprehension, payable on his delivery either to the police magistrate at Kororareka or Auckland, while anyone found assisting, harbouring or concealing him would be charged.[24] A week earlier FitzRoy had offered £50 each for the apprehension of three other chiefs held responsible for a series of robberies in both the Bay of Islands and at Matakana.[25] With insufficient troops to deal with the renewed emergency, FitzRoy once again wrote to Gipps, requesting at least 200 troops for his 'struggling colony'. On this occasion he explained that he couldn't hope to be able to return this force in less than three months, and he now believed that a permanent military force was necessary to prevent 'plunder and murder' in the colony.[26] Gipps duly dispatched two companies of the 58th Regiment, consisting of two captains, four subalterns, one medical officer and 200 rank and file.[27]

Meanwhile, FitzRoy ordered a new flagstaff to be made and erected without delay. The lower section, up to about eight feet from the ground, would now be guarded by iron bars, hoops and chain to render it axe-resistant.[28] But to no avail: it too was felled in little over a week, and re-erected on 22 February. Pushed to 'the utmost limit of forbearance and moderation', the governor now adopted a different course. He warned that a blockade of the Bay of Islands might be necessary, in which case 'Individual interest must yield to state necessity'. He also recommended to Lieutenant-Colonel Hulme, commander of the troops in the country, that portable blockhouses should be constructed in Auckland and taken north on the *Hazard*.[29] Beckham swore in fifty special constables and handed out arms and ammunition. Settlers needed to decide what to do, but in the event of an attack the only assistance or protection the government could provide was in Kororareka. And something that would shortly have major implications for many local property owners was FitzRoy's warning that there could be no compensation for any loss or damage.[30]

By late February, after being held up by heavy rain, Heke was at Kaikohe where he was joined by a force of 200 from the Hokianga. He was now reported to be preparing to march to Kawakawa to be joined by Kawiti, now an ally, and his 200 men. An attack on Kororareka was expected to follow. Defensive measures included the selection of Joel Polack's house and the town lock-up as places of refuge for women and children, both buildings being considered safely out of range of the *Hazard*'s guns in the event of a bombardment. Alarmed local settlers were now coming into the town, and a wooden stockade was constructed around Polack's property to provide cover for troops from enemy fire. Concern mounted when a number of robberies in the neighborhood were attributed to Kawiti's tribe, while three houses near Okiato were plundered and burned to the ground.[31]

It is generally accepted that the flagstaff on Maiki Hill was erected and felled on four occasions, but there have been claims for an additional staff. Benjamin Turner, who admitted he was not too good with historical facts, referred to five, as did the *New Zealand Spectator and Cook's Straits Guardian*. According to information received in 'private letters', it revealed that this one, allegedly the fourth, was produced by a contracted carpenter and taken to the top of Maiki Hill, and had disappeared by the time a party of men arrived to erect it. Naturally, Heke was suspected, but enquiries revealed that another local chief was to blame. He claimed to have been born under the very tree from which this latest flagstaff had been made, and was concerned that if Heke were to cut it down – which seemed highly likely – then he would also die. To prevent this outcome he took the flagstaff back to the security of his own pa. At this point FitzRoy decided to avoid further offence to local Maori by purchasing a suitable spar from a ship in harbour. A mizzen-mast was obtained from a Chilean man-o'-war, it being safely assumed that no New Zealand chief could claim to have been born under the tree from which it had been made.[32]

On 22 February 1845 Police Magistrate Beckham advised FitzRoy that although 'nothing of consequence' had happened over the last few days, matters had now assumed such a 'critical position' that a 'collision' seemed inevitable.[33] Less than two weeks later, on 3 March, hostilities moved within two miles of Kororareka when a party of Kawiti's men attacked property belonging to Benjamin Turner at Uruti Bay, south of Matauwhi Bay. A force of men from the *Hazard*, armed with muskets and cutlasses, was dispatched but arrived to find that Turner's house had been destroyed and two horses had been stolen from Captain Brind's paddock nearby. The attacking force of some 300 was pursued in the vicinity of Pomare's pa with an exchange of fire, and it now seemed that the Maori were determined to have war. Although he had recently declared the Bay of Islands a free port, FitzRoy now considered issuing 'passports' for chiefs and imposing an embargo on all canoes whose owners lacked such documentation. The systematic Henry Williams had also recommended the keeping of a register of 'good and bad natives'.

With an attack on Kororareka expected, a detachment of the 96th Regiment was stationed at an upper blockhouse on Maiki Hill to protect the vulnerable flagstaff. Below that was the lower blockhouse, equipped with three cannons, the barracks and Polack's now stockaded house. At the southern entrance to town, Matauwhi Pass, was the one-gun battery, which was intended to provide warning of an attacking force rather than to check its advance, while HMS *Hazard* lay waiting in the harbour.[34] Local residents were now being organised and drilled under the supervision of Lieutenant George Phillpotts of the *Hazard*. Beckham had requested about fifty muskets and ammunition, along with shot and cartridges; FitzRoy sent him forty stand (a stand being a complete set for one soldier, consisting of a musket, bayonet, cartridge box and belt) and a thousand rounds of ball cartridge.[35]

The arrival of British 'redcoat' troops, with their scarlet tunics, white straps, elegant headdress and other military paraphernalia brought a new sartorial dimension to the Bay of Islands. Known as 'The Bendovers', the 96th Manchester Regiment of Foot had been dispatched to Australia in 1841, and from there its tour of duty was extended to New Zealand before it sailed for India in 1849.[36] But in May 1844 two members of this regiment may have had reservations about being posted to the looming crisis in the far north. They deserted and a £2 reward was offered for their recapture, but they would not have been difficult to spot if they were still in uniform. It was reported that their dress at time of desertion was 'red shell jacket, black cloth trousers, leather stock, forage cap, and regimental boots'.[37]

In February 1845 Bishop Selwyn was rounding the East Cape on the *Hazard* when a violent storm forced the ship to dump seven of its guns overboard. On reaching Auckland he heard news of 'collisions' in the north and was concerned for the safety of the missions. He arrived at the Bay of Islands on the morning of 9 March on the schooner *Flying Fish*, and as he neared Kororareka he observed such a 'solemn stillness, that every ripple upon the rocks was distinctly heard'. The ship had just anchored when a lieutenant from the *Hazard* nearby came on board and advised that an attack was expected. Everywhere there was a sense of foreboding that the expected conflict was about to happen.[38] At Waimate the following night, the Rev. Burrows reported that there was much restlessness and talking among the Maori camped around the mission, and no one got much sleep. Those who did were awoken early next morning by the sounds of gunshots coming from the direction of Kororareka.[39]

ATTACK BY STEALTH

A SUCCESSION OF UNTOWARD EVENTS

The town was attacked in three places by parties consisting
of, I should think, not less than 200 men each; their mode
of warfare entirely strange to us . . .[1]

In the early morning of 11 March 1845 Kororareka was enveloped in a
thick fog and an eerie silence, perhaps broken by the occasional call of the
morepork. Despite appearances, there was plenty going on beneath nature's
convenient cover. Pre-dawn military precautions were already underway, for
the European settlers now suspected an attack was imminent. But the town's
fate had already been determined that very morning by Hone Heke at an
assembly of some 600 men at nearby Uruti. To make good his intention to
remove the symbol of British authority from the region, the chief had
engineered a multi-pronged attack in which three war parties would
approach Kororareka simultaneously from different angles.[2]

The plan was for Kawiti to make his way towards the town from Matauwhi,
while a group from Kapotai pa in the Waikare inlet would approach through
a gully from Oneroa Bay (Long Beach) on the opposite side of the peninsula.
Heke himself would lead an attack from Tapeka to the north, with the
primary aim of securing Maiki Hill and dealing once again to the flagstaff.
The strategy unfolded according to plan when Kawiti's force of some 200,
moving northwards along the Matauwhi road, encountered a party from the
Hazard. Some time before 4 a.m. the ship's acting commander, David

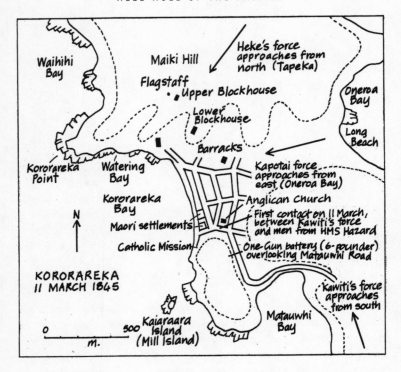

Waihihi Bay

Maiki Hill

Heke's force approaches from north (Tapeka)

Flagstaff

Upper Blockhouse

Lower Blockhouse

Oneroa Bay

Long Beach

Barracks

Kororareka Point

Watering Bay

Kapotai force approaches from east (Oneroa Bay)

Kororareka Bay

Anglican Church

N

Maori settlements

First contact on 11 March, between Kawiti's force and men from HMS Hazard

Catholic Mission

One-Gun battery (6-pounder) overlooking Matauwhi Road

KORORAREKA
11 MARCH 1845

Kawiti's force approaches from south

Matauwhi Bay

0   500   Kaiaraara Island (Mill Island)

m.

Robertson, had landed some forty-five 'small-arm men', seamen and marines, on Kororareka Beach. Conditions were 'thick and hazy' as they trudged to the heights overlooking Matauwhi Bay with the intention of constructing breast-work (a low temporary defence) on the face of a hill. As they reached the spot, the sentry at the one-gun battery at the southern entry to Kororareka was heard to challenge and fire at Kawiti's approaching party. The two forces met near the south-east corner of the church, and Robertson gave the order to engage. Hand-to-hand fighting took place around the church property, its wooden fence sustaining a few direct hits. Robertson was dangerously wounded, shot through both legs and one arm and his temple grazed by a pistol shot. Acting Lieutenant Morgan assumed command. Six men from the *Hazard* were killed in this brief skirmish, including a sailor who managed to spike the six-pound gun. Although the

Maori were repulsed and forced to retreat to the heights above the town, their objective had been achieved.[3]

Meanwhile, Heke's party had been making its way up the slopes of Maiki Hill, moving stealthily though the scrub and fog, and now lay in wait. Ensign Campbell of the 96th then led five men out from the upper blockhouse, armed and equipped with spades in order to work on a defensive trench on the hills overlooking Oneroa Bay. They had just begun digging when they heard the commotion in the gloom below. The crack of pistol shots as Kawiti's force countered the charge of the men from the *Hazard* had created the intended distraction. Campbell immediately retreated to a point on Maiki Hill, about 200 yards from the blockhouse, while the other fifteen men who were off-duty and asleep inside were now rudely awakened. They hastily armed themselves and dashed outside, crossing the surrounding ditch to investigate the cause of the disturbance. This response was what Heke had hoped for. He and his men now converged on the vacated blockhouse. Fighting took place but the soldiers were unable to regain entry to their post. Four were killed attempting to retake it, and the others were forced to retreat down the slopes to the safety of the lower blockhouse. When Campbell and his detachment hastened to the scene of the action they also ran the risk of being cut off by a second party of warriors, and had no option but to fall back to the lower position. Thanks to the upper blockhouse being left largely unattended, Heke had been able to take Maiki Hill far more easily than he could have imagined. Soon the flagstaff fell for the fourth time, although on this occasion it required some excavation to overcome its protective iron sheathing.[4]

The third group of assailants to attack Kororareka was the Kapotai party. As they were approaching from the east, Lieutenant Barclay of the 96th Regiment went to the barracks, located between the lower blockhouse and the beach, to rouse the detachment there as a precautionary measure. The men had slept 'armed and accoutred' and had just formed up when word arrived of fighting near the church. Barclay led the men out to provide assistance, for the Maori force were said to be keeping up a 'galling fire'. At that point the Kapotai party were advancing over the hills from Oneroa Bay, and the soldiers soon found themselves being fired upon from the heights. With the breaking dawn came another awful realisation: both the flagstaff and the upper blockhouse had fallen into enemy hands. By now both the

Hazard's men and Barclay's force were running out of ammunition, and so soldiers and sailors retreated to Kororareka Beach and from there made for the safety of the stockade.

Relocated in the lower blockhouse, Ensign Campbell and his party checked the advance of the Maori attacking from the surrounding hills and the intervening gullies where they lay scattered and concealed in the thick scrub. Seamen from the *Hazard*, assisted by the redoubtable Cornthwaite Hector and others, operated two guns from a small platform in front of the blockhouse. A steady fire was kept up between the two sides, the settlers relying on fresh supplies of ammunition brought up from the stockade. The lower blockhouse was now pivotal, affording protection for the townsfolk sheltering in the stockade below. Without it the Maori may have been able to make a general rush on that lower position, using nearby houses for protection. Lieutenant Phillpotts now took command of the operation, directing firing from the lower blockhouse – also known as Fort Phillpotts – and the stockade on to the upper blockhouse and the barracks, both of which had now been abandoned.[5]

From the relative safety of the *Flying Fish*, Bishop Selwyn had been watching events unfold on shore since early morning. His attention was drawn to activity on Maiki Hill when he heard shouting ring out across the water, exclaiming that the Maori had taken possession of the flagstaff. He saw soldiers retreating down the hill to the safety of the lower blockhouse, and then watched as the *Hazard* opened fire on the upper blockhouse. The observant Bishop noted that the ship's gunners managed to achieve only ineffective near-misses. Between salvoes a warning voice could be heard: 'Kia tupato ki te pu huriwhenua!' ('Beware of the earthquake gun!') A 'tremendous' fire was kept up until about 10 a.m. when the Maori retreated. Fighting resumed briefly about an hour later, and around midday the Maori hoisted a flag of truce, allowing the wounded of both sides to be removed to safety.[6]

Polack's house and its cellar were crowded with women and children and it was now decided that they should be sent on board the ships in the harbour. Soon after this had been successfully carried out, at about 1 p.m., the day's second calamity occurred. For some reason the magazine in the stockade exploded, completely destroying the building and wounding several inhabitants, two fatally. According to some versions of events, Polack himself was dragged unscathed from the smoking ruins of his own property.[7] But if the earlier loss of the upper blockhouse had not already determined the outcome of the day, this explosion most certainly did. With all the available ammunition now prematurely expended, the stockade no longer afforded protection. While some were keen to retain the lower blockhouse, at least until the evening, a council held on board the *Hazard* agreed that the town should be evacuated, and so a 'general retreat to the shipping' ensued.[8] The townsfolk went first, followed by the party of military in the blockhouse, but they now made the journey without the benefit of covering fire, for someone – even Phillpotts didn't know who – had ordered the guns to be spiked. With Kororareka now abandoned to the attacking Maori forces, plundering began and houses were set on fire. The residents might be out of immediate danger on board the ships but could take little comfort, for there were fears that even the vessels in the harbour might be attacked that evening.

After allowing the inhabitants time to retrieve what property they could, Phillpotts ordered regular shelling of the town from the *Hazard*, and 'whenever the natives made their appearance'.[9] At one point the ship had to take evasive action when the Maori responded with musket fire to a volley from its twelve-pounder. During the evening the ship's surgeon grew concerned for the large numbers of wounded and the confined conditions of the lower deck, and so the commander decided to sail south as soon as practicable. Other incentives to leave the Bay were a shortage of water and reports that Maori forces were marching towards the capital. The residents of Kororareka – estimated at about 500 – were placed on board five ships, the US warship *St Louis*, the English whaler *Matilda*, the schooner *Flying Fish*, the government brig *Victoria* and the *Hazard*.[10] The latter carried a total of seventy-seven passengers, consisting of two officers and thirty-six corporals, sergeants and privates of the 96th Regiment, and thirty-nine civilians, one of whom died on board.[11] There were seven boys and eight girls from five local families, who for victualling purposes were each given '¼ allowance'. Among the nine women were the mothers of the children and two 'domestics', each of whom were granted '½ allowance', although some wag had appended the entry in the muster book with the instruction 'spirits excepted'.[12] If the now homeless residents of Kororareka did manage to get some sleep on board that night, they awoke next morning to the sight of their town in ruins. Phillpotts described it as being 'burnt nearly level with the ground' and saw the disaster in naval terms, equating the loss of a flagstaff to that of a ship.[13] The day had been a series of 'melancholy occurrences' to say the least.[14]

Among the refugees from Kororareka were at least two animals. Four-year-old Catherine Flowerday was making her way down to the beach, carrying her pet cat, when it escaped into the raupo bordering the creek. A while later it reappeared with a dead bird in its mouth and was reunited with its owner for the voyage to Auckland. One of the sailors on board happened to be an amateur taxidermist and he now stuffed and mounted the bird and placed it in a glass case. Years later Catherine's daughter, Mrs Elsie Wilkinson of Hikurangi, presented the specimen – a spotless crake, and member of the rail family – to the Russell Museum where it is now on display. Some 140 years

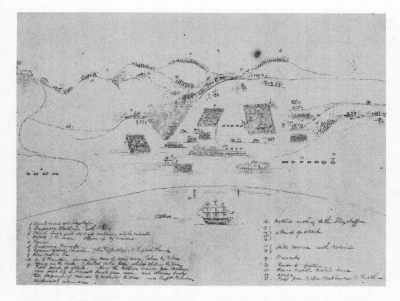

'View of the attack upon the settlement of Russell by the natives on Tuesday morning at 1/4 to 5' by William Bambridge, 1845. This charming and somewhat bird's-eye view of events recorded Joel Polack's stockaded house 'containing all the portable property of the town. Blown up by accident' and the hills above the town 'covered with natives'. Bambridge was a missionary and teacher based at Waimate until late 1844 when he moved to Auckland. *Alexander Turnbull Library, Wellington, New Zealand, MS-0130-249*

after the sacking of Kororareka, that incident involving Catherine Flowerday's cat and the bird was the inspiration for the children's story *Come Back Ginger*, written by Dorothy Butler and illustrated by Lyn Kriegler.[15]

One summary of the events of 11 March is the on-the-spot account in the *Hazard*'s logbook (transcribed here with only some modified punctuation): '3.30 Sent pinnace to the beach. 4.30 Heard firing of muskets in the direction of the Protestant Church. 4.45 Heavy firing. Received order by the pinnace to fire in the direction of the Church and School house. The commander acting Lieutenant Morgan with the small arms men and marines being severely engaged with the natives. Daylight Observed the natives in possession of every height except Fort Phillpotts. Marines and small arms men beat the natives back from the Church School. Observed the natives enter the block house without opposition. Hove in the stream cable. Opened fire on the block house. The natives cut the flag staff down. The firing increasing in many directions, soldiers and seamen having possession of Fort Phillpotts and the stockade. Laid the ship broadside to the town and commenced firing shot and shells at the natives on the heights. Fort Phillpotts keeping up a steady fire. Sent supplies of ammunition to the stockade. About 6.30 a shore boat bought the commander alongside having been dangerously wounded in many places while driving the natives out of the Church when Colour Sergeant McArthy, Alex. May (marine) and William Lovell were killed and others wounded. Sent to the US sloop *St Louis* for medical assistance and to request their assistance in embarking women and children from the immense number of natives attacking the defences & every probability of their taking the town before dark and firing shot and shell. Fort Phillpotts and the stockade keeping up a steady fire. Boats from the US *St Louis* and small vessels embarking women and children. About noon the firing ceased the natives showing a white flag for both sides to take their dead. Sent a supply of powder and all ready made ball cartridge except 500 to the stockade for Fort Phillpotts. Also a supply of meat, bread and spirits for troops. About 1 o'clock Mr Polack's house which was inside the stockade was blown up. On the smoke clearing away the house was down and the neighbouring houses on fire. Mr E Morgan, Acting Lt., 2 seamen, 1 marine being slightly wounded. Many town people dangerously so by the explosion. The last supply of ammunition intended for Fort Phillpotts having been lost in the stockade and their ammunition nearly expended, Mr Beckham, Police Magistrate,

Lieutenant G Phillpotts, Sgt. Barclay of the 96th Regt. after the loss of ammunition and stockade, the natives appearing on every height, considered it proper to embark all the people and abandon the town before dark. The English ship *Matilda* arrived and embarked many of the town people. About 4pm all the troops, seamen and marines with town people embarked. Observed the natives in the town and plunder it. The ship not firing, many town people having gone on shore again to endeavour to save their goods. The ship in her present position being exposed to the fire of musketry from the heights ... Gov. brig *Victoria* sailed for Auckland. Rt Rev G A Selwyn went on shore and buried the dead seamen and marines ... Lost by the explosion of stockade bread 182 lbs, beef salt 90 lbs, pork 90 lbs, rum 6 gallons. Midnight calm and clear.'[16]

Some sense of the state of Kororareka before its destruction began was provided by resident Captain George Thomas Clayton, one of a number of ships' masters who had visited the town and stayed, establishing businesses and families. Clayton ran a store at the north end of the beach, with his house nearby, and sketched the town on the morning of 11 March, suggesting an assemblage of some fifty buildings. Clearly identifiable were Polack's two houses inside their stockade at the north end of the beach and the Anglican Church, Turner's Row (or Terrace) and the Catholic mission complex at the other. Also apparent are two palisaded Maori communities toward the southern end of the beach, and several flags fluttering from the signal station on Maiki Hill. Clayton's sketch shows several canoes and boats hauled up on the shingle, and what looks like a quay or jetty built parallel to the beach with a small vessel tied up alongside.[17]

The next morning some residents returned to the town to salvage any remaining goods, while the *Hazard* continued its fire in an attempt to deter looters. Bishop Selwyn and Henry Williams also went ashore to recover and bury the dead, fearing a revival of a 'certain barbarous custom, now almost extinct'. Instead, they found the town's attackers perfectly civil and inoffensive, guiding them to where bodies lay. Selwyn buried six in the church ground, near where they fell, while Williams collected five bodies on Flagstaff Hill; these were buried at Paihia the next day. After the withdrawal of the troops, the natives 'carried on their work of plunder with perfect composure'. Selwyn observed, with sorrow, that many of the natives were wheeling off casks of spirits, although he was allowed to turn the tap of one

'Kororarika, Bay of Islands; formerly the seat of government of New Zealand (burnt by natives)' by Theodore Morton Jones, 1851. Jones was a lieutenant and artist on the survey ship HMS *Pandora* which visited New Zealand in 1851. This sketch, one of three which make up a panorama of Kororareka, shows shows houses (on left) and the Catholic mission complex with the printery (now Pompallier) at centre rear. *Alexander Turnbull Library, Wellington, New Zealand, C-003-002-3*

and empty the contents. Looting of the abandoned buildings continued, and by afternoon most of the town, apart from the church and mission houses, was up in flames, with the loss of an estimated £50,000 worth of property. After the burial service at Paihia, Selwyn rode to the mission station at Waimate, and as he approached the settlement the sky was 'lighted up with a lurid glare'. From a hill the bishop could see the outline of Kororareka, some twenty-three kilometres distant, illuminated by its burning houses.[18]

At Waimate, on the morning of the attack, the Rev. Burrows had a hasty breakfast and climbed a nearby hilltop. Through his telescope he could see that the *Hazard*'s guns were directed towards Maiki Hill, but the flagstaff was nowhere to be seen. He later saw a large plume of smoke rise from one end of the town, the result of the explosion in the stockade. About 2 p.m. a messenger brought a hastily written note from Henry Williams, advising that the flagstaff had been cut down and that the Maori were in possession of Maiki Hill. Selwyn arrived at Waimate shortly afterwards and suggested there was a certain irony in the situation, for some of the very individuals engaged in the destruction of Kororareka had entrusted their daughters to the care of the mission school. Burrows was anxious for further news of the disaster and left early on the 14th for Paihia, reaching Kororareka to find its houses were still being plundered and burned. He spoke to two or three looters who were 'at their work of destruction'. One declined Burrows' thoughtful offer to 'knock the head in' of a cask of spirits he was rolling away, while another who had a jar of sweets under his arm did offer the reverend some of his booty.[19]

12

AFTERMATH

THE NORTHERN WAR

Whoever doth this staff displace
Must meet Bob FitzRoy face to face.[1]

A fortnight after the fall of Kororareka, Governor Robert FitzRoy turned to the unenviable task of explaining the situation to his superiors in London. On 26 March 1845 it was his 'painful duty' to report to Colonial Secretary Lord Stanley that a 'disastrous calamity' had befallen New Zealand: 'A succession of untoward events happened in the doomed settlement, for which no foresight could have prepared.' As recently as the day before, an attack had seemed unlikely, but because the settlers were fatigued by 'constant drilling and labouring at temporary works of defence', they were 'thrown off their guard'. First to be thrown were those in the upper blockhouse, and FitzRoy explained that this was lost when all but four of the men stationed there were away from their post and made no attempt to 'rally and retake it'. Next to fall was the flagstaff, 'the key to our position'. But thanks to the 'occasional well-directed' fire of the *Hazard*'s guns, the whole population had been safely placed on ships in the harbour, leaving the town to be plundered and burned, with only the missionaries' houses and churches spared. As for the 'rebellious' Maori, FitzRoy suggested that European troops 'would not have behaved better, nor shown less vindictiveness', for the attackers had exhibited 'acts of a chivalrous nature' and a remarkable forbearance, especially towards the missionaries. The beleaguered governor described the hills around the town as 'a place most easy to attack, most difficult to defend', and reported the day's losses as thirteen British killed and twenty-three wounded, while thirty-four Maori were known to have been killed and at least sixty-eight wounded.

Just in case Lord Stanley was under the impression that the whole disaster might have been prevented had all the available military force ('small as it is') been concentrated at Kororareka, FitzRoy pointed out it had been necessary to maintain troops at Wellington, which was also under threat. In addition, had there been no troops left in Auckland, Heke may have made feigned attacks on Kororareka and then sent his main body south to the defenceless capital.[2]

There was no shortage of opinion of what had gone wrong at Kororareka. Although Captain J Everard Home of the HMS *North Star* was not actually there at the time – his ship arrived at Auckland eleven days after the event, bringing officers and 150 men of the 58th Regiment from Sydney – he attributed the 'ill success of that day' to two factors. First, there had been a lack of knowledge of 'the peculiar mode of warfare adopted by these brave and sagacious savages' and, second, a lack of experience on the British side. While Ensign Campbell might well have displayed better judgement and restraint when the first alarm was sounded, such qualities might not be expected from an officer of barely two years' service.[3] At a subsequent court martial, Campbell and Lieutenant Barclay were charged with abandoning their positions, the first being found guilty but receiving only a reprimand, and the other being acquitted on the grounds that he had been outnumbered and overpowered.[4]

Historian James Cowan blamed the disastrous outcome on a lack of co-ordination between the operations of the naval, military, police and civilian forces, with each giving orders and acting independently. In his view Beckham was over-cautious and Phillpotts too impulsive, and there might have been a happier outcome had the spirited Cornthwaite Hector been given more responsibility after Robertson was injured. Hector had offered to attempt to retake Flagstaff Hill with a force of volunteers, but his bold initiative was not allowed to proceed.[5]

There were widely varying estimates of the number of Maori involved in the attack on Kororareka, ranging from 600 to more than 2000.[6] George Phillpotts put the figure at 1200 at least, and a force that was 'as well armed as ourselves, if not better' on account of many having long American rifles, which were no doubt a benefit of trading with visiting whalers. He considered the attackers' mode of warfare 'entirely strange', for the bush on the surrounding hills was filled with 'armed men lying in ambush', and it was impossible to flush them out of their cover and engage them in the open.[7]

From the British point of view, the disastrous outcome at Kororareka was due to at least two monumental blunders, beginning with the loss of the upper blockhouse. Although the Maori insurgents had then gained the highest point above the town, it is possible that the settlers could have held out below and mounted a Gallipoli-type assault on the summit, as Hector had proposed. But if they had retaken the upper blockhouse and restored some honour by reinstating the flag, their continued resistance would have been spectacularly terminated with the next big blunder, the loss of the ammunition supply in the stockade. Phillpotts did not know whether this untimely explosion occurred by 'accident or treachery' for there were reports of both, although he suspected the former.[8] According to at least three historians, it was the result of a spark from a pipe, in which case smoking, rather than drinking or licentiousness, was the real downfall of Kororareka.[9]

One year on, a reflective Robert FitzRoy – now no longer governor – claimed that the events of 11 March had astounded every one, including even the Maori. He believed the attackers were 'as much astonished at their own success, as the whole colony was at so unthought-of a disaster'. For even though an attack by Heke had been expected, the possibility of the place being destroyed had 'entered no man's mind'. It was a 'singularly unfortunate affair' for several reasons, one being that it represented the first occasion in the colony's history that troops had been engaged with Maori – 'and had failed'. The imagined superiority of the British forces was now gone, balanced by a rise in the daring and self-confidence of the Maori, and their increasing disrespect for the enemy. FitzRoy excused the performance at Kororareka on the grounds that because many of the men of the 96th Regiment were 'very young' and had not previously been under fire, they were not able to cope with hardy and battle-tested warriors.

When three large ships were seen sailing into Auckland's Waitemata Harbour in the late evening of 16 March it was presumed they were bringing troops from Sydney or England. But the nervous public's joy at this arrival soon changed to 'deep gloom' when it was discovered that they were the

Hazard, the *St Louis* and the *Matilda*, and all three were crowded with fugitives from the Bay of Islands.[10] Aucklanders panicked, realising they were only a four-day journey from the victorious Heke's pa in the north. Defensive measures were quickly attended to. Britomart Point, the elevated promontory above the harbour, was fortified and became Fort Britomart, while St Paul's church, situated on the point, had its windows planked and loopholed with narrow slits in case the firing of muskets became necessary. On 22 March the *North Star* brought 162 officers and men from Sydney and further reinforcements arrived in the following weeks.[11] But by then the capital was considered to be out of danger, for Waikato chief Te Wherowhero had offered to provide protection from his old enemies, the Nga Puhi. Nevertheless, at about 2 a.m. on 1 April, Aucklanders heard musketry firing and suspected an attack was imminent. There was a good turnout of the military and volunteer force, including the crew of the *Hazard* who hastened on shore, but it proved to be a false alarm. Maori had been firing shots a short distance from the town, 'as is their custom, in consequence of the death of the wife of a chief'.[12]

The humiliation of defeat at Kororareka took its toll in various ways, and was even offered as a defence at the Auckland Supreme Court. Four soldiers of the 96th Regiment were charged with rioting, intent on demolishing a house in Shortland Crescent, and had been urged on by a large crowd with such exhortations as 'Go it 96' and 'Knock the house down'. Colonel Hulme spoke of the good character of the soldiers, noting that they had been 'much slandered and insulted since the affair at Kororareka'. Nevertheless, the jury found two of the men guilty, and they were sentenced to eighteen months' imprisonment with hard labour.[13]

The Auckland-based governor was now coming under increasing criticism and, not surprisingly, the most stinging of this originated from Wellington. Recent events at the Bay of Islands presented the *New Zealand Spectator and Cook's Straits Guardian* with further grounds to both attack FitzRoy's policies and question his personal competence. When the government brig *Victoria* arrived at Port Nicholson with 'intelligence of the most afflicting and calamitous nature' regarding Kororareka, the paper reminded readers that it had predicted FitzRoy's 'timid vacillating policy' would have just such consequences. The governor was portrayed as a man hell-bent on destruction, and one who had placed the colony in a situation of 'unexampled difficulty and distress'. Much to the displeasure of Wellingtonians, in a recent speech he had made no mention of the colony's southern settlements, as if they didn't exist. He had also, and somewhat prematurely, described the 'Aborginal [sic] population' as displaying self-restraint and 'wonderful' tranquillity, and was confident of their loyalty towards Her Majesty and the settlers generally. But within a week of this announcement, the 'entire destruction of one of the oldest settlements in New Zealand' had taken place, and now there were 500 persons 'entirely ruined'. The governor had thus earned an unenviable reputation, and like 'Eratostratus' (Herostratus), who destroyed the Temple of Diana of Ephesus, he would be chiefly remembered for 'the ruin of which he has been the author'.

According to the same newspaper, Governor FitzRoy heeded only 'one sided and biased opinions', mainly those from missionaries. Of them, the paper could not 'trust' itself to describe the conduct of the Rev. Henry Williams, the chorus-leader of 'missionary land sharks'. It was alleged that Kororareka had been lulled into a sense of false security after Williams had spoken to the disaffected Maori and decided there was no real cause for fear. The paper hoped there would now be an inquiry into the conduct of this 'false prophet', 'Arch traitor' and 'Reverend Imposter' who had cried peace. What's more, on the night before the attack when he declared there was no danger, he derided residents for putting their personal property on ships, but at the same time took care to ship his own. As a result, thundered the *New Zealand Spectator and Cook's Straits Guardian*, 'deluded inhabitants, misled by his perfidious advice' had lost all they owned.[14]

In the weeks following 11 March, Kororareka lay abandoned, reduced to ashes and with little left to be plundered or pilfered. But the south end of the beach was about to be witness to an event that may have been, in its own way, as remarkable as any in that town's short and turbulent history. Details of this were recorded, albeit somewhat later and second-hand, by Father Walter McDonald, private secretary to Bishop Pompallier. He travelled extensively on the bishop's behalf, and while in Rome in 1860 he wrote to the Directors of the Work of the Propagation of the Faith in France giving details of an incident back in the Bay of Islands that appeared to involve deliverance from certain death.[15]

Although there would later be suggestions to the contrary, letters written by Pompallier before the destruction of Kororareka indicate that he wished to avoid the impending conflict. In late January 1845 he advised chief 'Jean

Heke' of his love for all Maori people, including those who had 'engaged blindly in Protestantism' and those who had not embraced any religion at all. He was aware of Heke's attacks on the British flag at Kororareka, and warned him of the might of Britain, which had 'millions' of soldiers overseas. Because he claimed not to represent any foreign power, Pompallier assured Heke he would work for the salvation of his people, whether they submitted to the British government or remained independent.[16] And although Heke offered to take him and his flock to safety, the bishop felt that no such secure place existed this side of heaven.[17] He was well aware that the recent 'prey of bloody disorders' had been instigated by Heke, who just happened to be 'one of the first disciples of the Protestant ministers' and a nephew of Hongi Hika, whom he described as a 'sort of Attila'.[18]

Before Heke's attack, Pompallier was advised by the warring Maori chiefs that his house would be safe as long as he did not leave it. His establishment was left intact, as promised, along with a number of neighbouring houses, for he had managed to convince the attackers that they could not burn those without endangering his own. All others were reduced to ashes and dispersed by the wind, leaving nothing but nails and a forest of chimneys. The bishop stayed put for three weeks, then learned that a large force of armed Maori – consisting of Protestants and pagans – intended to attack his establishment at dawn the following day. They had determined to destroy what little that still remained of Kororareka, and the bishop's life and those of his household were to be sacrificed to avenge chiefs who had died in the previous battle.

As threatened, war canoes were seen on the harbour at dawn. There were about six, some carrying more than thirty warriors, and their war cries made their intentions clear. The bishop advised his companions to prepare for their fate, if that was God's will. As he walked in front of the house, reciting his rosary, a Catholic chief from the district informed him that a force of local Maori would come to his defence. As Pompallier learned of this last-minute offer of support, the canoes advanced towards the beach. It was then that Péata, the twenty-four-year-old whom the Bishop had earlier baptised and who was the first Maori woman received into the Catholic church, hastened to the water's edge. She addressed the assailants in the canoes, now only fifty yards distant, welcoming them if they came as brothers but warning them they would be opposed if their intentions were otherwise. The canoes slowed, and the leading chief asked how many men were on shore to resist their landing. Péata responded that she alone stood between them and the bishop's house. Realising that their path was barred by a princess, and that to proceed would be just cause for war, the warriors diverted to a spot some distance from the mission. As they came ashore they were approached by the force Pompallier had been told about, some 150 men armed with guns who had concealed themselves during the night to watch the enemy's arrival. They now confronted the landing party, but violence was averted and peace prevailed. Speeches followed, and the chief of the would-be assailants presented Pompallier with a dog-skin cloak and a double-barrelled rifle. After a feast the two sides left for their respective districts.[19]

Kororareka then returned to its previously deserted state. The bishop's own account, published forty-three years after the event, made remarkably little mention of the destruction of the town, and none of the pivotal role of Péata. He wrote that on 11 March 1845 he and his fellow clergy passed their time in prayer, 'in the middle of cinders', while 'the ravages of the pest of war' passed over their heads. As a security, he had stowed church records and other valuables on board the schooner *Russell*, to be taken to the safety of Auckland and other mission stations. When the fighting began he and others retreated to the ship, where 'balls whizzed over [their] heads like hailstones'. After the explosion in the stockade they watched their town 'delivered up to the horrors of war, of pillage, and of burning'.[20]

Following their success at Kororareka, Heke and Kawiti remained in the town for about a week before they too departed. Heke went to Pakaraka and then to Te Ahuahu, a small pa to the north-east of Lake Omapere; Kawiti went south to Waiomio. The two chiefs would shortly join forces again.

In order to deal with 'certain disaffected natives', on 26 April FitzRoy imposed martial law on all parts of the northern North Island within a radius of sixty miles from Russell. At the same time he reminded the colony that it was at war, and Maori in the Bay of Islands who wished for peace and commerce were advised to stear clear of 'ill disposed natives'. They were not to approach ships, soldiers or military camps without a missionary or an equivalent 'protector' carrying a white flag, or they might be fired on by mistake. FitzRoy also required that all boats and other property that had been plundered at Kororareka be returned to certain authorised persons.[21]

On the day following these proclamations, the British campaign was re-activated when 470 officers and men in three ships sailed north from

Auckland. In addition to the 58th and 96th regiments there were some fifty volunteers, most of whom were previous residents of the Bay of Islands, led by Cornthwaite Hector. With considerable pomp and ceremony, Lieutenant-Colonel Hulme raised the flag on Kororareka Beach. Plans were then made for the military campaign to follow.

The *North Star* moved around to Otuihu and anchored offshore from Pomare's pa. Although the chief himself had played no part in the recent uprising, some of his men were involved and he was suspected of harbouring anti-government sentiments. Pomare was now lured on board the *North Star* and taken prisoner, while his fortified village, which had long been recognised as a festering den of iniquity, followed the fate of Kororareka and was sacked and burned. The three British ships were then joined by the *Hazard*, which had arrived from Auckland, and they moved across the Bay to the shelter of Kent Passage, a narrow gap between the mainland and Moturoa Island. On 3 May 1845 some 400 men went ashore at the beach at Onewhero Bay and began the first march inland of British troops in New Zealand.[21]

The first conflict in the campaign took place when Hulme's forces engaged Heke's at Puketutu, near the eastern shores of Lake Omapere. After an ineffective artillery barrage, including the use of rockets and considerable hand-to-hand fighting, the attack on the pa was called off. In June Colonel Henry Despard, who had arrived in New Zealand with two companies of the 99th Regiment, set out to attack Kawiti's new fortification at Ohaeawai. This well-designed pa held the combined forces of Kawiti and Heke: underground bunkers and protective screens enabled it to withstand a week-long bombardment which was augmented by a gun from the *Hazard*. On 1 July Despard gave orders to storm the stockade and the men rushed forward 'in the most gallant and daring manner'. They encountered heavy fire and a few managed to get through the outer defences, but they suffered heavy casualties and the retreat was sounded. The following day the despondent Despard advised FitzRoy of his failure to take the pa, and hoped that the character of the British would not be 'tarnished' on this occasion. Of his 600 men engaged in the eight-day operation, seventy-three were wounded and forty-one were killed, among them Lieutenant George Phillpotts of the *Hazard*, shot dead while forcing his way through the stockade.[23] ('Toby' Phillpotts was a colourful and excitable character who went into battle at Ohaeawai wearing a monocle and cotton underpants in place of the regulation black trousers.[24] Earlier, in 1844, he had taken exception to adverse comments by the editor of the *Auckland Times* concerning the war in the north. A duel was arranged, in which the editor took a bullet through his coat tail while Phillpotts lost a button from his uniform.)[25]

Following the embarrassment of Kororareka and the severe setback at Ohaeawai, the Colonial Office resolved to recall FitzRoy, who was now accused of displaying a lack of judgement and resolve in his handling of 'the native question'. His replacement was George Grey, whose first contact with this part of the world was two exploratory expeditions in north-western Australia in 1837 and 1839. Earlier, he had sat on a House of Commons committee looking into transportation and asked a number of questions regarding the large number of escaped convicts who had stowed away on ships at Sydney and absconded to New Zealand. He learned that once there they had led Maori to 'the commission of great violence upon one another, and . . . are even accused of stimulating them to violences upon the Europeans'.[26]

Grey arrived in New Zealand on 18 November, and his immediate concern was the state of violence in the Bay of Islands. He was there within a week and announced to a conference attended by a large number of Maori that after a period of inactivity the war would continue. He considered Kororareka to be an unsuitable location for a camp, being a distance from the rebel Maori and accessible only by water. Grey also ordered that the Bay of Islands be blockaded in an attempt to cut off the rebels' supplies of gunpowder. But the Hokianga Harbour remained open to overseas shipping, and the valuable commodity still managed to find its way through.[27] Grey also planned another inland expedition involving more than 1100 men with the objective of taking Ruapekapeka, a new pa built by Kawiti south of Kawakawa. Following a heavy bombardment, the stockade was breached and the pa was found to have been deserted, although fighting took place in the bush behind. This battle gave neither side a victory, but shortly afterwards Heke and Kawiti agreed to peace terms.

While governor, FitzRoy had suspected Pompallier and others of fomenting anti-British feelings among the Maori. Aware of this accusation, the bishop wrote to Everard Home of the *North Star* protesting that he wished nothing but 'peace and happiness both to the white man and the native', and asking Home to convey his letter to the governor.[28] FitzRoy had also written to Lord Stanley at the Home Office in London, suggesting that 'Frenchmen as well as Americans' had instigated the native resistance to British authority, and offering as evidence of this complicity Pompallier's contact with the French corvette *Rhin*, which had visited the Bay of Islands the previous January. This was in spite of the bishop's claim to have been a positive influence at Kororareka, when 'about fifteen houses' of English residents were not set on fire by the attacking Maori for fear that the Catholic mission would have also been destroyed.[29] But when Grey replaced FitzRoy, he wrote to Stanley vindicating Pompallier and his priests. Although the new governor admitted an initial prejudice against Pompallier and his clergy, he now believed Her Majesty had no more loyal subjects than the Maori who had sided with British troops, and a considerable proportion of them happened to be Roman Catholics. Grey also knew the captain of the *Rhin* to be an 'amiable officer', who would not promote any outrages in this country. Far from accusing the Catholics of stirring up trouble, Grey suggested that it may have been the Church of England missionaries who contributed to the unsettled state, for their large and contentious purchases of land from Maori hardly enhanced their image.

Cleared of any suggestions of disloyalty or mischief-making, Pompallier could now abandon his contingency plan, for had he been expelled from New Zealand he had intended seeking refuge in the suitably named Friendly Islands.[30] He also had big plans for Kororareka, in the form of a cathedral and a college for the education of Maori. But from the early 1840s it was increasingly apparent that it would no longer be the main settlement in the country, and any hopes for a revival were dashed by the events of March 1845. The following year Pompallier left for Auckland where he would realise his schemes with the consecration of St Patrick's Church in 1848, and the establishment of St Mary's College at Takapuna.

For those who had been residents of Kororareka in March 1845 there was the matter of compensation. They would soon have an ally in a weekly newspaper, *The New-Zealander*, launched in Auckland to champion the interests of the average citizen, both European and Maori. In its first issue on 7 June it took up the cause of the 'sufferers of the Bay of Islands, and other parts to the Northward', a matter then being considered by the governor. It claimed many of those that had suffered worst had already left the colony 'with the remnant of their broken fortunes', and many others would do likewise if only they could afford to do so. The paper strongly recommended assistance for those who were now bereft of their land and other property, and by doing so the government would be sending a clear message that it really had the 'advancement, happiness and prosperity of the Colony at heart'.[31]

But it obviously hadn't as far as one group of citizens was concerned, who eleven years later still sought compensation for losses resulting from the 'Government Wars with the Natives'. In 1856 Benjamin Turner headed a petition to the House of Representatives on behalf of himself and twenty other one-time settlers from Kororareka. Between them they had lost thirty-three houses in the destruction of the town, Turner losing the most with eight (one of which was used as barracks for the troops), while George Thomas Clayton claimed his store as well as a house. The signatories were in no doubt as to who was responsible for the events which had brought them 'poverty and ruin'. In the first instance, the acting governor Willoughby Shortland had not taken decisive action following the June 1843 massacre of twenty-two Nelson settlers at Wairau by Maori under the 'unbridled and furious' leaders Rangihaeta and Te Rauparaha. When FitzRoy became governor seven months later he merely offered Te Rauparaha a pardon, and it was this, according to the disaffected Kororareka property owners, that encouraged a contemptuous attitude towards British authority in the northern part of the North Island. As a result, on 4 July 1844 Hone Heke and followers arrived in Kororareka and 'behaved insultingly' to British settlers, plundering some of their stores, killing their pigs and cutting down the flagstaff. FitzRoy was advised against dealing with Heke by a missionary, which only heightened the ridicule and contempt for British authority. His Excellency demanded muskets as payment but returned them to their owners. At the same time the troops were sent back to Sydney, for the whole matter was apparently settled.

The memorialists recorded that after Heke had cut down the flagstaff for the third time, FitzRoy dispatched soldiers to the town and certain buildings were taken over for military purposes. Turner claimed that the largest of these was his own, which was used as barracks. He had undertaken 'expensive alterations' for the purpose and had received neither payment nor compensation. The petition stressed official incompetence: that the blockhouse was taken as a result of the mismanagement of the officer in command, and the flagstaff was then levelled for the 'fifth' time. The fight lasted about two hours,

after which the 600 inhabitants of the town – now 'homeless . . . disheartened
. . . deprived of every earthly possession' – were taken to Auckland. The value
of plunder taken by the victors, along with other losses, was put at upwards
of £40,000. In conclusion, this disaster had been the result of an 'obnoxious
display of authority' and the repeated reinstatement of the unprotected
flagstaff. The government of the day had failed to deal with the 'turbulent
spirit' of the Maori, yet the petitioners pointed out that at Kororareka there
had long been an 'amicable interchange' between European settlers and the
original New Zealanders.[32]

Only three of the twenty-one petitioners now listed their present abode as
the Bay of Islands, with ten 'absent' and four resident in Auckland. It appears
they received no satisfaction from the government, and eight years later the
matter was again raised in the House of Representatives, now stimulated by
the decision to compensate Taranaki settlers £200,000 for their losses during
more recent hostilities. Hugh Carleton, member for the Bay of Islands,
claimed that those who had suffered as a result of 'Heke's War' were even
more entitled to compensation than the Taranaki settlers. In his view the
latter had 'courted war', while the disaster at Kororareka had been about the
flagstaff, the 'emblem of Government'. Besides, when martial law was
proclaimed, northern settlers were sworn in as special constables and had
been 'menaced with prosecution if they refused to take the oath'. They had
lost everything, but Carleton was confident there would be no difficulty
estimating the extent of their losses. A property tax had been levied only a few
days prior to 11 March 1845, and people were 'not in the habit of overrating
their property when it was about to be taxed'.

While Carleton had some support in the House, William Colenso, now the
member for Napier, had no sympathy for his old near-neighbours at
Kororareka. Not only did he feel the time for compensation had passed, but
those settlers had shown 'a want of personal courage', leaving their property
and not behaving 'as Englishmen on that occasion'. Another member
recommended that the matter of compensation be deferred until the present
disturbances were over, fearing there would be 'no end of petitions' and the
colony would not be able to meet the claims in full.[33] Nine months passed,
and Carleton again reminded the House of the losses at Kororareka. While he
accused the government of 'sacrificing' that town, there were other
suggestions as to who was at fault. The American consul at the Bay of Islands

was blamed for telling Heke that American whalers would not visit as long as the British flag was 'waving' there, while another member felt responsibility for the disaster lay with the 'home' rather than colonial government. Carleton commended the bravery and determination of the Kororareka settlers, telling the House how the women had torn up their petticoats to make cartridges, and how 'a boy carried up those cartridges [to the soldiers] through a cross-fire'. He concluded by suggesting that the out-of-pocket settlers would be happy to accept compensation in land – something he felt the government would soon have much of 'at their disposal'.[34]

In mid-1867, after another twenty-one months had elapsed, the persistent Carleton raised the matter yet again. He had no wish to 'embarrass' the government, but felt it better if his 'unfortunate clients' were to learn there was no hope rather than to suffer from 'hope deferred'. In response Premier Edward Stafford pointed out it was one thing to pass a resolution, but it was another to put up the money. No such fund had been set aside, but at least a select committee would now be appointed.[35] A report was expected in three weeks, but – like the reply to Turner's petition eleven years earlier – it did not appear to eventuate.[36] Soon afterwards the House did learn that payments had been made for losses sustained in the war by settlers in the Auckland province, although there was no specific mention of Kororareka. Even so, those claims were later re-investigated and the awards were reduced, with settlers receiving one-third in cash and the balance in scrip to be used to purchase land. Responding to criticism of the value of that scrip, Stafford now stated that the government had done all it could in this matter.[37]

Among those Kororareka residents who had sought compensation back in 1856 was Joel Polack, who claimed for one house destroyed. Apart from the structure itself, another great loss for the town and New Zealand generally may have been the personal items within it. Polack's books, artefacts, writings, sketches and paintings all went up in smoke when his property, requisitioned as a munitions store, was spectacularly destroyed on the afternoon of 11 March 1845.[38]

13

BACK IN BUSINESS

TAKING LIBERTIES ASHORE

Come breast the bars, bullies, an' heave her away,
Soon we'll be rollin' her 'way down the Bay,

We're outward bound for Vallipo Bay,
Get crackin', m' lads, 'tis a hell o' a way![1]

By the end of January 1846 the Northern War was over and the Bay of Islands' main settlement lay mostly destroyed and depopulated. One year earlier, thanks to the efforts of the New Zealand Company, Wellington had been the most populous of the colony's twelve districts and settlements, with 4347 persons (only Europeans were counted at that stage), followed by Nelson (3036), Auckland (2754) and Taranaki (1155). Fifth on the list was the Bay of Islands, with 534 – down from 669 in 1843. But by the following year it had plummeted to just a token ten, while Auckland's European population had risen accordingly to 3970. At least the Bay had bottomed, and would enjoy a slow but steady rise, creeping up to 200 by 1850. By then a pattern had emerged: Auckland was the most populous region – and would stay that way until the discovery of gold in Otago in the early 1860s – with 8301, followed by Wellington. A similar story was revealed by the amount of customs revenue collected at the colony's seventeen ports. In 1840 the Bay of Islands was the main – if not sole – earner in this regard, but by the following year it had been overtaken by both Auckland and Wellington. All three ports enjoyed

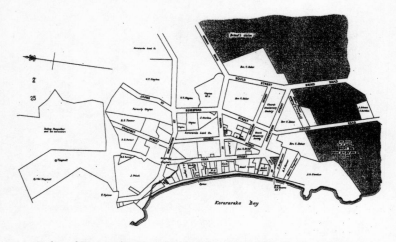

A plan of Kororareka (Russell) drawn by Murray V Hedges based on an
1863 plan, 'shewing the original streets and alterations proposed by
[pioneer surveyor] Mr [Thomas] Cass also the original boundaries of
claims and of the lands granted . . .' *Reproduced with the kind permission
of Mrs Jocelyn Chisholm and Mrs M V Hedges*

spectacular growth in 1842, but the Bay then went into rapid decline. Not
surprisingly, it had no such income to declare for the 1845 year, and while the
situation began to improve subsequently, it did not reach the 1840 level again
until 1852. By now Auckland was the main port, collecting nearly forty per
cent of the colony's customs revenue, followed by Wellington with nearly one-
third.[2]

As these statistics suggest, some of the former residents did drift back to
Kororareka. Apart from possibly having nowhere else to go, they still owned
properties, such as they were. The men tended to return first, to carry out
necessary repairs in advance of their wives and children. Eventually, most
of the houses were either restored or rebuilt, but without any official
assistance or government compensation.[3] Before abandoning Kororareka,
residents had buried some of the more valuable possessions they were
unable to take with them on the ships to Auckland. One such item was a large
framed engraved print of Queen Victoria's coronation in 1838, the property
of Samuel Stephenson, who had set up business as a chandler in Kororareka
in 1830. Carefully wrapped and buried, it was later disinterred, and is now on

display in the Russell Museum, lent by the granddaughter of its original owner.[4]

In April 1846 a chief constable was reinstated at Kororareka, but there was now another unsettling undercurrent when some of the less respectable European residents resented the employment of temporary Maori police to patrol the streets.[5] However, there was the reassuring presence of an army detachment, based at Te Wahapu until 1857, and locals now had a neighbour in Nga Puhi leader Tamati Waka Nene. He had taken the government side during the 1845–46 war, and his loyalty was rewarded with an annuity and a whare on the Kororareka waterfront.

Kororareka residents who had difficulty re-establishing themselves up north may have been lured away by the promise of gold in California in 1849, or Australia a few years later. They may have then returned when New Zealand had a rush of its own. By the end of the 1840s Auckland was home to about thirty-seven per cent of the colony's European population, and at the same time had taken over from Kororareka as the main concentration of its undesirables.[6] In the opinion of newspaper editor, artist, explorer and politician William Fox – he was also a New Zealand Company agent, so would hardly be unbiased – the main problem with Auckland was its people: as an example of colonisation the place was both 'rotten' and 'Algerine', the latter term being a comparison with Algeria implying 'piratical'. The population in that northern city was rootless, as was proved when 'some hundreds' packed up and rushed to California in search of gold. By comparison, Fox claimed that barely half a dozen persons in the Wellington region were 'moved by that bait'. The main activity of the then capital seemed to be shopkeeping, and while it had 'one or two very good streets', other parts were as filthy as the naval towns of Deptford and Wapping.[7]

As any good New Zealand Company agent would maintain, the first colonisation of New Zealand was 'rude and irregular' with all the usual runaway sailors, escaped convicts and shorewhalers, until a more systematic approach began in Wellington in 1839.[8] In Fox's view, Auckland consisted largely of individuals from Sydney or Tasmania, which was reflected in the crime statistics and further illustrated the need for organised colonisation. In the year ending December 1847 there were 1083 criminal cases dealt with at Auckland, 994 of which involved only Europeans; of the 857 convictions, 529 were for drunkenness. On this basis, one in six Aucklanders was convicted of one crime or another, as compared to the Wellington figure of only one in forty.[9]

The Bay of Islands entered the 1850s on a more respectable and scientific note with the arrival of HMS *Rattlesnake* on 16 May. After leaving Australia the ship found it had sprung a leak so put in to Kororareka for recaulking. Assistant surgeon Thomas Huxley took advantage of the stopover to make an excursion up the Kerikeri River to the missionary establishment at Waimate. Like his friend Charles Darwin fifteen years earlier, he was impressed by the 'quiet, unpretending, straightforward folks' he found there. Although he didn't comment on Kororareka, he was generally more positive about New Zealand than his colleague had been, admitting he 'liked the look' of the place. [10]

Whaleships continued to scour the Pacific, and in 1845 the American 'fisheries' consisted of 650 vessels totalling 193,000 tons and manned by 15,000 officers and men. With an eye on this valuable industry – the value of the stores required by these ships on each voyage amounted to about $10.6 million – a Wellington newspaper recommended that smaller and faster ships should be built and fitted out in New Zealand. And, not surprisingly, Port Nicholson was seen as the ideal port where whalers could obtain all the necessary supplies 'at the most reasonable rate'.[11] In fact, while Kororareka would face competition from other 'resorts', Port Nicholson was hardly one of them. Of the New Zealand ports, Auckland was the one that lured most of the maritime trade away from the Bay of Islands, and as a growing city it offered much of interest to sailors. With some of these distractions in mind, including the possibility of crews being 'shangaied', some captains preferred to stick to the northern port, where there were still adequate facilities for refitting and repairing and a ready supply of water.[12] And if the accounts of one whaler who visited Kororareka in the early 1850s can be believed, some of that town's old habits hadn't changed.

Nelson Cole Haley was born in 1832 in New Bedford, Massachusetts, and ran away to sea at the age of twelve. In 1849 he departed as a boat-steerer, or harpooner, on the *Charles W Morgan* on a voyage that took him to New Zealand. He experienced all aspects of whaling, the animal's life and death, and provided some highly detailed and original descriptions of the chase, capture and processing. There was little time for sentimentality in that business, as when a day-old calf nudged up to Haley's boat, mistaking it for its mother. Any sympathy for the harpooned juvenile was short-lived, for not only did it give up about two barrels of oil but it also provided a useful lesson in anatomy that assisted future catches. Recalling Jonah's experience, Haley wrote that whale jaws opened wide enough for an ox team to drive in. The harpoon was attached to some 220 fathoms (400 metres) of manila rope, which lay coiled and ready for action in a tub in the bottom of the whaleboat.[13] Along with whaling's other cordage requirements, it amply illustrated why such high hopes were held for New Zealand's flax industry.

The *Charles W Morgan* rounded the Cape of Good Hope and sailed eastwards across the Indian Ocean into the South Pacific. In mid-January 1850 it entered the Bay of Islands, winding between 'green-clad islets' and 'reefs of rocks', while Haley observed the 'little white cottages' of settlers and their free-ranging cattle. Shortly the ship approached a sandy beach, behind which rows of houses extended 'for a mile or more' and included the sort of 'gin mills' (taverns) found in English and American settlements. The sails were furled, the rigging coiled, and the captain reported to the custom house. But he returned to the ship that evening in a 'towering rage', for while he was ashore his boat-steerer had taken the other men into a public house, and they later had great difficulty rowing back to the ship. The *Charles W Morgan* lay off Kororareka for about two weeks, taking on some 300 barrels of water and receiving a repaint. When the men went ashore they 'spent most of their time, and all their money' in the public houses, and as a result had 'roaring headaches'. Some of Haley's fellow sailors ventured into the Maori settlement at Kororareka, and reported that the women there – especially the 'half-breeds' – were 'rather pretty'.[14]

The ship left the Bay of Islands and headed north-east in search of whales. It encountered the *Christopher Mitchell* of Nantucket doing likewise, and its captain told of a remarkable incident at sea. When that ship was off the coast of Peru a sailor contracted a fever and retired to bed, and a shipmate detected something unusual. This sailor had displayed 'refinement and deportment' seldom seen in the forecastle of a whaler, and while able to pull oars and furl sails with the best of them, had a feminine quality that had not passed unnoticed. The captain was hailed and when he peered into the sick sailor's berth he was astonished to see a 'beautifully formed woman'. Her cover blown, she confessed that it had all been an attempt to track down a man who had deserted her after promising marriage. She had followed him to New York where he had shipped as a whaler, and in the hope that she might find him she passed herself off as a 'green boy' and went to sea. She had a boyish figure, and by wearing a form-fitting garment of 'topgallant duck' to flatten her bust she had managed to pass herself off as a man for eight months. Even so, some of the crew had had their suspicions, noting her propensity to blush and the fact that she seemed 'broader across the transom' than other sailors. The captain decided to take her to the American consul at Lima and she now deferred to her feminine side, making do with clothes donated by the crew. The men were startled by the transformation, the captain recording that the boat-steerer's black broadcloth trousers 'fit[ted] her form without a wrinkle'. After an emotional farewell she left the ship at Lima, and from there returned to New York. The captain of the *Christopher Mitchell* had been to sea 'man and boy, for over forty years' and had never seen nor heard of anything like it.[15]

Perhaps with that experience in mind, Haley continued his narrative of his voyage, describing how the wind filled out the sails like 'well-formed woman's breasts, and almost as graceful'.[16] On a return visit to the New Zealand ground the *Charles W Morgan* sailed for a month without sighting anything, until a gale sprang up and there were 'whales to the windward, whales to the leeward, whales ahead, whales astern, whales everywhere'. They tumbled about and shot down the sides of waves, 'like a boy sliding down the side of a snow bank on a sled', and approached the ship apparently without fear. If this seemed contrary to Charles Wilkes' claim that whales were becoming more wary, Haley was aware from first-hand experience that these remarkable animals knew that during such a gale no boat would attempt to attack them.[17]

In the vicinity of the Three Kings Islands, fifty kilometres north-west of the northern tip of the North Island, the ship was party to another of the sea's mysteries. Haley was aloft early one morning, the rising sun appearing like 'a vast golden cheese', when he saw some large and indistinct objects in the water. Although unable to get any other crew members to confirm his sighting, he was convinced he had seen a trio of 'submarine denizens', the giant squid. He was well positioned to view those leviathans, and using the known length of the ship for comparison he estimated their lengths at up to 300 feet.[18]

No other monsters of the deep were sighted, not even whales, and the ship put into Kororareka. Since the previous visit the town had gained an extra public house, which Haley felt was hardly necessary for a population he put at no more than 200. The *Charles W Morgan* took on wood and water, and the men went ashore. There were other ships in the harbour at the time, so the three public houses drove a 'rattling trade'. The drink – a 'vile concoction' – inevitably led to fighting, and spread 'from one end of the beach to the other'. Haley suggested that there was more 'fun' per square inch than one might have thought possible, while baton-brandishing policemen 'dancing around like performing monkeys' were bowled over by some of the revellers.[19]

Haley was more abstemious in his habits, which may explain why he was responsible for rounding up the crew after a day's leave. By that stage some could barely crawl, and needed the added inducement of a whipping to get them aboard. They were then taken in by sympathetic shipmates who undressed them and put them in their bunks. Some had learned the hard way how the rules regarding alcohol were enforced on the ship, for if once aboard a drunken man made the slightest noise or caused trouble he was dragged aft and thrown in irons. If he persisted in being a disturbance, stiffer punishments followed, such as having his mouth stuffed and muffled and his head trussed with rope. Haley attested to the efficacy of such desperate measures, for drunken sailors tended to fall uncharacteristically quiet when their boat approached the ship.

On a liberty day Haley and some of his fellow crew were rowing up one of the rivers that empty into the Bay. Passing a grove of fruit trees and keen to sample the produce, they approached the nearby house of an elderly Englishman and his wife. The owners insisted that the men help themselves, so they all repaired to the orchard, accompanied by the couple's daughter, who Haley guessed was aged about sixteen. This young lady wore a short dress and no shoes or stockings, and as a result 'a fair share of her lower works showed' when she stooped to gather fruit. Some of men later confessed that this 'stern view' was enough to make them want to desert ship and settle down nearby.[20]

While the *Charles W Morgan* was in port its crew were involved in what Haley described as one of the most 'desperate fights' that ever took place on Kororareka Beach. He qualified it by noting that it was 'between foreigners', so he may have been aware of The Girls' War of some twenty years earlier. This latest disturbance erupted on a Sunday afternoon in front of one of the public houses, and the combatants were quickly joined by patrons from the others. Haley watched the 'entertainment' from the ship, which lasted for about two hours and involved 150 to 200 men, until soldiers arrived and with fixed bayonets cleared the battle zone. A large number of men from the *Charles W Morgan* were locked up in an old wooden building, as the jail was full. But it couldn't hold the sailors, who broke out and took to the beach, followed by a full evacuation back to the ship. Haley described some of his crewmates' heads next morning looking 'as though a horse had trod on them with shoes on'. But some were not so lucky, for when an officer came on board to arrest those involved in the fracas – unsuccessfully, for none would admit to having been ashore – he reported that two or three men had been killed.[21]

In early January 1853 the *Charles W Morgan* was back in the Bay of Islands, but with no whales to its credit. For this reason the captain chose to anchor further round at Te Wahapu, where there were several ships known to have had successful catches. He had the further ignominy of agreeing to take on board another ship's oil, so the latter could take another cruise north to the whaling grounds. Such arrangements were not uncommon, and the transfer of about one thousand barrels took a week. The *Charles W Morgan* also took on some 250 barrels of water, along with several tons of kauri gum destined for the varnish industry in the United States.[22]

On the morning of 8 February 1853 the crew heaved on the windlass, the anchor was raised and the *Charles W Morgan* was underway. Haley recorded that welcome moment as it headed for home and the hills above Kororareka were alive, if not with the sounds of music, at least with the hearty strains of 'High, Randy, Dandy', 'Oh Off She Goes, Off She Must Go', 'Jigger in the Bum Boat' ('or words to that effect') and 'Sally in our Alley'. Next stop was Valparaiso, or as it was known to sailors, 'Valipo' or 'Vallipo Bay'.[23]

Thanks to the whaling business, Waikouaiti, Cloudy Bay and others had joined Kororareka as localities with certain reputations. But however bad they were, there would be worse on the other side of the Pacific following the discovery of gold in California in 1849. For some idea of what went on in San Franscisco we are indebted to an author with a fascination for the seamy side of America. In 1933 Herbert Asbury painted a remarkable picture of goings-on in that gold-smitten town. Although it was written long after the event, and drew heavily on anecdotes and newspaper reports, if only a fraction can be believed the place was an undisputed hell-hole. And if Kororareka and Sydney felt outdone by the latecomer's excesses, the latter could at least take some credit for contributing to its condition. Asbury noted that 'ruffianly larrikins' and escaped convicts and ticket-of-leave men (convicts permitted, subject to conditions, to go at large prior to the completion of their sentences) from Australia's penal settlements gave the 'whorish quarter' of the San Francisco waterfront its particular character. This wave of 'undesirable immigration' was '100 per cent criminal', and before long the district where it congregated became known as Sydney-Town. Its inhabitants were referred to as Sydney Ducks, or Sydney Coves, and occupied a squalid slum section much like The Rocks back home. This 'Alsatia of dives, dance-halls, and depravity' was a maze of dark alleys and cul-de-sacs, with such uninviting names as Murder Point and Dead Men's Lane, the haunts of cut-throats, thieves, good-time girls and gamblers. Of its saloons and vice dens, two of the toughest were the Billy Goat – run by an Irish woman known as 'Pigeon-toed Sal' – and the Bull Run, which operated under the motto 'Anything Goes Here'. Then there was the Fierce Grizzly, which kept a live bear chained beside the door, and a couple of establishments owned by a Sydney ticket-of-leave man with the formidable name of Hell Haggerty.[24]

According to Asbury, some 2000 women, most of them harlots, poured into San Francisco in the first six months of 1850 alone. Before long every country in the world was represented here by at least one practitioner of the oldest profession.[25] No nationality or predilection was overlooked, and for skinflints and 'new hands' there was even breast-fondling, the going rate being 10 cents for one and 15 cents a pair.[26] While the scale of operations no doubt outstripped those back in the south-western Pacific, there were some similarities. The reign of terror imposed by the Sydney Ducks drove a group of concerned citizens to form a Vigilance Committee. This American version of rough justice went much further than Kororareka's deterrent of tarring and feathering, as its punishment for miscreants extended to public hangings.[27] There was another Australian connection here, resulting from the fact that many of the cooks on ships arriving in New South Wales in the early 1800s were Chinese. It has been suggested it was they who invented chop-suey, and later when local 'coves' left The Rocks for San Francisco they took their appetite for this new dish with them.[28] The Australian influence later became less apparent when Sydney-Town was renamed the Barbary Coast, presumably on account of its resemblance to the pirate-infested coasts of Africa.[29]

On the basis of Asbury's lurid depictions, San Francisco would have exceeded Kororeraka for wickedness, but one thing the two places did share was a spectacular climax. Following a gigantic earthquake on the morning of 19 April 1906, devastating fires caused by ruptured gas mains raged out of control all over San Francisco and any remnant of that 'mile of vice' and 'cesspool of rottenness' was wiped from the face of the earth. It may have gone but not before it enriched the language, for a San Francisco journalist described members of a local street gang as 'noodlums', the name inspired by reversing that of their leader, one Muldoon. When this went to print a compositor mistook the 'n' for an 'h', and so the word 'hoodlum' was born.[30] But Kororareka can claim that its own immoral behaviour had already added to the language – New Zealand's, at least – when Henry Williams first referred to those young Maori women who sought a 'good or profitable time' with seafarers as 'ship-girls'.[31]

Another cause for concern, and contender for hell-hole status, in the latter half of the nineteenth century was Hawaii. Following the whalers, and the pattern established elsewhere in the Pacific, these islands were first visited by New England missionaries in 1823, bringing a printing press and western culture, and preaching the evils of nudity, erotic dancing and heathen religion. The whalers began coming north to avoid the Bay of Islands, made uneconomic since the establishment of British authority. Hawaii also had the attraction of being closer to the rich 'off Japan grounds' and the Arctic waters, as whales became depleted in the warmer ocean to the south. The whaling era was at its peak there from 1840 until the late 1850s, when petroleum was proving better and cheaper than whale oil. In its heyday, more than 400 whaling ships visited Hawaii in one season – far more than ever visited the Bay of Islands. Each had a crew of twenty-five to thirty-five and tended to stay for four to five months, engaging in much drinking and prostitution. The ships crowded the harbour here twice a year, preparing for their voyages to the fishing grounds to the north in March, and the warmer waters further south in November and December.[32]

Port authorities at Honolulu introduced a sliding scale of punishments for the sort of offences whalers might get up to. At the lower end was a $1 fine for a first-time desecration of the Sabbath, while 'hallooing' or making a noise in the streets at night brought $1–$5. For sexual activity, it was $5 for fornication and $30 for adultery. On-shore disturbances between crews and locals were likely to involve the much-feared 'Sidney [sic] Rangers', originally from Australia and noted for their brutality and lawlessness. In 1844, following a certain Saturday night affray involving seamen, American whaling masters petitioned the governor of Maui. In their opinion the problem was the 'unprincipled' owners of grog-shops rather than the drunken sailors, and they suggested that if the legal sale of ardent spirits continued they could not be held responsible for the conduct of their crews. They regarded liberty ashore as vital to the well-being of crews, who were likely to be at sea for upwards of eight months.[33]

Although the halcyon days of whaling (and its associated revelry) were now over, Kororareka at least looked more like a maritime town when it acquired its first substantial jetty. This facility was in place by 1858 when the Reverend John Kinder, master at the Church of England Grammar School in Auckland, paid a visit.

In January that year Maiki Hill also received a replacement flagstaff following an offer by Maihi Paraone Kawiti, youngest son of chief Kawiti.[34] A suitable tree was felled and squared at Waikare and taken to Kororareka Beach, and after a ceremony on the waterfront it was carried to the top of Maiki Hill by 400 men in two teams. The flagstaff was then set up and formally presented to Thomas Gore Browne, who had replaced Sir George Grey as governor of New Zealand and was visiting at the time. The staff was named Whakakotahitanga o Nga Iwi, translated as 'the unification of two races' or 'being at one with the Queen'. But it was a case of history repeating itself in 1915 when an out-of-control gorse fire raced towards the hill. The flagstaff was felled once again, but not for long, for its charred exterior and lower rotted section were removed and a shorter and more slender version reinstated. Then, after suffering five human attacks – four intentional and one accidental – it was nature's turn in the 1970s, when the flagstaff was struck by lightning, and although not felled it was reduced in length by several feet.[35]

John Kinder painted the view from the top of Maiki Hill in 1858, and would have clambered over the remains of the trenches that had failed to restrain Heke thirteen years earlier. The reverend recorded a peaceful day in the Bay, with smoke curling from a cottage chimney in the foreground, a three-masted ship at anchor, and canoes and boats drawn up on the beach on either side of the new jetty. The beach frontage was occupied by two-storey gable-end wooden buildings, with smaller dwellings at the rear of the town towards the swamp. Dominating this view was the church, with a glimpse of Matauwhi Bay beyond, and what was once the Catholic mission complex at the south end of the beach.[36]

Kororareka received a second jetty in the mid-1860s, when it was still a favoured port for American whalers in the South Pacific. The first half of 1860 saw visits from forty-five ships, the greatest number for over a decade, but the trade was soon in decline.[37] Apart from the rise of the petroleum industry, whales were becoming fewer and more difficult to catch, which meant voyages that needed to be longer and therefore less economic. As for the ships themselves, many were captured and destroyed in the American Civil War (1861–65), or sunk and used to blockade harbours. The much-reduced industry was further hit in 1872 when thirty-two ships were abandoned in the Arctic Ocean after being crushed in the ice.[38]

No longer the hell-hole of the past, bypassed and somewhat out of the way, Kororareka still managed to exhibit some of its old traits. There was always alcohol, and a population with its fair share of individuals who might be down on their luck, or perhaps opportunists, while the port still retained some appeal for deserters. In spite of the town's history, one of the worst things that could now be said of a resident of Kororareka was that they had been a convict or were the offspring of one. To either expose or imply such an Australian connection could be extremely offensive indeed.

The Williams brothers, the reverends Henry and William, had been well-known about the Bay of Islands, but there was another pair of siblings with the same surname who had reputations for rather different reasons. In 1861 Kororareka resident Robert Evans claimed that Thomas and John Williams had turned up at his back door one morning and demanded, 'Come out here, you bugger.' Thomas accused Evans of saying something about his father, but before he could reply John had grabbed him by the shirt. Thomas then instructed his brother to 'Give it to the bugger', whereupon Evans was punched under the ribs and beaten with a stick, and then thrown alongside the pump by his back door. It seems that the plan to form a local cricket club was one reason for the bad blood, with Evans accusing John Williams of being a 'hot tempered fellow' and admitting he was one himself, and therefore wisely concluding that they should not belong to the same organisation. In addition, John Williams was agent for Benjamin Turner, Evans' landlord, and the tenant had sublet his property contrary to an agreement. John Williams admitted there was 'no love' between himself and Evans, who had called him 'a convict's offspring'. That, according to Williams, 'would excite any person'. John Williams was found guilty of assaulting and beating Evans and sentenced to one month's imprisonment.[39] It was a busy time for the Williams brothers, for that same year they applied for publican's licences, and Thomas was fined £3 for selling liquor at the National Hotel at Kororareka on a Sunday. A number of people were seen inside drinking, and another lying outside in a state of drunkenness, and Williams' only defence was that he 'could not help it if he could not keep them out'.[40]

There was another domestic disturbance in the town in 1861 when one Ellen Parker was sitting at her dinner table and heard talking outside. Going to investigate, she encountered her neighbour, named Baker, who addressed her: 'Oh you damned scoundrel. You are rearing up your children to robbing and plundering: what you rob at night you eat in the day time.' Parker also alleged that Baker had told her she was a 'damned whore' and that her children would be 'hung or transported for being thieves'. In his defence Baker explained that one of his fowls had been killed recently, and because his own sons had denied any responsibility, he presumed it had been one of the neighbours. He had therefore called out to Mrs Parker that if her children killed any more of his fowls he would come over and thrash them. At that point, according to Baker, Mr Parker came out and called him 'an old wretch, and a thief' and that he would put the payment 'up my backside'. The mutual abuse continued across the back fence with Mrs Parker calling Baker a 'Hobartown convict', an 'old wretch and a whoremaster'. Baker told her to 'pull her head in' and informed her he had heard her husband call her 'a bad woman' and had seen him running around with an axe. Robert Evans – presumably the same individual involved in the other altercation with the Williams brothers – told the court he had heard Parker (whom he suspected was drunk) call his wife a whore, and had also seen him chasing another man with an axe, which he dropped while climbing a fence. In the end each party was given a caution and ordered to pay costs.[41]

In 1863 there was something of a return to the language of the past when an 'outrage' was reported at Matauri on the east coast, north of the Bay of Islands. The offender, a Maori youth, had 'perpetrated' an assault on the daughter of a European settler, although he did not succeed 'in his base design'. The matter was reported to Edward M Williams, son of Henry Williams, and resident magistrate at Waimate, who passed it on to George Clarke, civil commissioner, also at Waimate, and it ended up on the desk of Edward Shortland, native secretary at Auckland. Williams investigated the matter and a court found the youth guilty as charged. The penalty required by law on a European for such a case was imprisonment, and it was requested that the youth be given up. But the tribe resisted, offering instead to pay for the crime, even begging Williams to accept the money. Aware that there had been instances where Maori women had been 'roughly handled' by Europeans and no imprisonment had resulted, the Maori were strongly opposed to the youth's imprisonment. Williams adjourned the case and after consulting the resident magistrate at Russell decided that 'in the present excited state of the colony' it would be unwise to do anything that might provoke a disturbance. He returned to Matauri, but after two days' discussion it was apparent that the youth would not be given up so it was agreed that a fine of £50 would be levied.

This incident was put into context with the publication of a list of all the cases between Europeans and Maori that had been tried in the Magistrate's Court at Russell in the period 1 January 1860 to 30 September 1863. Of the thirty-four, most involved licensing breaches (thirteen), assault (eight), felony (five) and desertion from the armed forces (three), and Europeans were defendants in all but five. Similarly, in returns for civil cases at this time, Europeans were defendants in all ten in which they were involved with Maori. It was pointed out that this particular return 'did not include cases between Maoris only', and in fairness it should be noted that it did not include cases between Europeans only either, which on the basis of the foregoing statistics might have been considerable.[42]

A decade later, the Williams brothers – Thomas and John – were still getting into trouble. In November 1873 photographer Henry Wright complained that the pair had used provoking and insulting language in his presence on Kororareka Beach. They were heard to utter: 'There goes the damned chairman who contaminated the meeting', 'the damned skunk', and 'There goes the devil with the white hat', while the word 'thrashing' was also mentioned. In his defence John Williams said there were other people who wore white hats and were chairmen of meetings, and if his words were applicable to Mr Wright then 'he was welcome to make use of them'. He explained that he had been 'pretty annoyed' by the complainant's sundry remarks about his character and the house he was living in. On this occasion the defendants were required to keep the peace for three months and pay costs.[43] But the matter was hardly settled, for shortly afterwards Wright accused one of the Williamses of calling him a 'damned scoundrel' in regard to a letter he had recently had published in the *Herald*, and also of threatening to thrash him with a stick. As before, the defendant was cautioned and required to pay costs.[44]

By the 1870s, some three decades after it had been officially ordained, Russell was finally replacing Kororareka as the commonly used name of the town. In 1866 it had gained a hotel, the Cricketers' Arms, which claimed to be 'superior' and suitable for lady lodgers, and there was now a third addition to the foreshore, in the form of the government wharf.[45]

Whaleships were now infrequent callers, but some continued the old tradition of not always leaving with a full complement. In October 1873 Mrs Isobella Donald of Russell committed a breach of the Foreign Seaman's Act by harbouring two sailors from the *Adeline*, a ship that had already played a small and dramatic part in New Zealand maritime history. In late 1839 it was refuelling with wood and water at Kapiti Island when its boat was forcibly taken by the crew of another whaler, who threatened 'instant death' to anyone who resisted. The captain of the *Adeline* pursued his captured boat and found it at a shore-whaling station, along with thirty to fourty armed and 'desperate-looking wretches'. He cautioned them against acts of piracy, and was informed that if he attempted to take back the boat his brains would be blown out with a pistol.[46] Thirty-four years later, one of the two deserters from the *Adeline* now told the court that they had taken refuge in an empty house in Russell. When Mrs Donald came to the door and asked if they were 'the two chaps that have run away from the ship' they admitted they were, and told her they were going to give themselves up to the police. The hospitable Mrs Donald plied them with bread, butter and cake, and suggested that they 'hold out longer'. She was fined £10, but complained she had been 'used as a tool' by the local constable in his attempt to arrest the runaways.[47]

Louisa Worsfold was born in 1872 and from an early age was aware of the twice-yearly arrivals of the whaling ships at Russell. The local population – which she then put at only 150 – knew there were whalers in the harbour around daybreak, when they heard the tapping sound of the ship's cooper assembling new casks from bundles of staves. The completed casks were then roped together and floated ashore, and stood under a small waterfall that ran over a rocky ledge at 'Watering Bay'. A crew member attended to their filling, directing water by means of a 'shoot' (possibly 'chute'). The casks were then towed back to the ship, their tops just visible above the water line, and hauled aboard. Once emptied of water they would be used for carrying that other precious commodity, whale oil. The young folk of Russell also had good reason to welcome the visiting whaling ships for they would be invited aboard and treated to an all-American breakfast of hot muffins, cornbread porridge, buckwheat cakes and maple syrup, and fruit from the Pacific Islands.[48]

The number of whaling ships calling at Russell each year had dropped to single figures by the 1880s. Within another decade or so they were gone altogether, and one of the last to visit was an old regular, the *Charles W Morgan*. Apart from boat-steerer Haley's remarkable exploits, the ship had also managed to survive a mutiny, a lightning strike and a fire at sea.[49] The 113-foot long and 314-ton vessel was launched at New Bedford, Massachusetts, in 1841, and its Pacific voyages in search of sperm whales kept it away from home for an average of forty months. The last surviving American whaleship, it was laid up in 1913. In 1938 it entered the museum at Mystic Seaport, Connecticut, and went on public display three years later.

Kororareka's original church survived the events of 1845, although the paling fence on its southern boundary suffered some hacking and splintering from the cutlasses and bayonets of the men from the *Hazard*. When that ship bombarded the town with grapeshot and cannnonball, the church took a number of superficial hits. But its most dramatic modification came in 1871 when the original hipped roof was considered inappropriate and replaced with a tall gable in mock Gothic style, and a porch was attached to its previously plain front. This new roof proved unstable, and supporting buttresses had to be added to the sides of the building. Then in 1873, after nearly forty years without a name, it was decided that this place of worship would be officially known as Christ Church. The building later became noticeably shaky, structurally speaking, and there were plans to replace it with something more stable. But the public demanded it be retained and in March 1936 a morning service marked the completion of its first century. Four years on, when the nation celebrated its own centennial, the church saw a re-enactment of the 'Governor' reading his proclamations. In 2001 New Zealand's oldest surviving church was given a new shingle roof, and its walls were stabilised with steel beams, while its bullet holes remain a tourist attraction.

In the shadow of Christ Church are graves recalling the early days of Kororareka, among them six fatalities – four seamen and two marines – from the *Hazard*. They were preceded here by their captain, Charles Bell, who suffered from malaria in Auckland and came north to recuperate. In August 1844 he fell overboard and drowned in the Bay, whereupon David Robertson assumed command of the *Hazard*. There are also whalers who did not return home: a man from the *Mohawk*, Nantucket; another from the *Lancaster*, New Bedford, who was suffocated while his ship was being fumigated for rats; and the fourth mate of the *Rainbow*, Massachusetts, fatally stabbed in a waterfront brawl.[50] In 1871 this also became the resting place of Tamati Waka Nene. While his wooden house on the waterfront has gone, its chimney bricks have been converted into a seat beside the Russell Museum. The nearby Walker Passage also honours the chief, who chose his baptismal name Tamati Waka in memory of an English supporter of the mission. The churchyard is the resting place for another local identity, Dr Samuel Hayward Ford. During the turbulent days of 1845 he and his wife left Te Wahapu – after which their house was burned – and went to Auckland, but three years later they returned to Kororareka. The doctor continued to practise and offer his own home for recovering patients who had nowhere else to go. When he was buried here in 1876, ships in the Bay lowered their flags as a mark of respect. Ford and Nene had been good friends and arranged to be buried next to one another, the story being that the chief would knock on the doctor's coffin if he required any further treatment.[51]

Overlooking them all from Maiki Hill is the flagstaff Whakakotahitanga. Administered by the Department of Conservation on twelve days of the year, it flies the Maori Confederated Tribes flag of 1834, recalling important dates in the history of the north. They are: 10 and 11 January (battle of Ruapekapeka, 1846), 16 January (re-erection of the flagstaff in 1858), 6 February (Waitangi Day, 1840), 11 March (sacking of Kororareka, 1845), 20 March (adoption of the Maori Confederation of Tribes flag by twenty-five representative northern chiefs at Waitangi, 1834), 5 May (death of Kawiti,

1854), 8 May (battle of Puketutu near Lake Omapere, 1845), 16 May (battle at Waikare, at pa of Kapotai, 1845), 1 July (battle at Ohaeawai, 1845), 6 August (death of Hone Heke at Kaikohe, 1850), and 28 October (declaration of the United Tribes of New Zealand, Waitangi, 1835).[52]

14

HELL ON EARTH?

ROMANCING ON THE BEACH

What an air of olden romance clings around this well-
named Bay of Islands! The Sleepy Hollow of North
New Zealand, it lies serene and untroubled of the outer
world. Very beautiful, very quiet, is the island-strewn gulf
as seen from the flagstaff on the historic Maiki Hill, above
the little township of Russell – this lofty white signal-
staff stands on the spot where its three predecessors
were cut down by Hone Heke's warriors. For miles and
miles stretch the heavenly-blue waters, lapping
pohutukawa-fringed beaches of finest sand and creeping
into bay and cove innumerable – the delight
of yachtsmen and campers-out.[1]

On 13 March 1845 Bishop Selwyn made an early start, leaving Waimate at
2 a.m. so he could catch the tide at a creek on his way to Paihia. Just before
sunrise he reached the summit of a hill overlooking the entrance to the
Bay of Islands. The surface of the bay was calm and glassy, reflecting the
dark outline of the hills and the straw-coloured light of the eastern sky above.
The *Hazard* sat motionless in mid-channel, between Paihia and what was
left of Kororareka and beneath a pall of smoke. The bishop observed: 'All that
had been devoted to Mammon was gone.' He also noted that 'heathen
vengeance' had spared the 'patrimony of God', for the two churches and their

associated houses were still standing. He was aware of what might be interpreted as another instance of Providence at work when Maori decided against burning down a house belonging to Benjamin Turner because it was uncomfortably close to that of Bishop Pompallier. They pulled it down instead, and in so doing discovered a cache of coins believed to have been worth £2000.[2] It was reported in the press that Turner had secreted the money behind panelling in various parts of the building, before sailing for Sydney on his schooner.[3]

Another person not sad to see the destruction of Kororareka was Governor FitzRoy. Although his first official reaction had been to describe it as a 'disastrous calamity',[4] he came to regard the event as a visitation of Divine Providence, effectively removing 'the most blighting house of corruption in the colony'.[5] But as much as he despised the place for being 'extremely immoral and addicted to low vices', he conceded that it was no different from a number of English seaports.[6] FitzRoy's abbreviated term as governor coincided with that of the United States Consul to New Zealand, John Williams, who saw even less hope for the Bay of Islands: its residents were 'vile persons, concupiscent and licentious'. Its 'Splendid Sin' could not go unpunished and he wondered if retribution was not already underway, as reflected in the falling population.[7] That change was, of course, due to something much more basic, the general drift south to Auckland.

While some might insist that Kororareka deserved to suffer the fates of Sodom and Gomorrah, the question is just how bad the place really was. As a sailor's town and once the largest European settlement in New Zealand, it naturally attracted a commanding share of the grog and prostitution trades and allied activities. Thus equipped, it became known as the hell-hole of the (South) Pacific, a reputation that however justified appears to have originated with a misunderstanding. Nevertheless, the missionaries across at Paihia had much to gain from seeing it as synonymous with evil, for it made any of their achievements in the face of such competition seem all the more creditable. Opinions on the state of the place were fairly subjective, and visiting sailors, far from being offended, may have been comforted by the fact that it was not much different from their other favourite ports of call. 'Hell' on earth was a popular term at the time, commonly applied to dungeons, prisons and gambling houses. But however unruly and debased Kororareka actually was, its condition was largely the outcome of positive attributes – its sheltered harbour and natural (including human) resources, and its location beyond the reach of the law. It was therefore in stark contrast to certain other places which had also acquired dire reputations, but whose existence was entirely due to British government policy.

If the Mr Jameson who visited Kororareka in the late 1830s can be believed, crime against property was rare. Instead, lawless activity was more likely to involve moral lapses, mostly fuelled by alcohol, and, apart from communicable diseases, was largely self-inflicted. From a missionary perspective such activity was hellish enough, but there was much worse available at Macquarie Harbour and Port Arthur, for example, where viciousness and inhumanity truly knew no bounds.

With the demise and destruction of such spots as Kororareka, fact was frequently another casualty, subject to imaginative retellings and exotic comparisons. The excessive but extremely quotable John Williams had nothing positive to say about the inhabitants of Kororareka, but did manage to find beauty in its abandoned pa site, likening it to ancient ruins from Tangiers or Carthage.[8] A decade and a half later, Arthur S Thomson suggested that in 1832 the town had been 'the Cyprus of the Southern Ocean', where life was 'one unceasing revel' and the Bay polluted by 'floating brothels'. He also felt the missionaries had exaggerated the goings-on, and estimated the European population there in 1838 at 'a thousand souls' – most of whom were no doubt beyond redemption in the eyes of the missionaries.[9] Four decades later, William Pember Reeves reflected on the Bay of Islands as a 'beautiful haven' where only man was vile, in fact, 'very vile indeed'. In his view, the beach at Kororareka had been a 'sort of Alsatia', inspired in this instance by the area in seventeenth-century London between the Strand and the Thames, notorious for its criminal element.[10] Another writer around this time also detected this resemblance – originally to Alsace in Germany – with Kororareka 'a marine Alsatia, a Bohemia of villainous license . . . where, on occasion, as many as a thousand whites indulged in unbridled and brutalising debauchery . . .'[11]

The annexation of New Zealand by Britain brought an end to what Duncan Mackay has termed the coastal phase of the country's frontier. Following the decline of whaling, other extractive industries took over. The population of the goldfields settlement at Hokitika in Westland peaked at nearly 6000 in 1867, qualifying it as the sixth largest centre and one of the richest and busiest ports in the country. Thames was not much smaller, with 5000 at that time – and many of those fortune-seekers had now decamped from Auckland. Both Thames and Hokitika were said to have more than 100 hotels each in their heyday, with the latter's mile-long, and aptly named, Revell Street alone claiming eighty-four, not to mention its brothels. Aside from the miners' activities, there was filth of a much more palpable nature. While there do not appear to be any references to Kororareka's sanitary arrangements, it was reported that early Hokitika residents used their beach as a toilet, and nightsoil dumped there returned on the next 'high' tide.[12]

In 1932, on the occasion of the gift of the Waitangi estate to New Zealand by the Governor-General Lord Bledisloe and Lady Bledisloe, a newspaper review of the nation's history described how the Bay of Islands had become the favourite resort of South Pacific whalers by 1825. The town of Kororareka was inhabited by 'a few respectable families' but for the most part by individuals who were now affably portrayed as 'picturesque ruffians and adventurers who for one reason or another had turned their backs on civilisation'.[13] A few years later, and nearly a century after Heke had levelled its most obvious symbol, New Zealand turned its mind to appropriate means of marking the establishment of British sovereignty. On 6 February 1940, some 10,000 people gathered at Waitangi for a re-enactment of the signing of the Treaty of Waitangi. *Nga-Toki-Matawhaorua*, the 120-foot (36.5-metre) war canoe built by northern tribes for the occasion, escorted 'Hobson' and his entourage to shore, manned by 150 warriors 'clad to the last detail in the garb of their ancestors'. All the main historical figures were there in period dress, with the Rev. Henry Williams and the Maori chiefs being represented by their own descendants. The main authority for the correctness of the speeches and 'incidentals' was the writings of William Colenso. A week earlier, a modest ceremony at Russell marked Hobson's first landing there in 1840 and, as it would happen, the beginning of the end for Kororareka.[14]

Of all the accounts of Kororareka, whether fact, fiction or a healthy mixture of both, none may be more vivid than that by novelist Edith Lyttleton. Born in Tasmania in 1873, she moved with her family to Rakaia at the age of six. In 1909 she went to London, and later became a prolific writer of popular colonial fiction under the pseudonym G B Lancaster. Her second historical novel, *Promenade*, published in 1938, opened in England ninety-nine years earlier and quickly moved to the Bay of Islands. It referred to actual figures and events – Hobson, Busby, Waka Nene, 'big Bishop Selwyn', the ships *Herald* and *Hazard*, 'scarred whaling-ships, smelling of their trade', and the Lynch Law League and its sticky practices. Some of *Promenade*'s characters seem to have been inspired by real residents such as Corny Fleet (Cornthwaite Hector?) and Nick Flower (the Flowerday family?), while the 'small trader' Robinson may have owed something to Joel Polack. Lancaster likened Kororareka Beach to a 'randy girl', 'effervescing in the most unsavoury manner'. It was *Gulliver's Travels* and *Genesis* 'walking hand in hand', with *Revelations* imminent. There were sea captains in monkey jackets and sallow ear-ringed sailors from the Spanish Main, along with English, Norwegian, Negro and Yankee seamen, 'nuggety little breeds from Quebec' and Maori looking like Highlanders with their flax-kilts, worn – at missionary insistence – over 'bulging tweed trousers'.[15]

An understanding of Kororareka's past is assisted by material turned up by the archaeologist's trowel. But despite the digging of numerous trenches through the town in recent years, no prehistoric material has been found, nor have any deposits of midden (refuse, such as shell and fish deposits) been identified. This suggests that the Maori village encountered here by the first European visitors may have come into existence in response to the trading opportunities offered by the whaling fleets.[16] At the southern end of the beach the Department of Conservation Visitor Centre now sits on the site of a pa, said to have been constructed in the late 1700s by the chief Tara. Known as Kororareka pa, it was occupied in the early 1800s by chief Te Whareumu, and then had a succession of owners. Kiwikiwi, who left in 1830, was followed by Rewa, and surviving descriptions suggest that by the late 1830s it covered a considerable area and incorporated European houses, grog-shops and other buildings. Later it was either abandoned or lost its importance during the events of 1845, and by 1852 had passed out of Maori ownership.[17]

Archaeological excavations, supported by historical accounts and illustrations, suggest that there had been a number of palisaded enclosures along Kororareka Beach, and what became known as Rewa's pa was the last of these to survive. There is no evidence of a very early occupation of the site, nor have any fragments of human bone been found, as might be expected had it operated during the turbulent decade from 1820. However, the material that has been found does reflect a momentous period in Maori history, linking the prehistoric past to early European settlement. Alongside chert and obsidian flakes, a complete greywacke adze and a section of a patu, archaeologists have unearthed muzzle-loading rifle parts, leftovers from the musket wars that had a devastating effect on this area. One of nine gun-flints found was of French origin, and may date from Laplace's visit in 1831 when he presented guns and powder to Rewa. As well as two eighteen-millimetre balls for Brown Bess muskets, gun parts and files suggest that firearm repairs were carried out on this site. Other signs of European influence were 351 clay pipe fragments and shards of early gin and beer bottles, while two religious trinkets, including a medal handed out to Maori converts by Marist missionaries, represent the arrival of a more spiritual influence.[18] On the basis of these humble relics, archaeologist Simon Best concludes: 'The 400 metres or so of front beach ridge at Russell contain archaeological evidence of the earliest substantial European settlement in New Zealand.'[19]

The Bay of Islands has been variously termed the 'cradle of New Zealand' and the 'cradle of New Zealand civilization';[20] according to naturalist Ernst Dieffenbach, it was a 'small cove in the bay'.[21] But more than just a cradle, cove or even hell-hole, the settlement was also known as the Devil's Playground and Blackguard's Beach.[22] In 1843 Henry S Chapman, a Wellington Supreme Court judge, accused it of having once been a 'moral pest-house' on account of harbouring outcasts from other colonies,[23] and ninety-three years later historian J C Beaglehole looked back on it as an '*al fresco* thieves' kitchen'.[24] Perhaps the only thing regarding all this alleged wickedness that can be said with any certainty is that it would have fluctuated wildly according to whether the ships were in. Coincidentally, the main hell-raisers came because they were either in pursuit of something (whales) or in avoidance of something (authority and justice). For its sins, Kororareka's ways bore no resemblance to the hellish punishment meted out in penal institutions across the Tasman, and it may never have been as busy as San Francisco or Honolulu in their respective heydays. But it certainly had its moments, and as far as New Zealand was concerned there was probably no place like it.

For the last word on that town, there is none more colourful than G B Lancaster's description of its destruction in March 1845. As the inhabitants took to the safety of ships, they witnessed something in the harbour more apocalyptic than even Selwyn or FitzRoy could have imagined, with the added irony of its demise being fuelled by the very industry that had made the town what it was in the first place. In her account, Kororareka was overwhelmed by a 'great and terrible sunset . . . galloping with blue and scarlet tongues'. It was 'biting all the houses into bits; tossing their limbs up under exploding oil-barrels; running in glowing rivers to the sea'.[25]

REFERENCES

CHAPTER 1

1 John Hawkesworth, *An account of the voyages undertaken by the order of His present Majesty for making discoveries in the southern hemisphere ... drawn up from the journals which were kept by the several commanders and from the papers of Joseph Banks, esq.*, W Strahan and T Cadell, London, 1773, vol. 3, p. 439.

2 Randall R Reeves, Brent S Stewart, Phillip J Clapham and James A Powell, *National Audubon Society Guide to Marine Mammals of the World*, Alfred A Knopf, New York, 2002, p. 12.

3 Graeme Stevens, Matt McGlone and Beverley McCulloch, *Prehistoric New Zealand*, Heinemann Reed, Auckland, 1988, p. 23.

4 Ernst Dieffenbach, *Travels in New Zealand*, John Murray, London, 1843, vol. 1, pp. 45–6.

5 J C Beaglehole, ed., *The Journals of Captain James Cook*, vol. 1, Hakluyt Society, Cambridge University Press, 1955, pp. 165, 167.

6 'The *Endeavour* Journal of James Cook', 20 November 1769, National Library of Australia, manuscript 1, pp. 156, 158.

7 'The *Endeavour* Journal of James Cook', 2 December 1769, manuscript 1, p. 158. Note: The details relating to the punishment of the men for drunkenness was crossed out in the original journal.

8 'The *Endeavour* Journal of James Cook', 5 December 1769, manuscript 1, p. 160.

9 Beaglehole, *The Journals of Captain James Cook*, vol.1, p. 259.

10 Ronald C S De Braganza and Charlotte Oakes, eds, *The Hill Collection of Pacific Voyages*, University Library, University of California, San Diego, 1974–83, p. 139.

11 Beaglehole, *The Journals of Captain James Cook*, vol.2, pp. 111, 114, 122.

12 Ibid., p. 135.

13 Ibid., p. 119.

14 Ibid., p. 302.

15 Ibid., pp. 482, 581.

16 Ibid., p. 319.

17 John Marra, *Journal of the Resolution's voyage in 1772, 1773, 1774 and 1775, on discovery to the southern hemisphere, by which the non-existence of an undiscovered continent between the equator and the 50th degree of southern latitude is demonstratively proved*, F Newbery, London, 1775. Marra was a gunner's mate on the *Resolution*.

18 Hawkesworth, p. 438.

19 Granville Allen Mawer, *Ahab's Trade: The Saga of South Seas Whaling*, Allen and Unwin, Australia, 2000, pp. 77–83.

20 Robert McNab, *From Tasman to Marsden: A History of Northern New Zealand from 1652 to 1818*, J Wilkie and Co, Dunedin, 1914, p. 95.

21 Robert McNab, *Historical Records of New Zealand*, Government Printer, Wellington, 1914, vol. 2, pp. 509, 518–20.

22 Rhys Richards, *Jorgen Jorgenson's Observations*, Paremata Press, Wellington, 1996, p. 56.

23 Robert Falla, lecture to Auckland University College, reported in *New Zealand Herald*, 20 June 1935.

24 Robert Hughes, *The Fatal Shore*, Pan, London, 1988, p. 247.

25 Ibid., p. 246.

26 Trevor Bentley, *Captured by Maori: White Female Captives, Sex and Racism on the Nineteenth-century New Zealand Frontier*, Penguin, Auckland, 2004, p. 26.

27 Eugene Grayland, *Coasts of Treachery*, A H and A W Reed, Wellington, 1963, pp. 28–34.

28 Ibid., pp. 64–9.

29 Arthur S Thomson, *The Story of New Zealand: Past and Present – Savage and Civilized*, John Murray, London, 1859, p. 291.

30 John Savage, *Some Account of New Zealand, Particularly the Bay of Islands and Surrounding Country*, reprinted with notes in A D McKinlay, *Savage's Account of New Zealand in 1805 together*

with Schemes of 1771 and 1824
for Commerce and Colonization,
L T Watkins, Wellington, 1939,
p. 5.

31 McKinlay, pp. 14, 16–7.

32 Ibid., p. 21.

33 Ibid., pp. 86–7, 91.

34 Ibid., pp. 87–8.

35 Ibid., p. 90.

36 Bentley, pp. 19–21.

37 McKinlay, p. 91.

38 Ibid., p. 88.

39 Wises New Zealand Guide, Wises
Publications, Auckland, 1987,
p. 180.

40 Wade Doak, The Burning of the
'Boyd': A Saga of Culture Clash,
Hodder and Stoughton,
Auckland, 1984, p. 76.

41 Hawkesworth, p. 439.

42 'Report of the Commission of
Inquiry on the State of
Agriculture and Trade in the
Colony of New South Wales',
House of Commons, 13 March
1823.

43 Hughes, pp. 371–2, 400.

44 Ibid., pp. 332–3.

45 Ibid., p. 60.

46 Angela Ballara, Taua, Penguin,
Auckland, 2003, p. 188.

47 Ibid., pp. 171–7.

48 Ibid., p. 189.

49 Dumont d'Urville, Jules-
Sebastian-Cesar, An Account in
Two Volumes of Two Voyages to
the South Seas by Captain (later
Rear-Admiral) Jules S-C Dumont
D'Urville to Australia, New
Zealand, Oceania 1826–1829 in
the corvette Astrolabe and to the
Straits of Magellan, Chile,
Oceania, South East Asia,
Australia, Antarctica, New
Zealand and Torres Strait 1837–
1840 in the corvettes Astrolabe
and Zélée, trans. and ed. Helen
Rosenman, vol. 1, Melbourne
University Press, Melbourne,
1987, pp. 103, 106.

50 Dumont d'Urville, vol. 1,
pp. 105–6.

CHAPTER 2

1 Letters from the Bay of Islands:
The Story of Marianne Williams,
ed. Caroline Fitzgerald,
Penguin, Auckland, 2004, p. 185.

2 Letter from Governor Phillip
King to Earl Camden, in McNab,
Historical Records of New
Zealand, vol. 1, pp. 254–5.

3 Missionary Register: Containing
the Principal Transactions of the
Various Institutions for
Propagating the Gospel, with the
Proceedings, at Large, of the
Church Missionary Society,
London, 1820, p. 61.

4 Missionary Review: Containing
an Abstract of the Proceedings of

the Principal Missionary and
Bible Societies Throughout the
World. London, 1814, vol. 2,
p. 463.

5 Missionary Review, 1814, vol. 3,
p. 105.

6 Missionary Review, 1814, vol. 3,
p. 156.

7 Missionary Review, 1814, vol. 3,
p. 158.

8 Missionary Review, 1814, vol. 3,
p. 162.

9 J L Nicholas, Narrative of a
Voyage to New Zealand,
including a description of the
country . . . and the soil, climate
and productions of the island,
James Black and Son, London,
1817, vol. 1, p. 21.

10 Missionary Review, 1814, vol. 2,
p. 463.

11 Ibid., p. 264.

12 Ibid., p. 267.

13 Nicholas, vol. 1, pp. 31–3.

14 William Pember Reeves, The
Long White Cloud Ao Tea Roa,
Senate, Middlesex, 1998, p. 129.

15 Nicholas, vol. 1, pp. 15, 23.

16 Ibid., p. 38.

17 Ibid., pp. 44–5.

18 Ibid., pp. 46–7.

19 Ibid., pp. 47, 66.

20 Ibid., pp. 113–4.

21 Ibid., p. 171.

22 Ibid., pp. 171–2.

23 Ibid., pp. 203–6.

24 Missionary Register, 1816, p. 470.

25 Ibid., p. 470.

26 Nicholas, vol. 1, pp. 208–9.

27 Ibid., pp. 210, 229.

28 Ibid., p. 184.

29 Ibid., pp. 213–8.

30 Ibid., pp. 187–8.

31 Ibid., p. 201.

32 Ibid., pp. 342–7.

33 Nicholas, vol. 2, p. 147.

34 Missionary Register, 1817, p. 346.

35 Nicholas, vol. 2, p. 153.

36 Missionary Register, 1820, p. 307.

37 Missionary Register, 1819, p. 464;
Missionary Register, 1829,
pp. 465–6.

38 Reprinted in New Quarterly
Review or Home, Foreign and
Colonial Journal, London, 1844,
p. 487.

39 Missionary Register, 1831, p. 54.

40 Missionary Register, 1824, p. 408;
Fitzgerald, p. 57.

41 Fitzgerald, p. 60.

42 Ibid., p. 85.

43 Augustus Earle, Narrative of a
Residence in New Zealand &
Journal of a Residence in Tristan
da Cunha, ed. E H McCormick,
The University Press, Oxford,
1966, p. 29; Fitzgerald,
pp. 97, 100.

44 Dumont d'Urville, vol. 1, p. 104.

45 Missionary Register, 1826, p. 618.

46 D U Urlich 'The Introduction
and Diffusion of Firearms in New

Zealand 1800–1840', *The Journal of the Polynesian Society*, vol. 79, no. 4, 1970, p. 400.

47 *Missionary Register*, 1829, p. 461.

48 Fitzgerald, p. 110.

49 Fitzgerald, p. 111.

50 Jocelyn Chisholm, *Brind of the Bay of Islands*, J Chisholm, Wellington, 1979, pp. 9, 15.

51 Ibid., p. 17.

52 Ibid., p. 21.

53 *Missionary Register*, 1822, p. 538.

54 *Missionary Register*, 1829, pp. 286, 467; 1830, p. 869.

55 Fitzgerald, pp. 115, 118.

56 Fitzgerald, pp. 121, 162.

57 Marie King, *A Most Noble Anchorage*, Northland Historical Publications Society, Kerikeri, 1992, pp. 138, 185.

58 Fitzgerald, pp. 125–6.

59 Chisholm, *Brind of the Bay of Islands*, p. 20.

60 Ibid., p. 53.

61 *Missionary Register*, 1830, p. 376.

62 Fitzgerald, p. 186.

63 Fitzgerald, p. 198.

64 *Missionary Register*, 1831, p. 58.

65 *Missionary Register*, 1830, pp. 374–6.

66 Ballara, pp. 201–3.

67 Fitzgerald, p. 179; *Missionary Register*, 1833, p. 284.

68 Peter Bays, *A Narrative of the Wreck of the Minerva*, B Bridges, Cambridge, 1831 (facsimile edition, Kiwi Publishers, 1997), p. 159.

69 Ibid., pp. 144–5, 147.

70 Ibid., p. 151.

71 Ibid., p. 162.

72 Ibid., p. 165.

73 Ibid., p. 169.

74 Chisholm, *Brind of the Bay of Islands*, p. 67.

75 Jocelyn Chisholm, 'Brind, William Darby 1794?–1850', *Dictionary of New Zealand Biography*, updated 31 July 2003, URL: http//www.dnzb.govt.nz/

76 Keith Sinclair, *Laplace in New Zealand, 1831*, Heritage Press, Waikanae, 1998, p. 64.

77 Ibid., p. 30.

78 Ibid., p. 101.

79 Ibid., p. 30.

80 Ibid., p. 99.

81 Ibid., p. 100.

82 Ibid., p. 98.

83 Ibid., pp. 105, 107.

84 *Missionary Register*, 1822, p. 257.

CHAPTER 3

1 Lieutenant Charles C Wilkes, *Narrative of the United States Exploring Expedition*, Wiley and Putnam, London, 1845, vol. 2, p. 371.

2 Earle, p. 15.

3 Ibid., pp. 35, 56, 66.

4 Ibid., p. 66.

5   Ibid., pp. 81–2.

6   Ibid., pp. 18, 85–6.

7   Ibid., p. 141.

8   Ibid., p. 157.

9   Ibid., p. 129.

10 Ibid., p. 18.

11 Ibid., pp. 23, 25.

12 Ibid., p. 154.

13 Ibid., pp. 100, 104.

14 *Missionary Register*, 1828, p. 614.

15 Earle, p. 81.

16 Ibid., p. 156.

17 Ibid., p. 150.

18 Painting in collection of Alexander Turnbull Library, Wellington.

19 P Dillon, *Voyage in the South Seas*, Hurst Chance and Co, London, 1829, vol. 2, p. 332; *The Letters and Journals of Samuel Marsden*, ed. J R Elder, Otago University Council, Dunedin, 1932, p. 438.

20 Earle, p. 121.

21 F W Nicholas and J M Nicholas, *Charles Darwin in Australia*, University of Cambridge, Cambridge, 2002, p. 5.

22 Conrad Martens, *Journal of a Journey from England to Australia*, transcribed by Michael Organ, State Library of New South Wales Press, Sydney, 1994, pp. 51–2.

23 *The Bay of Islands, New Zealand* by Conrad Martens, 1835.

This painting is reproduced in *Conrad Martens: The Man and his Art*, Lionel Lindsay, Angus and Robertson, Sydney, 1920.

24 Charles Darwin, *The Voyage of the 'Beagle'*, Dent, Everyman's Library, London, 1983, pp. 401–2.

25 Ibid., pp. 402, 405.

26 Ibid., pp. 402, 409.

27 Ibid., p. 404.

28 Letter from Charles Darwin to George Grey, 13 November 1847, Auckland Central Library, George Grey Correspondence, GL-D8(2).

29 Darwin, p. 414.

30 Ibid., p. 410.

31 Nicholas and Nicholas, pp. 21–2.

32 Ibid., p .140.

33 Ibid., p. 139.

34 Wilkes, vol. 1, p. 134.

35 Herman Friis, ed., *The Pacific Basin: A History of its Geographical Exploration*, American Geographical Society, New York, 1967, p. 268.

36 Wilkes, vol. 2, p. 370–1.

37 Ibid., p. 374.

38 Ibid., pp. 375–7.

39 Ibid., p. 413.

40 Ibid., vol. 5, p. 502.

CHAPTER 4

1   'Psalm CVII, From an Improved Metrical Version of the Psalms

of David, Proposed for Use of
the Presbyterian Church in
Australia and New Zealand.
Written Wholly at Sea' in
Colonial Advertiser, E Alcock,
Sydney, vol. 1, 7 October 1841–
31 December 1842, p. 3.

2 John Ward, *Information Relative
to New Zealand, Compiled for
the Use of Colonists*, John W
Parker, London, 1840, pp. 108–9.

3 Thomson, vol. 1, p. 284.

4 Polack, *Manners and Customs of
the New Zealanders*, vol. 2,
James Madden and Co, London,
1840, p. 279.

5 Richard S Hill, *Policing the
Colonial Frontier: The Theory
and Practice of Coercive Social
and Racial Control in New
Zealand, 1767–1867*, Historical
Publications Branch,
Department of Internal Affairs,
Wellington, 1986, part 1, p. 85.

6 *An Encyclopaedia of New
Zealand*, ed. A H McLintock,
Government Printer,
Wellington, 1966, vol. 2, p. 216.

7 *Missionary Register*, 1833, p. 384.

8 Ibid., 1834, p. 550.

9 Ibid., 1833, p. 460.

10 Ibid., p. 469.

11 Ibid., p. 550.

12 Ibid., p. 59.

13 Ibid., p. 622.

14 Ibid., p. 513.

15 Jocelyn Chisholm, *Captain
Cattlin Towards New Zealand*,
J Chisholm, Wellington, 1994,
p. 18.

16 'Christ Church, Kororareka
Russell', Christ Church
Committee, Russell, 1997 (pages
not numbered).

17 'Subscriptions for the Purpose
of Erecting a Chapel at
Kororarika for the Benefit of
European's and Natives to be 40
feet by 20', handwritten book,
collection of Russell Museum.

18 'Christ Church, Kororareka
Russell', (pages not numbered).

19 *Missionary Register*, 1839, p. 267.

20 Temperance Society poster,
printed at the press of the
Church Missionary Society,
Paihia, by William Colenso,
4 May 1836.

21 Edward Markham, *New Zealand
or Recollections Of It*, edited
with an introduction by E H
McCormick, Government
Printer, Wellington, 1963,
comment on front flap.

22 Ibid., p. 25.

23 Ibid., pp. 63, 65.

24 Ibid., p. 40.

25 Ibid., p. 41.

26 Ibid., p. 52.

27 Ibid., p. 50.

28 Ibid., pp. 40, 54.

29 Ibid., p. 64.

30 Ibid., p. 74.

31 Ibid., p. 77.

32 Ernest S Dodge, *New England and the South Seas*, Harvard University Press, Cambridge, Massachusetts, 1965, p. 38.

33 'New Zealand (1834)' from the *Independent*, reprinted in *New Zealand in the 1830s*, Victorian New Zealand Series, no. 5, Hocken Library, University of Otago, Dunedin, 1979, pp. 30–7.

34 Joel Polack, *New Zealand: Being a Narrative of Travels and Adventures*, Richard Bentley, London, 1838, vol. 1, pp. 116–7; Polack, *Manners and Customs*, vol. 2, p. 201–2.

35 Ibid., pp. 201–2.

36 Polack, *New Zealand*, vol. 2, p. 343.

37 Ibid., p. 51.

38 Ibid., pp. 145–6.

39 *Missionary Register*, 1838, p. 218.

40 *Missionary Register*, 1841, p. 234.

41 Mawer, p. 169.

42 Ibid., p. 170.

43 *Missionary Register*, 1839, p. 545.

44 Angela Middleton, 'Early Nineteenth Century Globalisation: A Maori Response in the Bay of Islands, New Zealand', paper presented at the 2nd annual doctoral students' conference of the Association of Pacific Rim Universities, Auckland, 2001.

45 William Wade, *A Journey in the Northern Island of New Zealand*, George Rolwegan, Melbourne, 1842, p. 70.

46 Ibid., p. 73.

47 Ibid., pp. 71–2.

48 Alfred K Newman, 'A Study of the Causes Leading to the Extinction of the Maori', *Transactions and Proceedings of the New Zealand Institute*, vol. 14, 1881, pp. 459–77.

49 Phillip Houghton, *The First New Zealanders*, Hodder and Stoughton, Auckland, 1980, p. 134.

50 Newman, 'Extinction of the Maori', p. 271.

51 Ibid., p. 470.

52 Ibid., p. 475.

53 Ibid., p. 477.

54 Alfred K Newman, 'Is New Zealand a Healthy Country?', *Transactions and Proceedings of the New Zealand Institute*, vol. 15, 1882, pp. 509–10.

55 McNab, *Historical Records of New Zealand*, vol. 2, p. 401.

56 Richard Cruise, *New Zealand One Hundred Years Ago*, Brett Printing and Publishing Co, Auckland, 1921, pp. 153–4.

57 D Ian Pool, *The Maori Population of New Zealand*

1769–1971, Auckland University Press, Auckland, 1997, p. 93.

58 Cruise, pp. 153–4.

59 James McNeish, *Tavern in the Town*, A H and A W Reed, Wellington, 1957, pp. 33–8.

60 *An Encyclopaedia of New Zealand*, vol. 2, p. 818.

61 Polack, *New Zealand*, vol. 2, pp. 40–1.

62 *The Whaling Journal of Captain W. B. Rhodes: Barque Australian of Sydney 1836–1838*, introduction and notes by C R Straubel, Whitcombe and Tombs, Christchurch. 1954, pp. 49–50.

63 *An Encyclopaedia of New Zealand*, vol. 3, p. 71.

CHAPTER 5

1 John Carne Bidwill, *Rambles in New Zealand*, W S Orr, London, 1841, p. 3.

2 Polack, *Manners and Customs*, vol. 1, p. xxxiv.

3 Newsletter of Canterbury Genealogy Discussion Group, New South Wales, February 1998.

4 *An Encyclopaedia of New Zealand*, vol. 2, p. 189.

5 Polack, *New Zealand*, vol. 2, p. 211.

6 *Dictionary of National Biography*, ed. Sidney Lee, Smith, Elder and Co, London, 1896, vol. 46, p. 18.

7 Joceyln Chisholm, 'Polack, Joel Samuel 1807–1882', *Dictionary of New Zealand Biography*, updated 31 July 2003, URL: http//www.dnzb.govt.nz/.

8 Polack, *Manners and Customs*, vol. 1, p. xx.

9 Polack, *New Zealand*, vol. 2, pp. 337, 363.

10 Ibid., p. 422.

11 Ibid., vol. 1, pp. 370–2.

12 Joel Polack, Letters to his brother 1834–35, Auckland War Memorial Museum Library, MS 245.

13 Polack, *New Zealand*, vol. 1, p. 35.

14 Ibid., vol. 2, pp. 205–8.

15 Polack, *Manners and Customs*, vol. 1, p. xxvii.

16 Land Claim 288b, *New Zealand Government Gazette*, no. 14, 20 October 1841.

17 Polack, *New Zealand*, vol. 1, p. 292; Polack, *Manners and Customs*, vol. 2, p. 279.

18 *An Encyclopaedia of New Zealand*, vol. 1, p. 500.

19 Eric Ramsden, *Busby of Waitangi*, A H and A W Reed, Wellington, 1942, p. 174.

20 *Dictionary of New Zealand Biography*, ed. G H Scholefield,

Department of Internal Affairs, Wellington, 1940, vol. 2, pp. 404–5.

21 *Daily Southern Cross*, 9 May 1871.

22 Ibid., 24 May 1871.

23 Ibid., 14 June 1871.

24 Ibid., 28 June 1871.

25 Ibid., 6 October 1876.

26 *Dictionary of New Zealand Biography*, vol. 2, pp. 404–5.

27 Chisholm, 'Polack, Joel'.

28 Ormond Wilson, *Kororareka and Other Essays*, John McIndoe, Dunedin, 1990, p. 79.

29 Hazel P Harris, 'Ghosts May Attend the Celebrations', *Northland Regional Magazine*, no. 6, March 1959, p. 12.

30 Fergus Clunie, 'Mission at Kororareka', *New Zealand Historic Places*, no. 44, November 1993, p. 11.

31 *Sydney Herald*, 20 March 1837, in Edward Gibbon Wakefield, *The British Colonization of New Zealand: being an account of the principles, objects, and plans of the New Zealand Association . . . and native inhabitants of New Zealand*, John W Parker, London, 1837, pp. 148–9.

32 Polack, *New Zealand*, vol. 2, p. 342.

33 Ibid.

34 Marie King, *A Most Noble Anchorage*, p. 172.

35 *Sydney Herald*, 3 August 1837, 6 November 1837, and 20 November 1837, in 'Decisions of the Superior Courts of New South Wales, 1788–1899', Macquarie University Division of Law, Sydney.

36 R A A Sherrin and J H Wallace, *Early History of New Zealand*, H Brett, Auckland, 1890, p. 470.

37 Thomson, p. 47; William Pember Reeves, *New Zealand*, Horace Marshall and Son, London, 1898, p. 47.

38 Polack, *New Zealand*, vol. 2, p. 343.

39 Bidwill, pp. 2–4.

40 David Caughey, 'In Search of Samuel Ford 1811–1876', paper presented to Auckland Medical Historical Society, 3 July 2003.

41 Sherrin and Wallace, p. 472.

CHAPTER 6

1 Jean Baptiste François Pompallier, *Early History of the Catholic Church of Oceania*, H Brett, Auckland, 1888, p. 41.

2 *Dictionary of New Zealand Biography*, vol. 1, p. 207.

3 *A Life on the Ocean Wave: The Journals of Captain George Bayly 1824–1844*, eds Pamela

Statham and Rica Erickson, Melbourne University Press, Melbourne, 1998, pp. 4–5.

4 Ibid., pp. 62–3.

5 *Dictionary of New Zealand Biography*, vol. 1, p. 208; *A Life on the Ocean Wave*, p. 5.

6 A J Harrop, *England and New Zealand: From Tasman to the Taranaki War*, Methuen and Co, London, 1926, p. 101; *Dictionary of New Zealand Biography*, vol. 1, p. 208.

7 *The Letters and Journals of Samuel Marsden 1765–1835*, p. 439.

8 A Grove Day, *Adventurers of the Pacific*, Meredith Press, New York, 1969, p. 213.

9 Ibid., pp. 223–4.

10 *Dictionary of New Zealand Biography*, vol. 1, p. 208.

11 Pompallier, p. 12.

12 Ibid., p. 16.

13 Ibid., pp. 35–6, 40.

14 Ibid., pp. 40–2.

15 Ibid., p. 43.

16 Ibid., p. 44.

17 Ibid., pp. 46, 51, 58.

18 Ibid., p. 58.

19 *Missionary Register*, 1839, p. 553.

20 Pompallier, p. 59.

21 Deed of sale, Kororareka Beach, (South End), Bay of Islands District, from 'Kivie Kivie' to John Johnston [sic] no. 79, 29 December 1827; Clunie, 'Mission at Kororareka', pp. 10–11.

22 Pompallier, p. 59.

23 *The Founding of New Zealand: The Journals of Felton Mathew, First Surveyor-General of New Zealand, and his Wife 1840–1847*, ed. J Rutherford, Auckland University College, Auckland, 1940, p. 27; E R Simmons, *Pompallier: Prince of Bishops*, Catholic Publications Centre, Auckland, 1984, p. 44.

24 Rutherford, p. 101.

25 *Missionary Register*, 1841, p. 514.

26 Ibid., 1842, p. 479.

27 Ibid., 1843, p. 383.

28 Ibid., 1844, p. 407; Ibid., 1845, pp. 106.

29 Pompallier, pp. 81, 83.

30 Fergus Clunie, 'Mission Printery', *New Zealand Historic Places*, no. 44, November 1993, pp.14–6; Ruth M Ross, 'Old Kororareka: New Russell' in *Historic Buildings of New Zealand: North Island*, New Zealand Historic Places Trust, Cassell, Auckland, 1979, pp. 32–3.

31 Fergus Clunie, 'A Building Resurrected', *New Zealand Historic Places*, no. 44, November 1993, p. 30.

32 Pompallier, p. 55.

CHAPTER 7

1 Rutherford, p. 26.
2 Adrian Desmond and James Moore, *Darwin*, Penguin, London, 1991, p. 495.
3 Hill, part 1, p. 126.
4 *An Encyclopaedia of New Zealand*, vol. 2, p. 790.
5 Rutherford, p. 26; Markham, p. 63.
6 Rutherford, p. 77.
7 Ibid., p. 78.
8 *Extracts from a Diary Kept by the Rev. R Burrows during Heke's War in the North in 1845*, 1886, pp. 3–4.
9 Dumont d'Urville, vol. 1, pp. 531, 534–8.
10 Wilkes, vol. 2, pp. 209–10.
11 Ibid., p. 215.
12 Ibid., p. 236; Jan Morris, *Sydney*, Penguin, London, 1992, p. 143.
13 Morris, p. 121; *Parade*, Invincible Press, Sydney, no. 120, November 1960, p. 2.
14 Morris, pp. 21, 58, 144; *Parade*, no. 120, November 1960, p. 2.
15 *Parade*, no. 48, November 1954, p. 38.
16 *Parade*, no. 120, November 1960, p. 2.
17 Wilkes, vol. 2, p. 221.
18 Wilkes, vol. 1, pp. 166–7.
19 Wilkes, vol. 2, p. 382.
20 Ibid., p. 384
21 Conrad Bollinger, *Grog's Own Country*, Price Milburn, Wellington, 1959, pp. 26–7.
22 A H McLintock, *The History of Otago*, Otago Centennial Historical Publications, Dunedin, 1949, p. 82.
23 Hill, part 1, p. 51.
24 Rev. W J Williams, *Centennial Sketches of New Zealand Methodism*, Lyttelton Times Co, Christchurch, (n.d. c.1922), pp. 69–70.
25 McLintock, *The History of Otago*, pp. 118–9.
26 Ibid., pp. 119–23.
27 Williams, pp. 71–2.
28 Edward Shortland, *The Southern Districts of New Zealand*, Longman, Brown, Green, and Longmans, London, 1851, p. 109.
29 Ibid., pp. 110–11, 300–1.
30 McLintock, p. 83.
31 Shortland, pp. 113–5.
32 Dumont d'Urville, vol. 1, p. 530.
33 McLintock, *The History of Otago*, pp. 82, 84.
34 A H McLintock, *Crown Colony Government in New Zealand*, Government Printer, Wellington, 1958, p. 28.
35 Rev. William Morley, *The History of Methodism in New Zealand*, McKee and Co, Wellington, 1900, p. 88.
36 Dieffenbach, vol. 1, pp. 36–8.
37 Ibid., pp. 40–1.

38 Ibid., pp. 52–3.
39 Errol Brathwaite, *Sixty Red Nightcaps and Other Curiosities of New Zealand History*, David Bateman, Auckland, 1990, p. 36.

CHAPTER 8

1 James R Clendon in McNab, *Historical Records of New Zealand*, vol. 2, p. 608.
2 Ruth M Ross, *New Zealand's First Capital*, Department of Internal Affairs, Wellington, 1946, pp. 14–5.
3 'Report from the Select Committee on New Zealand together with the Minutes of Evidence, Appendix and Index', House of Commons, 29 July 1844, p. 56.
4 King, *A Most Noble Anchorage*, pp. 26–7.
5 A H McLintock in *An Encyclopaedia of New Zealand*, vol. 2, p. 91.
6 'Report from the Select Committee on New Zealand together with the Minutes of Evidence, Appendix and Index', p. 56.
7 Jack Lee, 'Clendon, James Reddy 1800–1872', *Dictionary of New Zealand Biography*, updated 31 July 2003, URL: http// www.dnzb.govt.nz/

8 McNab, *Historical Records of New Zealand*, vol. 2, pp. 604–22.
9 Ibid., p. 607.
10 Ibid., pp. 609–11.
11 Ibid., p. 608.
12 Ibid., pp. 608–9.
13 Hill, part 1, p. 127.
14 Ross, *New Zealand's First Capital*, pp. 37–8, 47–8.
15 Hill, part 1, pp. 128, 150.
16 Ibid., p. 181.
17 *New Zealand Government Gazette*, no. 6, 11 August 1841, p. 52.
18 Ibid., no. 20, 1 December 1841, p. 144.
19 *The Journal of Ensign Best 1837–1843*, ed. Nancy M Taylor, Government Printer, Wellington, 1966, pp. 215–6.
20 Ibid., pp. 217–9, 405–7.
21 H Carleton, *The Life of Henry Williams*, Wilson and Horton, Auckland, 1877, vol. 2, pp. 21–2, quoted in Taylor, p. 408.
22 Taylor, pp. 407–8.
23 McNab, *Historical Records of New Zealand*, vol. 2, p. 618.
24 Lee, 'Clendon, James'.
25 McNab, *Historical Records of New Zealand*, vol. 2, p. 620.
26 *An Encyclopaedia of New Zealand*, vol. 1, p. 279.
27 *New Zealand Government Gazette*, no. 1, 7 July 1841, p. 7.
28 Ibid., no. 3, 21 July 1841, p. 34.

29 'Returns Relative to Claims for Land in New Zealand', House of Commons, 16 June 1845, p. 3.

30 *An Encyclopaedia of New Zealand*, vol. 1, p. 279.

31 *New Zealand Government Gazette*, no. 33, 17 August 1842, p. 285 (case no. 44).

32 Ibid., no. 14, 20 October 1841, p. 89 (case no. 295(a)).

33 Ibid., no. 17, 10 November 1841, p. 106 (case no. 299).

34 Ibid., no. 20, 1 December 1841, p. 132 (case no. 322).

35 Ibid., no. 19, 24 November 1841, p. 128 (case no. 317(g)).

36 Ibid., no. 19, 24 November 1841, p. 128 (case no. 317(j)) and no. 20, 1 December 1841, pp. 132–3 (case no. 327).

37 Ibid., no. 20, 1 December 1841, p. 133 (case no. 327(b)).

38 Ibid., no. 9, 8 September 1841, p. 67 (case no. 256).

39 Ibid., no. 21, 15 December 1841, p. 148 (case no. 337).

40 Ibid., no. 22, 22 December 1841, p. 163 (case no. 361).

41 Ibid., no. 21, 15 December 1841, p. 149 (case no. 340(b)).

42 John B Williams, *The New Zealand Journal*, Peabody Museum of Salem and Brown University Press, Providence, Rhode Island, 1956, pp. 3–6.

43 Ibid., pp. 36, 59.

44 Ibid., pp. 58, 65.

45 Ibid., pp. 65, 71, 86.

46 Roger Blackley, 'John Guise Mitford: A Topographical Painter of the 1840s', *Art New Zealand*, no. 27, 1983, pp. 46–51.

47 John B Williams, pp. 66, 70, 88.

48 Ibid., pp. 69–72.

49 Ibid., pp. 78, 93.

50 Ibid., pp. 82–3.

51 William Laird Clowes, *The Royal Navy: A History*, Sampson Low, Marston and Company, London, 1901, vol. 6, pp. 312, 318–21.

52 J J Colledge, *Ships of the Royal Navy: An Historical Index*, David and Charles, Newton Abbot, Devon, England, 1969, vol. 1, p. 259.

53 *New Zealand Government Gazette*, vol. 4, no. 2, 13 January 1844.

CHAPTER 9

1 *New Zealand Advertiser and Bay of Islands Gazette*, no. 14, 10 September 1840.

2 Herbert W Williams, *A Bibliography of Printed Maori to 1900*, Dominion Museum, Wellington, 1924, p. vii.

3 *Missionary Register*, 1835, p. 471.

4 W A Glue, *History of the Government Printing Office*,

Government Printer, Wellington, 1966, p. 16; R A McKay, ed., *A History of Printing in New Zealand 1830–1940*, Wellington Club of Printing House Craftsmen, Wellington, 1940, pp. 4, 16.

5 *Missionary Register*, 1835, p. 471.

6 Herbert W Williams, p. ix.

7 *Missionary Register*, 1836, p. 563

8 King, *A Most Noble Anchorage*, p. 13.

9 *Missionary Register*, 1836, p. 563

10 Ibid., 1840, p. 512; 1841, p. 519.

11 Glue, p. 16.

12 McKay, p. 12.

13 Peter Kennett, *Unsung Hero: Barzillai Quaife*, Dunmore Press, Palmerston North, 1991, pp. 33, 36.

14 *New Zealand Advertiser and Bay of Islands Gazette*, no. 14, 10 September 1840.

15 Ibid., no. 5, 9 July 1840.

16 Ibid., no. 15, 17 September 1840.

17 Ibid., no. 2, 19 June 1840.

18 Ibid., no. 3, 25 June 1840.

19 Ibid., no. 7, 29 July 1840.

20 Ibid., no. 26, 3 December 1840.

21 Ibid., no. 8, 30 July 1840.

22 Ibid., no. 12, 27 August 1840.

23 Ibid., no. 15, 17 September 1840.

24 Ibid., no. 16, 24 September 1840.

25 Ibid., no. 13, 6 September 1840.

26 Ibid., no. 8, 30 July 1840; no. 9, 6 September 1840.

27 Ibid., no. 13, 6 September 1840; no. 14, 10 September 1840.

28 Ibid., no. 20, 22 October 1840.

29 Ibid., no. 13, 6 September 1840.

30 Ibid., no. 19, 15 October 1840.

31 Ibid., no. 20, 22 October 1840.

32 Ibid., no. 18, 8 October 1840.

33 Ibid., no. 27, 10 December 1840.

34 Kennett, pp. 84–6.

35 Notice sent to subscribers of the *New Zealand Advertiser and Bay of Islands Gazette* and the public by the publishers, Eagar and Co, Kororareka, 15 December 1840.

36 Kennett, pp. 98.

37 Glue, pp. 17–8.

38 Ibid., pp. 19–20.

39 Kennett, pp. 150–1.

40 Ibid., p. 74.

CHAPTER 10

1 Letter from C Hector to FitzRoy, 8 July 1844, enclosure in 'Copy of a Letter from J Busby to G W Hope', 17 January 1845, in 'Copies of Letters from Mr Shortland, late Acting Governor, and Mr Busby, late Resident of New Zealand, and Mr Hope', House of Commons, 7 March 1845, p. 17.

2 'Report from the Select Committee on New Zealand

together with the Minutes of Evidence, Appendix and Index', p. 653.

3 James Cowan, *The New Zealand Wars: A History of the Maori Campaigns and the Pioneering Period*, vol. 1, Government Printer, Wellington, 1922, pp. 7–10.

4 *New Zealand Advertiser and Bay of Islands Gazette*, no. 6, 16 July 1840.

5 Letter from James R Clendon to John Forsyth, Secretary of State, Washington, 26 October 1839, in McNab, *Historical Records of New Zealand*, vol. 2, p. 608.

6 Burrows, pp. 4–5; Melville Harcourt, *The Day Before Yesterday: A Short History of the Bay of Islands*, A H and A W Reed, Dunedin, 1940, pp. 156–7.

7 Kelly Tarlton, ' Search for the Remains of the Hulk "Sourabaya" at Matauwhi Bay, Russell, January 1978', Auckland War Memorial Museum Library, Auckland, MS 1019.

8 Marie King, 'Tradition: A Veteran of Heke's War', *Russell Review*, vol. 2, no. 1, 1978, pp. 7–11; King, *A Most Noble Anchorage*, p. 65.

9 'Account And Papers: New Zealand', House of Commons, vol. 33, 4 February – 9 August 1845, p. 28.

10 King, *A Most Noble Anchorage*, p. 34.

11 Letter to FitzRoy, 8 July 1844, enclosure in 'Copy of a Despatch from Governor FitzRoy to Lord Stanley', 20 August 1844, in 'Account And Papers: New Zealand', House of Commons, vol. 33, 4 February – 9 August 1845, pp. 88–9.

12 Ibid., p. 89.

13 Letter from C Hector to FitzRoy, ibid., p. 16–9.

14 'Copy of a letter from J Busby to G W Hope', in 'Copies of Letters from Mr Shortland . . . and Mr Hope', pp. 14–6.

15 Letters from Andrew Sinclair and FitzRoy, 12 July 1844, enclosures in 'Copy of a Despatch from Governor FitzRoy to Lord Stanley', p. 92.

16 Note from O'Connell, 5 August 1844, enclosure in 'Copy or Extracts from any Recent Despatches from the Governor of New South Wales, Respecting Outrages by the Natives in the Bay of Islands, in New Zealand', in 'Accounts and Papers: New Zealand', p. 6.

17 *Sydney Morning Herald*, 3 August 1844; also in enclosure

in 'Copy of a letter from J Busby to G W Hope', p. 19.

18 Muster book, HMS *Hazard*, ADM 38/8248, National Archives, Kew, London.

19 *The New Zealander*, 7 June 1845.

20 Letter from John B Williams to Secretary of State, Washington, January 1944, Auckland Central Library, Auckland.

21 George French Angas, *Savage Life and Scenes in Australia and New Zealand*, Smith, Elder and Co, London, 1847, vol. 2, pp. 168–70, 173.

22 'Extract of a Letter from Thomas Beckham to Governor FitzRoy, dated Russell, 10 January 1845', in 'Copies or Extracts of Correspondence Relative to an Attack on the British Settlement at the Bay of Islands by the Natives of New Zealand', House of Commons, 15 July 1845, p. 4.

23 'Extract of a Letter from Thomas Beckham to Governor FitzRoy, dated Russell, 16 January 1845', in 'Copies or Extracts of Correspondence Relative to an Attack', p. 5.

24 'Proclamation', 15 January 1845, in 'Copies or Extracts of Correspondence Relative to an Attack', p. 4.

25 'Proclamation', 8 January 1845, in 'Copies or Extracts of Correspondence Relative to an Attack', p. 4.

26 'Extract of a Letter from Governor FitzRoy to Governor Sir George Gipps', 21 January 1845, in 'Copies or Extracts of Correspondence Relative to an Attack', p. 6.

27 'Extract of a Despatch from Governor Sir George Gipps to Lord Stanley', 17 February 1845, in 'Copies or Extracts of Correspondence Relative to an Attack, p. 3.

28 Letter from FitzRoy to Beckham, 12 February 1845, in 'Extract of a Despatch from Governor FitzRoy to Lord Stanley, dated Auckland, 26 March 1845', enclosure in 'Copies or Extracts of Correspondence Relative to an Attack', p. 9.

29 Letters from FitzRoy to Beckham, 15 January 1845, pp. 7–8; FitzRoy to Hulme, 20 January 1845, p. 8, enclosures in 'Extract of a Despatch . . . 26 March 1845'.

30 Letter from FitzRoy to Beckham, 22 February 1845, enclosure in 'Extract of a Despatch . . . 26 March 1845', p. 11.

31 Letters from Beckham to FitzRoy: 27 February 1845, p. 12; 28 February 1845, pp. 12–3; 1 March 1845, p. 13, enclosures

in 'Extract of a Despatch . . . 26 March 1845'.

32 *New Zealand Spectator and Cook's Straits Guardian*, 22 March 1845.

33 Letter from Beckham to FitzRoy, 22 February 1845, enclosure in 'Extract of a Despatch . . . 26 March 1845', p. 11.

34 T Lindsay Buick, *New Zealand's First War*, Government Printer, Wellington, 1926, p. 64.

35 Letters from Robertson to FitzRoy, 4 March 1845, p. 13; Morgan to Robertson, 3 March 1845, p. 13; Beckham to FitzRoy, 4 March 1845, pp. 13–14; FitzRoy to Beckham, 6 March 1845, pp. 14–15, enclosures in 'Extract of a Despatch . . . 26 March 1845'.

36 R H Montague, *Dress and Insignia of the British Army in Australia and New Zealand 1770–1870*, Library of Australian History, Sydney, 1981, p. 78; *An Encyclopaedia of New Zealand*, vol. 1, p. 245.

37 *New Zealand Government Gazette*, vol. 4, no. 16, 8 June 1844.

38 'New Zealand Part IV, A Letter from the Bishop of New Zealand, to the Society for the Propagation of the Gospel; Containing an Account of the Affray between the Settlers and the Natives at Kororareka', The Society for the Propagation of the Gospel, London, 1847, Project Canterbury, *Church in the Colonies*, no. 12, pp. 8.

39 Burrows, p. 11.

CHAPTER 11

1 Letter from Phillpotts to FitzRoy, 15 March 1845, enclosure in 'Extract of a Despatch . . . 26 March 1845', p. 18.

2 King, *A Most Noble Anchorage*, pp. 39–41.

3 Letters from E Barclay to Lieutenant-Colonel Hulme, 15 March 1845, p. 21; Phillpotts to FitzRoy, 15 March 1845, pp. 18–19, enclosures in 'Extract of a Despatch . . . 26 March 1845'; 'Christ Church, Kororareka, Russell', pages not numbered.

4 Letter from J Campbell to Hulme, 16 March 1845, enclosure in 'Extract of a Despatch . . . 26 March 1845'; King, *A Most Noble Anchorage*, p. 41.

5 Letters from E Barclay to Hulme, 15 March 1845, pp. 21–3; Beckham to FitzRoy, 17 March 1845, pp. 16–17, enclosures in 'Extract of a

Despatch . . . 26 March 1845'.

6 'New Zealand Part IV, A Letter from the Bishop of New Zealand', p. 9.

7 Marie King, *Port in the North*, Russell Centennial Historical Committee, Russell, 1940, p. 67; Harcourt, pp. 191–2.

8 Letter from Campbell to Hulme, 16 March 1845, enclosure in 'Extract of a Despatch . . . 26 March 1845', p. 23.

9 Letter from Phillpotts to FitzRoy, 17 March 1845, enclosure in 'Extract of a Despatch . . . 26 March 1845', pp. 19–20.

10 Letter from Phillpotts to FitzRoy, 15 March 1845, enclosure in 'Extract of a Despatch . . . 26 March 1845', pp. 18–19.

11 'A Return of Passengers', enclosure in 'Extract of a Despatch . . . 26 March 1845', p. 20.

12 Muster book of HMS *Hazard*, 38/8248, National Archives, Kew, London.

13 Letter from Phillpotts to FitzRoy, 15 March 1845, enclosure in 'Extract of a Despatch . . . 26 March 1845', p. 19.

14 Letter from Phillpotts to Beckham, 20 March 1845, enclosure in 'Extract of a Despatch . . . 26 March 1845', p. 24.

15 Information supplied by Russell Museum.

16 'Six-Monthly Log of HM Sloop *Hazard* 1 October 1844 – 31 March 1845', ADM 51/3613, and 'Log Book of the Proceedings of HM Sloop *Hazard*', ADM 53/2617, National Archives, Kew, London.

17 'Kororareka, sketched by Captain Clayton on the morning before the assault and destruction of the town', Mitchell Library, New South Wales.

18 'New Zealand Part IV, A Letter from the Bishop of New Zealand', pp. 10–11.

19 Burrows, pp. 11–3.

CHAPTER 12

1 *New Zealand Spectator and Cook's Straits Guardian*, 5 July 1845. This is a parody on lines 'Who dares this pair of boots displace / Must meet Bombastes face to face.' from the tragic opera *Bombastes Furioso*, 1813.

2 Letter from FitzRoy to Stanley, 26 March 1845, in 'Copies or Extracts of Correspondence Relative to an Attack', p. 6.

3 Letter from J Everard Home to Rear Admiral Sir T Cochrane, 25 March 1845, in 'Copies or

Extracts of Correspondence Relative to an Attack', pp. 24–5.

4 King, *A Most Noble Anchorage*, p. 57.

5 Cowan, *The New Zealand Wars*, vol. 1, pp. 30–32.

6 Letters from FitzRoy to Gipps, 20 March 1845, in 'Copies or Extracts of Correspondence Relative to an Attack', p. 15; Beckham to FitzRoy, 11 March 1845, p. 16.

7 Letter from Phillpotts to FitzRoy, 15 March 1845, in 'Copies or Extracts of Correspondence Relative to an Attack', pp. 18–9.

8 Letter from Phillpotts to FitzRoy, 15 March 1845, in 'Copies or Extracts of Correspondence Relative to an Attack', p. 19.

9 Cowan, *The New Zealand Wars*, vol. 1, p. 31; Buick, p. 72; King, *Port in the North*, p. 67.

10 Robert FitzRoy, *Remarks on New Zealand in February 1846*, W and H White, London, 1846, pp. 39–40.

11 Cowan, *The New Zealand Wars*, vol. 1, pp. 35–7.

12 *New Zealand Spectator and Cook's Straits Guardian*, 10 May 1845.

13 *New-Zealander*, 7 June 1845.

14 *New Zealand Spectator and Cook's Straits Guardian*, 29 March 1845.

15 E R Simmons, 'McDonald, James 1824–1890; McDonald, Walter 1830–1899', *Dictionary of New Zealand Biography*, updated 31 July 2003, URL: http//www.dnzb.govt.nz/

16 Letter from Pompallier to Heke, 31 January 1845, in J J Wilson, *The Church in New Zealand*, The New Zealand Tablet Printing and Publishing Co, Dunedin, vol. 2, 1926, pp. 16–7.

17 Letter from Pompallier to Heke, April 1845, in Wilson, vol. 2, pp. 17–9.

18 Letter from Pompallier to the Central Council of the Work of Propagation of the Faith, May 1845, in Wilson, vol. 2, pp. 19–21.

19 Letter from Father Walter McDonald, 2 Feb 1860, from Rome, Archives of the Propagation of the Faith, Auckland Catholic Diocesan Archives, SRC6, pp. 987–997; Lillian Keys, *The Life and Times of Bishop Pompallier*, Pegasus, Christchurch, 1957, pp. 301–4.

20 Letter from Pompallier to the Central Council of the Work of Propagation of the Faith, May 1845, vol. 2, pp. 19–21; Pompallier, p. 83.

21 *New Zealand Government Gazette*, vol. 5, no. 9, 3 May 1845, pp. 47–8.

22 Cowan, *The New Zealand Wars*, vol. 1, p. 34.

23 *New Zealand Government Gazette*, vol. 5, no. 18, 7 July 1845, p. 90.

24 J A B Crawford. 'Phillpotts, George 1814?–1845', *Dictionary of New Zealand Biography*, updated 31 July 2003, URL: http//www.dnzb.govt.nz/; King, *A Most Noble Anchorage*, p. 56.

25 *An Encyclopaedia of New Zealand*, vol. 1, p. 500.

26 'Report from the Select Committee on Transportation', House of Commons, 14 July 1837, p. 23.

27 King, *A Most Noble Anchorage*, p. 59.

28 Ralph M Wiltgen, *The Founding of the Catholic Church in Oceania 1825 to 1850*, Australian National University Press, Canberra, 1979, pp. 394–5.

29 Letter from Pompallier to 'Captain Hone', April 1845, in Wilson, vol. 2, p. 18.

30 Wiltgen, pp. 397–9.

31 *New-Zealander*, 7 June 1845.

32 'Petition of Settlers at Kororareka', 'Votes and Proceedings: House of Representatives', Session 4, 1856, E-no. 7.

33 New Zealand Parliamentary Debates, House of Representatives, 12 December 1864, pp. 178–9.

34 New Zealand Parliamentary Debates, House of Representatives, 7 September 1865, pp. 435–7.

35 New Zealand Parliamentary Debates, House of Representatives, 24 July 1867, pp. 152–3.

36 New Zealand Parliamentary Debates, House of Representatives, 30 July 1867, p. 243.

37 New Zealand Parliamentary Debates, House of Representatives, 16 August 1867, pp. 488–9.

38 Chisholm, 'Polack, Joel'.

CHAPTER 13

1 'Randy Dandy O!' – a traditional sea shanty.

2 Thomson, vol. 1, pp. 328–9.

3 King, *A Most Noble Anchorage*, pp. 66–7.

4 Information supplied by Russell Museum.

5 Hill, part 1, p. 190.

6 William Fox, *The Six Colonies of New Zealand*, John Parker and Son, London, 1841, p. 16.

7 Ibid., p. 40.

8 Ibid., p. 17.

9 Ibid., p. 42.

10 Adrian Desmond, *Huxley*, Penguin, London, 1997, pp. 139–140.

11 *New Zealand Spectator and Cook's Straits Guardian*, 10 May 1845.

12 King, *A Most Noble Anchorage*, p. 68.

13 *Whale Hunt: The Narrative of a Voyage by Nelson Cole Haley Harpooner in the Ship Charles W Morgan 1849–1853*, Robert Hale, London, 1950, pp. 9–16.

14 Ibid., pp. 55–7.

15 Ibid., pp. 57–69.

16 Ibid., p. 69.

17 Ibid., p. 202.

18 Ibid., pp. 229–31.

19 Ibid., pp. 233–7.

20 Ibid., pp. 239–43.

21 Ibid., pp. 245–8.

22 Ibid., pp. 298–9.

23 Ibid., pp. 110, 303.

24 Herbert Asbury, *The Gangs of San Francisco*, Arrow Books, London, 2004, pp. 49–52, 113 (originally published as *The Barbary Coast: An Informal History of the San Francisco Underworld*, 1933); *Parade*, no. 22, May 1952, pp. 54–5.

25 Asbury, pp. 33–4.

26 Ibid., p. 258.

27 Ibid., p. 65–8.

28 *Parade*, no. 48, November 1954, p. 39.

29 Asbury, p. 98.

30 Ibid., p. 151.

31 Journal entry of Sunday 22 April 1827 in *The Early Journals of Henry Williams, Senior Missionary in New Zealand of the Church Missionary Society, 1826–40*, ed. Lawrence Rogers, Pegasus Press, Christchurch, 1961, p. 53; *The Dictionary of New Zealand English*, ed. H W Orsman, Oxford University Press, Auckland, 1997, p. 727.

32 Dodge, pp. 40–3.

33 Mawer, pp. 204–6.

34 Kene Hine Te Uira Martin, 'Kawiti, Maihi Paraone 1807–1899', *Dictionary of New Zealand Biography*, updated 16 December 2003, URL: http//www.dnzb.govt.nz/

35 King, *A Most Noble Anchorage*, pp. 82–4, 116–7, 140.

36 *Kororareka, Bay of Islands* by John Kinder, 1858, collection of Auckland Art Gallery Toi o Tamaki, reproduced in Ron Brownson, *John Kinder's New Zealand*, Random House New Zealand and Auckland Art Gallery Toi o Tamaki, 2004, p. 18.

37 King, *A Most Noble Anchorage*, pp. 85–6.

38 Charles Barrett, ed., *The Pacific*

Ocean of Islands, N H Seward, Melbourne, (n. d.), p. 54.

39 BAVX 4817/76/13, Archives New Zealand, Mt Wellington, Auckland.

40 BAVX 4817/76/27 and BAZX 4817/76/19, Archives New Zealand, Mt Wellington, Auckland.

41 BAVX 4817/76/12, Archives New Zealand, Mt Wellington, Auckland.

42 'Papers Relative to An Outrage Committed by a Maori at Mataure', *New Zealand Appendix to the Journals of the House of Representatives*, Session III, October–December 1863.

43 BAVX 4817/306/31, Archives New Zealand, Mt Wellington, Auckland.

44 BAVX 4817/306/40, Archives New Zealand, Mt Wellington, Auckland.

45 King, *A Most Noble Anchorage*, pp. 88, 89.

46 Wilkes, vol. 5, p. 494.

47 BAVX 4817/306/28, Archives New Zealand, Mt Wellington, Auckland.

48 Louisa Worsfold, 'A Social History of Russell' in Papers 1939–40, Auckland War Memorial Museum Library, MS 340, pp. 7–8.

49 King, *A Most Noble Anchorage*, p. 109.

50 'Christ Church Kororareka', Russell, pages not numbered; *Christ Church Cemetery Trail*, Russell Trust Board, Russell, 1998, pp. 19–20.

51 Caughey.

52 Russell Museum, Russell.

CHAPTER 14

1 James Cowan, *New Zealand or Ao-Tea-Roa (The Long Bright World)*, New Zealand Government Department of Tourist and Health Resorts, Wellington, 1908, pp. 109–10.

2 'New Zealand Part IV, A Letter from the Bishop of New Zealand', pp. 11–12.

3 *New Zealand Spectator and Cook's Straits Guardian*, 29 March 1845; *Dictionary of New Zealand Biography*, vol. 2, p. 405.

4 Letter from FitzRoy to Stanley, 26 March 1845, in 'Copies or Extracts of Correspondence Relative to an Attack', p. 6.

5 Buick, *New Zealand's First War*, p. 96.

6 J M R Owens, in *The Oxford History of New Zealand*, ed. Geoffrey W Rice, Oxford University Press, Auckland, 1992, p. 48.

7   John Williams, p. 72.
8   Ibid., p. 77.
9   Thomson, vol. 1, pp. 284–5.
10 Reeves, *The Long White Cloud
    Ao Tea Roa*, p. 128.
11 Quoted in M F Lloyd Prichard,
    *An Economic History of New
    Zealand to 1939*, Collins,
    Auckland, 1970, p. 14.
12 Duncan Mackay, *Frontier New
    Zealand: The Search for
    Eldorado 1800–1920*,
    HarperCollins, Auckland, 1992,
    pp. 34, 73–84.
13 *New Zealand Herald*, 11 May
    1932.
14 *Weekly News*, 14 February
    1940; *New Zealand Centennial
    News*, 1 April 1940, no. 13,
    pp. 22–3.
15 G B Lancaster, *Promenade*,
    Angus and Robertson, Sydney,
    1938, pp. 26, 67.
16 Simon Best, 'Guns and Gods:
    The History and Archaeology of
    Rewa's Pa, Kororareka:
    Archaeological Investigations at
    the Department of
    Conservation Visitor Centre,
    Russell, Site QO5/1179',
    Department of Conservation,
    Northland Conservancy, July
    2002, p. 119.
17 Ibid., pp. 2–7.
18 Ibid., pp. 72, 113–9.
19 Ibid., p. 120.
20 Harcourt, back jacket; King, *Port
    in the North*, p. 198.
21 Dieffenbach, vol. 1, p. 258.
22 King, *A Most Noble Anchorage*,
    p. 186.
23 H S Chapman, *New Zealand
    Portfolio*, Smith, Elder and Co,
    London, 1843, p. 127.
24 J C Beaglehole, *New Zealand: A
    Short History*, George Allen and
    Unwin, London, 1936, p. 18.
25 Lancaster, p. 74.

BIBLIOGRAPHY

BOOKS, ARTICLES AND PAMPHLETS:

Angas, George French. *Savage Life and Scenes in Australia and New Zealand*, 2 vols, Smith, Elder and Co, London, 1847.

Asbury, Herbert. *The Gangs of San Francisco* (originally published as *The Barbary Coast: An Informal History of the San Francisco Underworld*, 1933), Arrow Books, London, 2004.

Ballara, Angela. *Taua*, Penguin, Auckland, 2003.

Barrett, Charles (ed.). *The Pacific Ocean of Islands*, N H Seward, Melbourne, (n. d.).

Bays, Peter. *A Narrative of the Wreck of the Minerva*, B Bridges, Cambridge, 1831 (Kiwi Publishers facsimile edition, 1997).

Beaglehole, J C. *New Zealand: A Short History*, George Allen and Unwin, London, 1936.

Beaglehole, J C (ed.). *The Journals of Captain James Cook*, 4 vols, Hakluyt Society, Cambridge University Press, 1955.

Begg, A Charles and Begg, Neil C. *James Cook and New Zealand*, Government Printer, Wellington, New Zealand, 1970.

Bentley, Trevor. *Pakeha Maori*, Penguin, Auckland, 1999.

Bentley, Trevor. *Captured by Maori: White Female Captives, Sex and Racism on the Nineteenth-century New Zealand Frontier*, Penguin, Auckland, 2004.

Bidwill, John Carne. *Rambles in New Zealand*, W S Orr, London, 1841.

Blackley, Roger. 'John Guise Mitford: A Topographical Painter of the 1840s', *Art New Zealand*, 1983, no. 27, pp. 46–51.

Bollinger, Conrad. *Grog's Own Country*, Price Milburn, Wellington, 1959.

Brathwaite, Errol. *Sixty Red Nightcaps and Other Curiosities of New Zealand History*, David Bateman, Auckland, 1990.

Brownson, Ron. *John Kinder's New Zealand*, Random House New Zealand and Auckland Art Gallery Toi o Tamaki, Auckland, 2004.

Buick, T Lindsay. *New Zealand's First War*, Government Printer, Wellington, 1926.

Burrows, Rev. R. *Extracts from a Diary Kept by the Rev. R Burrows During Heke's War in the North in 1845*, 1886.

Carleton, H. *The Life of Henry Williams*, 2 vols, Wilson and Horton, Auckland, 1877.

Chapman, H S. *New Zealand Portfolio*, Smith, Elder and Co, London, 1843.

Chisholm, Jocelyn. *Brind of the Bay of Islands*, J Chisholm, Wellington, 1979.

Chisholm, Jocelyn. *Captain Cattlin Towards New Zealand*, J Chisholm, Wellington, 1994.

Chisholm, Jocelyn. 'Brind, William Darby 1794?–1850', *Dictionary of New Zealand Biography*, updated 31 July 2003, www.dnzb.govt.nz/

Chisholm, Jocelyn. 'Polack, Joel Samuel 1807–1882', *Dictionary of New Zealand Biography*, updated 31 July 2003, www.dnzb.govt.nz/

'Christ Church, Kororareka Russell', Christ Church Committee, Russell, 1997.

Christ Church Cemetery Trail, Russell Trust Board, Russell, 1998.

Clowes, William Laird. *The Royal Navy: A History*, 7 vols, Sampson Low, Marston and Company, London, 1901.

Clunie, Fergus. 'A Building Resurrected', *New Zealand Historic Places*, November 1993, no. 44, pp. 30–3.

Clunie, Fergus. 'Mission at Kororareka', *New Zealand Historic Places*, November 1993, no. 44, pp. 10–12.

Clunie, Fergus, 'Mission Printery', *New Zealand Historic Places*, November 1993, no. 44, pp. 14–16.

Colledge, J J. *Ships of the Royal Navy: An Historical Index*, David and Charles, Newton Abbot, Devon, England, 1969.

Cowan, James. *New Zealand or Ao-Tea-Roa (The Long Bright World)*, New Zealand Government Department of Tourist and Health Resorts, Wellington, 1908.

Cowan, James. *The New Zealand Wars: A History of the Maori Campaigns and the Pioneering Period*, 2 vols, Government Printer, Wellington, 1922.

Crawford, J A B. 'Phillpotts, George 1814?–1845', *Dictionary of New Zealand Biography*, updated 31 July 2003, www.dnzb.govt.nz/

Cruise, Richard. *New Zealand One Hundred Years Ago*, Brett Printing and Publishing Co, Auckland, 1921.

Darwin, Charles. *The Voyage of the 'Beagle'*, Dent, Everyman's Library, London, 1983 (first published 1839).

Day, A Grove. *Adventurers of the Pacific*, Meredith Press, New York, 1969.

De Braganza, Ronald L S and Oakes, Charlotte (eds). *The Hill Collection of Pacific Voyages*, University Library, University of California, San Diego, 1974–83.

Desmond, Adrian. *Huxley*, Penguin, London, 1997.

Desmond, Adrian and Moore, James. *Darwin*, Penguin, London, 1991.

Dieffenbach, Ernst. *Travels in New Zealand: with Contributions to the Geography, Geology, Botany, and Natural History of that Country*, 2 vols, John Murray, London, 1843.

Dillon, P. *Voyage in the South Seas*, 2 vols, Hurst, Chance and Co, London, 1829.

Doak, Wade. *The Burning of the 'Boyd': A Saga of Culture Clash*, Hodder and Stoughton, Auckland, 1984.

Dodge, Ernst S. *New England and the South Seas*, Harvard University Press, Cambridge, Massachusetts, 1965.

Dumont d'Urville, Jules-Sebastion-Cesar. *An Account in Two Volumes of Two Voyages to the South Seas by Captain (later Rear-Admiral) Jules S-C Dumont d'Urville to Australia, New Zealand, Oceania 1826–1829 in the corvette Astrolabe and to the Straits of Magellan, Chile, Oceania, South East Asia, Australia, Antarctica, New Zealand and Torres Strait 1837–1840 in the corvettes Astrolabe and Zélée*, 2 vols, translated and edited by Helen Rosenman, Melbourne University Press, Melbourne, 1997.

Earle, Augustus. *Narrative of a Residence in New Zealand & Journal of a Residence in Tristan da Cunha*, E H McCormick, ed., The University Press, Oxford, 1966.

Elder, J R (ed.). *The Letters and Journals of Samuel Marsden*, Otago University Council, Dunedin, 1932.

Fitzgerald, Caroline (ed.). *Letters from the Bay of Islands: The Story of Marianne Williams*, Penguin, Auckland, 2004.

FitzRoy, Robert. *Remarks on New Zealand in February 1846*, W and H White, London, 1846.

Fox, William. *The Six Colonies of New Zealand*, John Parker and Son, London, 1841.

Friis, Herman (ed.). *The Pacific Basin: A History of its Geographical Exploration*, American Geographical Society, New York, 1967.

Glue, W A. *History of the Government Printing Office*, Government Printer, Wellington, 1966.

Grayland, Eugene. *Coasts of Treachery*, A H and A W Reed, Wellington, 1963.

Haley, Nelson Cole. *Whale Hunt: The Narrative of a Voyage by Nelson Cole Haley in the Ship Charles W Morgan 1849–1853*, Robert Hale, London, 1950.

Harcourt, Melville. *The Day Before Yesterday: A Short History of the Bay of Islands*, A H and A W Reed, Dunedin, 1940.

Harrop, A J. *England and New Zealand: From Tasman to the Taranaki War*, Methuen and Co, London, 1926.

Hawkesworth, John. *An account of the voyages undertaken by the order of His present Majesty for making discoveries in the southern hemisphere, and successively performed by Commodore Byron, Captain Wallis, Captain Carteret, and Captain Cook, in the Dolphin, the Swallow, and the Endeavour: drawn up from the journals which were kept by the several commanders and from the papers of Joseph Banks, esq.*, 3 vols, W Strahan and T Cadell, London, 1773.

Hill, Richard S. *Policing the Colonial Frontier: The Theory and Practice of Coercive Social and Racial Control in New Zealand, 1767–1867*, Historical Publications Branch, Department of Internal Affairs, Wellington, 1986.

Houghton, Phillip. *The First New Zealanders*, Hodder and Stoughton, Auckland, 1980.

Hughes, Robert. *The Fatal Shore*, Pan, London, 1988.

Jones, Steve. *Almost Like a Whale: The Origin of Species Updated*, Doubleday, London, 1999.

Kennett, Peter. *Unsung Hero: Barzillai Quaife*, Dunmore Press, Palmerston North, 1991.

Keys, Lillian. *The Life and Times of Bishop Pompallier*, Pegasus, Christchurch, 1957.

King, Marie. *Port in the North: A Short History of Russell, New Zealand*, Russell Centennial Historical Committee, Russell, 1940.

King, Marie. 'Tradition: A Veteran of Heke's War', *Russell Review*, 1978, vol. 2, no. 1, pp. 7–11.

King, Marie. *A Most Noble Anchorage: A Story of Russell and the Bay of Islands*, Northland Historical Publications Society, Kerikeri, 1992.

Lancaster, G B. *Promenade*, Angus and Robertson, Sydney, 1938.

Lee, Jack. *The Bay of Islands*, Reed, Auckland, 1996 (first published as *'I Have Named it the Bay of Islands'*, Hodder and Stoughton, 1983).

Lee, Jack. 'Clendon, James Reddy 1800–1872', *Dictionary of New Zealand Biography*, updated 31 July 2003, www.dnzb.govt.nz/

Lee, Sidney (ed.). *Dictionary of National Biography*, Smith, Elder and Co, London, 1896.

Mackay, Duncan. *Frontier New Zealand: The Search for Eldorado 1800–1920*, HarperCollins, Auckland, 1992.

McKay, R A (ed.). *A History of Printing in New Zealand 1830–1940*, Wellington Club of Printing House Craftsmen, Wellington, 1940.

McLintock, A H. *The History of Otago*, Otago Centennial Historical Publications, Dunedin, 1949.

McLintock, A H. *Crown Colony Government in New Zealand*, Government Printer, Wellington, 1958.

McLintock, A H (ed.). *An Encyclopaedia of New Zealand*, 3 vols, Government Printer, Wellington, 1966.

McNab, Robert. *From Tasman to Marsden: A History of Northern New Zealand from 1652 to 1818*, J Wilkie and Co, Dunedin, 1914.

McNab, Robert. *Historical Records of New Zealand*, 2 vols, Government Printer, Wellington, 1914.

McNeish, James. *Tavern in the Town*, A H and A W Reed, Wellington, 1957.

Markham, Edward. *New Zealand or Recollections Of It*, edited with an introduction by E H McCormick, Government Printer, Wellington, 1963.

Marra, John. *Journal of the Resolution's voyage in 1772, 1773, 1774 and 1775, on discovery to the southern hemisphere, by which the non-existence of an undiscovered continent between the equator and the 50th degree of southern latitude is demonstratively proved*, F Newberry, London, 1775.

Marsden, Samuel, *The Letters and Journals of Samuel Marsden, 1765–1835*, edited by J R Elder, Otago University Council, Dunedin, 1932.

Martens, Conrad. *Journal of a Journey from England to Australia*, transcribed by Michael Organ, State Library of New South Wales Press, Sydney, 1994.

Martin, Kene Hine Te Uira. 'Kawiti, Maihi Paraone 1807–1899', *Dictionary of New Zealand Biography*, updated 16 December 2003, www.dnzb.govt.nz/

Mawer, Granville Allen. *Ahab's Trade: The Saga of South Seas Whaling*, Allen and Unwin, New South Wales, Australia, 2000.

Melville, Herman. *Moby Dick*, Penguin, London, 1994.

Molloy, Les and Smith, Roger. *Landforms: The Shaping of New Zealand*, Craig Potton, Nelson, 2002.

Montague, R H. *Dress and Insignia of the British Army in Australia and New Zealand 1770–1870*, Library of Australian History, Sydney, 1981.

Morley, Rev. William. *The History of Methodism in New Zealand*, McKee and Co, Wellington, 1900.

Morris, Jan. *Sydney*, Penguin, London, 1992.

'New Zealand (1834)' from *The Independent*, reprinted in *New Zealand in the 1830s*, Victorian New Zealand Series, no. 5, Hocken Library, University of Otago, Dunedin, 1979.

Newman, Alfred K. 'A Study of the Causes leading to the Extinction of the Maori', *Transactions and Proceedings of the New Zealand Institute*, 1881, vol. 14, pp. 459–77.

Newman, Alfred K. 'Is New Zealand a Healthy Country?', *Transactions and Proceedings of the New Zealand Institute*, 1882, vol. 15, pp. 509–10.

Nicholas, F W and Nicholas, J M. *Charles Darwin in Australia*, University of Cambridge, Cambridge, 2002.

Nicholas, J L. *Narrative of a voyage to New Zealand including a description of the country, and incidental remarks on the manners, customs and political economy of the natives, together with supplementary observations on the origin of the people, and the soil, climate and productions of the island*, 2 vols, James Black and Son, London, 1817.

Orsman, H W (ed.). *The Dictionary of New Zealand English*, Oxford University Press, Auckland, 1997.

Polack, Joel. *New Zealand: Being a Narrative of Travels and Adventures,* 2 vols, Richard Bentley, London, 1838.

Polack, Joel. *Manners and Customs of the New Zealanders*, 2 vols, James Madden and Co, London, 1840.

Pompallier, Rt Rev. Jean Baptiste François. *Early History of the Catholic Church of Oceania*, H Brett, Auckland, 1888.

Pool, D Ian. *The Maori Population of New Zealand 1769–1971*, Auckland University Press, Auckland, 1997.

Prichard, M F Lloyd. *An Economic History of New Zealand to 1939*, Collins, Auckland, 1970.

Ramsden, Eric. *Busby of Waitangi*, A H and A W Reed, Wellington, 1942.

Reeves, Randall R, Stewart, Brent S, Clapham, Phillip J and Powell, James A. *National Audubon Society Guide to Marine Mammals of the World*, Alfred A Knopf, New York, 2002.

Reeves, William Pember. *The Long White Cloud Ao Tea Roa*, Senate, Middlesex, 1998.

Reeves, William Pember. *New Zealand*, Horace Marshall and Son, London, 1898.

Rhodes, Captain W B. *The Whaling Journal of Captain W. B. Rhodes: Barque Australian of Sydney 1836–1838*, introduction and notes by C R Straubel, Whitcombe and Tombs, Christchurch, 1954.

Rice, Geoffrey W (ed.). *The Oxford History of New Zealand*, (2nd edition) Oxford University Press, Auckland, 1992.

Richards, Rhys. *Jorgen Jorgenson's Observations*, Paremata Press, Wellington, 1996.

Rogers, Lawrence (ed.). *The Early Journals of Henry Williams, Senior Missionary in New Zealand of the Church Missionary Society, 1826–40*, Pegasus Press, Christchurch, 1961.

Ross, Ruth M. *New Zealand's First Capital*, Department of Internal Affairs, Wellington, 1946.

Ross, Ruth M. 'Old Kororareka: New Russell', *Historic Buildings of New Zealand: North Island*, New Zealand Historic Places Trust, Cassell, Auckland, 1979, pp. 32–3.

Roth, H Ling (trans.). *Crozet's Voyage to Tasmania, New Zealand and the Ladrone Islands, and the Philippines in the Years 1771–1772*, Truslove and Shirley, London, 1891.

Rutherford, J (ed.). *The Founding of New Zealand: The Journals of Felton Mathew, First Surveyor-General of New Zealand, and his Wife 1840–1847*, Auckland University College, Auckland, 1940.

Savage, John. *Some Account of New Zealand, Particularly the Bay of Islands and Surrounding Country*, reprinted with notes in A D McKinlay, *Savage's Account of New Zealand in 1805 together with Schemes of 1771 and 1824 for Commerce and Colonization*, L T Watkins, Wellington, 1939.

Scholefield, G H (ed.). *Dictionary of New Zealand Biography*, 2 vols, Department of Internal Affairs, Wellington, 1940.

Sherrin, R A A and Wallace, J H. *Early History of New Zealand*, H Brett, Auckland, 1890.

Shortland, Edward. *The Southern Districts of New Zealand*, Longman, Brown, Green, and Longmans, London, 1851.

Simmons, E R. *Pompallier: Prince of Bishops*, Catholic Publications Centre, Auckland, 1984.

Simmons, E R. 'McDonald, James 1824–1890; McDonald, Walter 1830–1899', *Dictionary of New Zealand Biography*, updated 31 July 2003, www.dnzb.govt.nz/

Sinclair, Keith V. *Laplace in New Zealand, 1831*, Heritage Press, Waikanae, 1998.

Statham, Pamela and Erickson, Rica (eds). *A Life on the Ocean Wave: The Journals of Captain George Bayly 1824–1844*, Melbourne University Press, Melbourne, 1998.

Stevens, Graeme, McGlone, Matt and McCulloch, Beverley. *Prehistoric New Zealand*, Heinemann Reed, Auckland, 1988.

Taylor, Nancy M (ed.). *The Journal of Ensign Best 1837–1843*, Government Printer, Wellington, 1966.

Thomson, Arthur S. *The Story of New Zealand: Past and Present – Savage and Civilized*, 2 vols, John Murray, London, 1859.

Urlich, D U. 'The Introduction and Diffusion of Firearms in New Zealand 1800–1840', *The Journal of the Polynesian Society*, 1970, vol. 79, no. 4, pp. 399–400.

Wade, William. *A Journey in the Northern Island of New Zealand*, George Rolwegan, Melbourne, 1842.

Wahlroos, Sven. *Mutiny and Romance in the South Seas: A Companion to the Bounty Adventure,* Salem House Publishers, Topsfield, Massachusetts, 1989.

Ward, John. *Information Relative to New Zealand, Compiled for the Use of Colonists,* John W Parker, London, 1840.

Wilkes, Lieutenant Charles C. *Narrative of the United States Exploring Expedition,* 5 vols, Wiley and Putnam, London, 1845.

Williams, Herbert W. *A Bibliography of Printed Maori to 1900,* Dominion Museum, Wellington, 1924.

Williams, John B. *The New Zealand Journal,* Peabody Museum of Salem and Brown University Press, Providence, Rhode Island, 1956.

Williams, Rev. W J. *Centennial Sketches of New Zealand Methodism,* Lyttelton Times Co, Christchurch, (n.d., c.1922).

Wilson, J J. *The Church in New Zealand,* 2 vols, The New Zealand Tablet Printing and Publishing Co, Dunedin, 1926.

Wilson, Ormond. *Kororareka and Other Essays,* John McIndoe, Dunedin, 1990.

Wiltgen, Ralph M. *The Founding of the Catholic Church in Oceania 1825 to 1850,* Australian National University Press, Canberra, 1979.

Wises New Zealand Guide, Wises Publications, Auckland, 1987.

NEWSPAPERS & PERIODICALS:

Colonial Advertiser, Sydney.

Colonial Magazine and Commercial-Maritime Journal.

Daily Southern Cross.

Missionary Register: Containing the Principal Transactions of the Various Institutions for Propagating the Gospel, with the Proceedings, at Large, of the Church Missionary Society.

Missionary Review: Containing an Abstract of the Proceedings of the Principal Missionary and Bible Societies Throughout the World.

New Quarterly Review or Home, Foreign and Colonial Journal.

New Zealand Advertiser and Bay of Islands Gazette.

New Zealand Centennial News.

New Zealand Government Gazette.

New Zealand Herald.

New Zealand Historic Places.

New Zealand Spectator and Cook's Straits Guardian.
New-Zealander.
Newsletter of Canterbury Genealogy Discussion group, New South Wales.
Northland Regional Magazine.
Parade.
Sydney Herald.
Sydney Morning Herald.
Weekly News.

PARLIAMENTARY RECORDS:
'Accounts And Papers: New Zealand'. House of Commons, 4 February–
    9 August 1845.
'A Collection of the Public General Statutes passed in the Fifty-seventh year
    of the Reign of His Majesty King George the Third: being the Fifth
    Session of the Fifth Parliament of the United Kingdom of Great Britain
    and Ireland'. London, 1817.
'Copies of Letters from Mr Shortland, late Acting Governor, and Mr Busby,
    late Resident of New Zealand, and Mr Hope'. House of Commons,
    7 March 1845.
'Copy or Extracts from any Recent Despatches from the Governor of New
    South Wales, respecting Outrages by the Natives in the Bay of Islands, in
    New Zealand', in 'Accounts and Papers: New Zealand'. House of
    Commons 4 February–9 August 1845.
'Copies or Extracts of Correspondence Relative to an Attack on the British
    Settlement at the Bay of Islands by the Natives of New Zealand'. House of
    Commons, 15 July 1845.
New Zealand Appendix to the Journals of the House of Representatives,
    1863.
'Papers Relative to New Zealand'. House of Commons, 4 February 1845.
'Report from the Select Committee on New Zealand together with the
    Minutes of Evidence, Appendix and Index'. House of Commons, 29 July
    1844.
'Report from the Select Committee on Transportation'. House of Commons,
    14 July 1837.
'Report of the Commission of Inquiry on the State of Agriculture and

Trade in the Colony of New South Wales'. House of Commons, 13 March 1823.

'Returns Relative to Claims for Land in New Zealand'. House of Commons, 16 June 1845.

'Votes and Proceedings: House of Representatives'. Session 4, 1856, E-no. 7.

ARCHIVES:

Archives New Zealand, Mt Wellington, Auckland.

Auckland Catholic Diocesan Archives, Auckland: Archives of the Propagation of the Faith.

Auckland Central Library, Auckland: George Grey Correspondence; United States Consulate letters.

Auckland War Memorial Museum Library, Auckland: Joel Polack, Letters to his Brother 1834–35, MS 245; Kelly Tarlton, 'Search for the Remains of the Hulk "Sourabaya" at Matauwhi Bay, Russell, January 1978, MS 1019; Louisa Worsfold, 'A Social History of Russell' in Papers 1939–40, MS 340.

Hocken Library, Dunedin: George Clarke MS Letters and Journals 1822–49.

Macquarie University, Division of Law, Sydney: 'Decisions of the Superior Courts of New South Wales, 1788–1899'.

National Archives, Kew, London: Muster Book of HMS *Hazard*, 38/8248; 'Six-Monthly Log of HM Sloop *Hazard* 1 October 1844–31 March 1845', ADM 51/3613; 'Log Book of the Proceedings of HM Sloop *Hazard*', ADM 53/2617.

National Library of Australia, Canberra: 'The *Endeavour* Journal of James Cook, 20 November 1769', manuscript 1.

Project Canterbury, Church in the Colonies, no XII, New Zealand, part IV.

Russell Museum, Russell: 'Subscriptions for the Purpose of Erecting a Chapel at Kororarika for the Benefit of European's and Natives to be 40 feet by 20'.

PAPERS:

Best, Simon. 'Guns and Gods: The History and Archaeology of Rewa's Pa, Kororareka: Archaeological Investigations at the Department of

Conservation Visitor Centre, Russell, Site QO5/1179', Department of
Conservation, Northland Conservancy, July 2002.

Caughey, David. 'In Search of Samuel Ford 1811–1876', paper presented to
Auckland Medical Historical Society, 3 July 2003.

Middleton, Angela. 'Early Nineteenth Century Globalisation: A Maori
Response in the Bay of Islands, New Zealand', paper presented at 2nd
Annual Doctoral Students' Conference of the Association of Pacific Rim
Universities, Auckland, 2001.

INDEX

capital of NZ, 107–8, 123; first
bank at, 109, 126; hospital at, 124;
housing 'boom' at, 125; land
claims, 114–5, 125; Marsden's
comparison with Paihia, 42–3;
naming of, 22; plan of, 1863, 170;
population of, 76, 84, 91, 99, 101,
131, 183; postal services to, 127;
Russell, included within, 118. *See
also* Russell
LAW AND ORDER: court cases at,
181–3; fight on beach, 175–6;
'The Girls' War', 43–5, 65, 109;
grog-shops in, 58, 59, 65, 69, 70,
76, 77, 78, 84, 85, 110, 131, 132;
Kororareka Association, 77,
81–3, 85, 98, 124; Maori
demands that prisoner Kihi be
handed over, 112–3; *New
Zealand Advertiser* reports of
lawlessness at, 124–7; police
headquarters at, 111–2, 132,
135, 136, 140, 171, 175; prison
at, 112; public houses at, 69,
126–7, 173, 175; referred to as
'hell', 45, 62, 98, 188; reputation
of, 25, 60, 62–3, 71, 76, 101, 106,
176, 178, 180, 188–9, 190, 192
MISSIONARIES: building of
church (Christ Church), 45, 55,
60–1, 184–5; Catholic mission,
91, 92–5, 132; Church of
England, 32, 35, 41, 60, 188
NORTHERN WAR: expectation of
attack by Maori, 136–7, 140–3;
fall of, 145–54, 155–61, 187–8;
former residents return to,
170–1; residents' claims for
compensation, 164–7
PORT AND SHIPPING: American
ships at, 109–11, 138–9;
anchorage at, 26; importance of
shipping and port to, 52, 58, 65,
72, 118, 169, 170, 172, 173, 180;
jetties at, 179, 180

VISITORS TO, AND OPINIONS OF:
George French Angas, 139–40;
Edward Ashworth, 132; Peter
Bays, 45; Alexander Berry, 23;
Robert Burrows, 99; Charles
Darwin, 54, 55; d'Urville, 100;
Augustus Earle, 50–3; Captain
Jacob, 59–60; Mr Jameson, 84–5,
189; John Kinder, 179–80;
Cyrille-Pierre-Théodore
Laplace, 46–7, 192; Edith
Lyttleton, 190–1, 192–3;
Edward Markham, 61–4;
Conrad Martens, 53; Felton
Mathew, 98–9, 108; Charles
Pharazyn, 133; William Pember
Reeves, 189; Arthur S Thomson,
189; Charles Wilkes, 56, 102;
John Brown Williams, 117, 188,
189
Kororareka Association, 77, 81–3, 85,
98, 124
Kororareka Land Company, 115

La Pérouse, Jean François, 88
Lady Nelson, 22, 30
Lancaster, G B, 190–1, 192–3
land commissioners, 114–5
land sales, *see* Maori land sales
Laplace, Cyrille-Pierre-Théodore,
46–7, 192
Laurasia, 11–2
Lavaud, Commodore, 124–5
law and order, *see* Bay of Islands, law
and order; Kororareka, law and
order
Le Mascarin, 68–9
Lee, Samuel, 37, 119
Lovell, William, 151
Lyttleton, Edith, 190–1, 192–3

McArthy, Alex, 151
McDonald, Walter, 159
McKay, Donald, 114
McKenny, John, 112

Polack, Joel: builds brewery, 58; donation to church building fund, 60; descriptions of impact of shipping, 64–5, 79–80; description of tribal warfare, 70; settlement and trade in Kororareka, 71–5, 77, 78, 191; land transactions, 72, 74–5, 115; duel with Turner, 75; house stockaded during attack on Kororareka, 141, 142, 150; house destroyed, 148–9, 151; claim for compensation, 167
police force, 98, 102, 111–2, 132, 135, 136, 140, 171, 175; Maori, 171
Pomare, 40, 51
Pomare II, 40, 44, 47, 65, 70, 84, 102, 109, 123, 139, 142, 162
Pomare's pa, *see* Otuihu
Pompallier, Bishop Jean Baptiste François, 89–95, 103–4, 124, 129, 159–61, 163–4, 188
Pompallier House, 94–5
population, New Zealand, 169, 171, 189–90; *See also* Kororareka, population
Port Arthur, 25
Port Jackson: convict settlement in, 18, 19, 20, 23, 35, 41, 99, 101–2, 109; Marsden advises whalers not to visit, 33; missionaries' opinion of, 38, 41, 42; preferred to Kororareka, 60. *See also* Sydney
Port Nicholson (Wellington), 102, 123, 131, 156, 158–9, 169, 171, 172
ports, New Zealand, 169–70. *See also* Bay of Islands, shipping; Kororareka, port and shipping
Poyner, John, 61, 77
printing presses: first book printed in NZ, 120; Kerikeri, 119; Kororareka, 94, 95; Mangungu, 120; Paihia, 91, 95, 119–21. *See also* newspapers
prostitution, 19, 27, 35–6, 41–2, 44, 45, 46, 47, 59, 63, 66–9, 102, 116, 117, 177, 178

public houses, 69, 126–7, 173, 175. *See also* alcohol; grog-shops
Puketutu, 163

Quaife, Barzillai, 122–8, 129, 134

Rangihoua, 31, 34, 36, 37, 41, 47, 50
Rattlesnake, HMS, 97, 98, 172
Raven, William, 18
Rawene, 113
Reeves, William Pember, 189
Resolution, 15, 16
Rewa, 43, 45, 46, 47, 59, 60, 92, 114, 191, 192
Rhin, 164
Rhodes, William B, 70
Richmond, 132
Riggs, Abimelech, 20
Ringa, Maria, 40
Roberton Island, 46, 125
Robertson, David, 145–6, 156, 185
The Rocks, Sydney, 101–2, 177
Rosanna, 41, 50
Ross, James Clark, 56
Roux, Lieutenant, 68–9
Royal Sovereign, 43, 45
Ruatara, 31, 32, 34, 35, 36, 37
Russell (schooner), 161
Russell (town): auction of town allotments, 125; capital established at, 108, 111, 123; constable employed to track escaped convicts, 111–2; hospital location debate, 124; Kororareka included within, 118; Magistrate's Court cases, 182; martial law imposed, 161; replacing Kororareka as commonly used name of town, 183; whaling ships at, 183–4; wharf at, 183. *See also* Kororareka; Okiato

San Francisco, 66, 176–8, 192
Santa Anna, 31
Savage, John, 21–2

Waitangi, 37, 75, 99, 108, 113, 135, 139, 190
Waka Nene, Tamati, 171, 185, 191
Ward, John, 57
Watkin, James, 103–5
Wellington (city – Port Nicholson), 102, 123, 131, 156, 158–9, 169, 171, 172
Wellington (ship), 41
Wesleyan Methodist Missionary Board, 103
Wesleyan mission, 90, 95, 103–5, 120
Whakakotahitanga o Nga Iwi, 179, 185
whales, 11, 12–3, 15, 16, 17
whaling: American, 55, 56, 66, 73, 110, 113, 123, 132, 167, 172–6, 180; Bay of Islands / Kororareka as port for, 20–1, 29–30, 58, 60, 63, 64, 65, 66, 67, 83–4, 99, 100, 110, 123, 169–70, 185; contact between whalers and Maori, 57, 63, 67, 139, 157, 173; demise of trade in Bay of Islands, 37, 169–70, 180; Hawaii, 178–9; missionaries and, 33, 39–40, 41–2, 47, 51, 63, 65, 110; shore, 20, 103–6, 171, 183; transport of convicts linked with, 17–8
Whangarei, 108
Whangaroa, 23, 31
whooping cough outbreak, 40
Wilkes, Charles C, 55–6, 101–2
Wilkinson, Elsie, 150
Wilkinson, F, 76
William and Ann, 18
Williams, Edward M, 182
Williams, Henry: arrival at Bay of Islands, 37–8; incident with Waikato's musket, 39; holds church services at Kororareka, 41; and whalers, 41–2; views on alcohol, 59; views on musket trade, 60; and church at Kororareka, 60, 61; Polack's opinion of, 65; views on Otuihu, 65; authority to grant

marriage licences, 66; and Polack's land at Kororareka, 72; assistance to John Wright and family, 80; health, 84; Felton Mathew's opinion of, 93; competition with Pompallier, 93; attempts to stop demolition of house in Kororareka, 110; land claim on behalf of CMS, 114; influence on Hone Heke, 134; meets with FitzRoy at Waimate, 137; suggests register of 'good' and 'bad' Maori, 142; buries dead after attack on Kororareka, 152; advises Selwyn that flagstaff cut down, 153–4; opinion of *New Zealand Spectator and Cook's Straits Guardian*, 159; first referred to 'ship-girls', 178; representation of, at re-enactment of Treaty of Waitangi signing, 190
Williams, Jane, 39
Williams, John, 180–1, 182–3
Williams, John Brown, 115–7, 138–9, 188, 189
Williams, Marianne, 37, 38, 41
Williams, Thomas, 180, 181, 182–3
Williams, William, 39, 41–2, 43, 51, 54–5, 65, 66, 120, 135
Wilson, William, 123
women: Marsden's classification of, in Port Jackson, 19
women, Maori: kidnapping by crew of *Venus*, 20; Markham's description of, 61, 63–4; Polack's description of, 73; ship-girls, 27, 35–6, 38, 41–2, 44, 45, 46, 47, 59, 63, 66–9, 116, 117, 178; temporary marriages with sailors, 66, 117
Worsfold, Louisa, 183–4
Wright, Henry, 182–3
Wright, John, 80

Yate, William, 58, 119, 123

Zélée, 100, 105